The Man With The Long Shadow

The "meeting of the waters" where the Greta meets the Tees, near the hamlet of Wycliffe

The Man With The Long Shadow

Clara H. Stuart

WinePress Publishing
MUKILTEO, WA 98275

To my good friend

ROBERT EAVENSON

*In appreciation for countless hours spent
patiently reading successive versions of the manuscript,
making corrections and offering valuable suggestions
which contributed much
to the accuracy and readability
of the final text.*

ACKNOWLEDGMENTS

A writer does not write alone, but must gather about her a "cloud of witnesses." I express thanks to many who assisted in researching this book. Of those in England I am deeply indebted to Lewis Lupton, whom I met in London and who became a fast friend. His own volume on Wycliffe, deeply researched, superbly written, and embellished with his own art work, was of inestimable value. He allowed me to borrow copies of articles from periodicals I would not otherwise have found. At Lambeth Palace Library, the British Library, and the Bodleian librarians permitted me to examine manuscripts dating from Wycliffe's time. Personnel at Darlington, Lutterworth, and Lincoln libraries located useful materials. Denis Coggins in the Antiquities Office of Bowes Museum at Barnard Castle copied articles and supplied photographs relevant to Wycliffe's life. Ethel Moores at Fillingham and Colin and Penny Jee at Ludgershall contributed items of local lore, legendary bits not easily found elsewhere. Mildred Hayes at Lutterworth introduced me to people with historical knowledge and continued, through correspondence, to answer my questions and to be on the lookout for anything related to my subject.

I am indebted to those in the United States, too numerous to name here, who helped in many ways. Throughout the research and writing my daughter Martha, by her unflagging interest and encouragement, kept me going. In England she produced the photographs which appear in the book. I have called attention in the Dedication to the vital assistance of Robert Eavenson.

CONTENTS

PART ONE
EARLY YEARS AT OXFORD: CHANGES AND GROWTH (1346–1360) 9
"What will I find at the turning?"

PART TWO
ENLARGED VIEWS AND BEGINNING OF CONTROVERSY (1361–1373) 43
"The system must change!"

PART THREE
MOUNTING CONFLICT WITH ECCLESIASTICAL POWERS (1374–1378) 123
"The battle has just begun!"

PART FOUR
MOVING INTO DEEPER WATERS (1378–1380) 213
"Truth is of more weight than custom."

PART FIVE
POINT OF NO RETURN (1381–1382) 263
"I will walk a lonely path."

PART SIX
HANDING ON THE TORCH (1382–1385) 297
"In the end it will all come to pass."

EPILOGUE 377

PART 1

Early Years at Oxford: Changes and Growth
(1346–1360)
"What will I find at the turning?"

1. September 1346—The Preparation

Too excited for sleep, yet with a certain apprehension, young John Wycliffe lay awake through the hours of the night. Leaving the house in the dimness of pre-dawn, he groped his way to the bridge which lay across the ravine.

"Tomorrow!" he whispered, drawing a deep breath that was almost a sob. "Tomorrow I will leave this place, perhaps forever." The spoken words helped bring the reality more sharply into focus. The time had come. "I want to go...yet I am torn within. How can I leave the place and people I love so dearly?"

He planned to spend this day in an effort to make peace with his conflicting thoughts and emotions, to overcome, if possible, a deep reluctance that dragged at him.

Above him the manor house grew out of the rocky cliff like a small castle. To the north the cliff pitched steeply down to the river Tees. Here on the south lay a deep ravine, spanned by this bridge, which gave access to the house and which could be defended against attack. A castellated wall and tower offered further protection from infrequent invasions by the Scots.

As the eastern sky brightened, John turned and made his way around the house through dew-drenched grass to the edge of the cliff. A splendid panorama spread out before him—grassy meadows and a forest of stately elms on the other side, the river moving along with slow majesty.

"The water," he murmured brokenly, "this water of the Tees—it belongs to me. Even my name, John de Wycliffe, 'John of the Cliff by the Water,' binds me to the cliff and to the water." Back in the mists of time an early British word "wye," meaning "water," had combined with the Saxon word "cliffe" to give both the manor and the family of its lord the name "Wye-cliffe," now Wycliffe. Sir Roger Wycliffe, John's father, was the latest in a long line of ancestors who had been lords of this manor since the time of the Conquest. His roots were so deep! How could he leave?

Returning to the bridge, he stumbled blindly across and descended to the footpath which lay along the river. Past the church, past the scattered cottages, up and down hill, westward he went, quickening his pace as he came within sound and then sight of his destination.

With a sharp intake of breath he gazed at the scene which never failed to elicit deep emotion. "The meeting of the waters"—the point at which the Greta bounded into the Tees. Warm tears welled up in his eyes.

"Surely," he whispered, "I shall never, wherever I may go, see anything so beautiful as this running water nor hear anything so lovely as its ever-changing music."

He stepped out on a slanting slab of stone at the water's edge and leaped to another, then to another, until he reached the great boulder in the middle of the stream. Perched above the roaring torrent, he could feel himself a part of it. As the morning mists lifted, sunlight sparkled on the water. He sat with arms encircling drawn-up knees.

"Just as the Greta joins the Tees and becomes part of it," he said, "so this place will always be a part of me."

Through the thunder of the river he seemed to hear again his father's voice from the past. "The priestly calling is the highest in human society. The study of theology, my son, that is the course you are to follow. When the time comes, you will go to Oxford to study at the university."

He had always taken his studies seriously. His hunger for learning seemed insatiable. The monks with whom he studied at nearby Egglestone Abbey had introduced him to great minds of the past, such as Augustine, Aquinas, and Grosseteste.

He had become familiar with names and some of the teachings of men still living. Excitement seized him even now as he whispered, "Is it possible I may find the noted Thomas Bradwardine and Richard Fitzralph lecturing at Oxford? May I actually come to know these men?"

Impulsively he rose and bounded once more with practiced agility to the bank. He would make a last visit to Egglestone. He loved the remoteness of the abbey's location. It nestled like a jewel of rare beauty in the midst of the sheltering forest, close to the sight and sound of his beloved river.

The wooded path opened into a clearing. Cows belonging to the abbey stood contentedly grazing in the pasture. A footbridge across a ditch led into the precincts of the abbey.

Silence reigned in the deserted church. Sunlight streaming through the west window brought the stained glass saints to radiant life. He became aware of a murmur. It was as if the walls, saturated with prayers offered here for a century and a half, were now whispering them back into the air. A holy moment! He did not fully understand, but he would treasure it forever.

As the sun neared the horizon he turned to retrace his steps. One more stop he must make—the parish Church of St. Mary. As he entered, the low-hanging sun sent its rays through the stained glass of the west window, imparting a soft glow to the Madonna and Child in its path. John paused to lay his hand upon the rough stone font in which he had been baptized.

Approaching the altar, he knelt to pray. Somehow the tightness around his heart loosened; cords which had bound him slipped away.

Daylight faded as he turned toward home. Stopping beside a stone wall, he gave a low whistle, and from

Church of St. Mary at Wycliffe where John Wycliffe grew up

across the pasture his favorite horses trotted up. The smaller one nuzzled his shoulder, to be pushed aside by his darker companion. He petted them both. "Tomorrow we begin a long journey," he said.

He paused once more upon the bridge and looked down into the chasm. This time he drew a breath of relief and anticipation. At last he was ready. Ready for the new, he had released his hold on the old. His life would move on just as the river.

"Tomorrow!" he said again. "Tomorrow I will round the bend and lose sight of beloved places, family and friends. What will I find at the turning?"

2. October 1346—The Beginning

In his sixteen years John Wycliffe had never traveled more than a few miles from home. Now his mother drew him into a last embrace. He could scarcely hold back the tears, but her brave smile helped. With a determined lifting of his shoulders he mounted his horse and followed his father down the narrow path. A trusted retainer came along behind them.

Sir Roger had arranged for John to travel from Richmond, eleven miles away, with a large party, which stood less chance of an attack by brigands or wild animals. By early afternoon the group had assembled. While John was making the acquaintance of others on their way up to the university, Sir Roger called the servant aside.

"See that you take good care of him. Remain until he is well settled. I will expect a full report upon your return."

At the moment of parting John bade his father farewell with no outward display of emotion. He turned just once to look back. His father stood watching. As the distance between them increased, John sought to swallow a troublesome lump in his throat.

After the first day or two of long hours of riding, the novelty wore off. Pouring rain removed any remaining enthusiasm. The journey seemed interminable. Day after day, day after day, through showers or blazing sunshine, they plodded on. Finally on the tenth evening, rain-drenched once more and overwhelmed with weariness, John Wycliffe made his first entry into Oxford. All he craved was a dry bed and sleep, which he was told he would find at the Mitre Inn.

By morning his earlier eagerness had partially returned. He set out at once to locate Balliol College, which his father had arranged for him to enter. He found it a short way outside the North Gate.

It was a busy place. People moved about briskly, and no one seemed to have time for him. With some difficulty he at last obtained a number indicating the room he was to occupy, but he still had no idea where he would find it.

Seeing his uncertainty, an older student came to his rescue. "Need a bit of help?" he asked.

"Oh, please!" said Wycliffe. "I only arrived last night. I have been assigned a room and a number, but I don't know its location."

The young man led him up a stairway and along a corridor. Halfway along he stopped, flung open a door, and stepped across the darkened room to unlatch the shutter of the one small window. "You'll find it a tight squeeze," he said.

In dismay Wycliffe looked at the tiny cell-like room. "I...I guess I can manage," he said in a shaky voice.

Dismay turned to shock when his guide said, "You understand you'll share this room with three other students. Not a place you'll want to spend much time in, for sure. New students get the worst accommodations."

Wycliffe murmured his uncertain thanks, and the man left him. He looked despairingly about the cramped space. "So little light!" he said. "And the heat...it's stifling. Where will I store my clothes and other possessions, few as they are?"

Turning to his servant with a frown, he said, "When you return home, tell Father..." Then with a shrug he broke off. "Tell Father nothing. I shall hardly be here except for sleeping, for which I shall probably have little enough time."

Sleep on his first night at Balliol did not come easily. The bed, hardly more than a narrow board attached to the wall, offered scant comfort. The air had cooled somewhat with nightfall, but there was little circulation. An oppressive odor permeated the air. "Too many bodies packed into too little space," he said. A wave of homesickness swept over him in the hours before sleep came.

His roommates, of whom he saw little, informed him that two meals a day were served in the hall, breakfast at mid-morning and dinner in late afternoon. As he headed into the hall on the first morning, he found the student who had helped him earlier. "I hope they serve a hearty breakfast," he said. "I don't know when I've been so hungry."

"Don't count on it. I was here last year, and I know."

Still Wycliffe was hardly prepared for the unappetizing bowl of watery oatmeal of which breakfast consisted. A tentative taste revealed a strong scorched flavor.

"Ugh!" said the lad next to him. "Someone in the kitchen let it boil too low before adding more water." But he continued to eat until his bowl was empty.

After forcing a few mouthfuls, Wycliffe pushed the bowl aside and left the hall with hunger pangs undiminished.

"I have to eat," he cried. He used a portion of his rapidly shrinking funds to purchase from the street market a dish of tripe and sausage. Not his favorite food, but cheap and filling.

The helpful student of the previous evening had followed. He offered a word of caution. "You'll soon discover more important uses for your money. Daylight hours are insufficient for study. You'll need candles, and they're expensive."

"I hadn't thought of that," said Wycliffe. "It's true I won't have much money."

"Even more, you'll want books. You should horde your funds for essentials."

Wycliffe had never gone hungry. The meagerness of the two meals a day was appalling. Lacking in both quality and quantity, the sameness of the fare grew monotonous. Oatmeal, an infinitesmal portion of boiled beef, an occasional turnip or a bit of cabbage. Realizing the need to sustain bodily strength, he determined to eat what was provided, unsatisfying as it was, but his thoughts wandered yearningly to his father's table.

The Michaelmas term opened formally, according to custom, on October 10 with a mass of the Holy Ghost at St. Mary's, the university church. Stately proceedings were all very well, but Wycliffe was eager for studies to begin.

Time seemed his scarcest commodity. To his deep satisfaction he was able to enter at once into the regular university program. The majority of young students had to complete preliminary studies before they could qualify for the university courses. "How grateful I am," he said, "for the instruction I received at Egglestone Abbey."

During the early weeks a sense of claustrophobia troubled Wycliffe. "I can't breathe," he exclaimed. "Buildings huddle against each other. There is no room.

Overhanging upper stories shut out the sunlight. Streets are mere alleyways. How can people live like this?"

Even worse was the filth which made walking precarious. Heavy rains flooded cobblestones and turned unpaved streets into bogs. Balliol Hall stood outside the North Gate across a ditch which became a river of mud. Pigs rooted about. The stench was overpowering.

He complained to a fellow student, who laughed and said, "You'll get used to it. London is much worse."

One day he could stand it no longer. "I've got to have some open space and fresh air," he cried. "I'm suffocating."

Leaving his studies aside, he headed for the river Cherwell. He wandered along its banks and into a nearby forest, reveling in the untainted air, listening to the crunch of fallen leaves underfoot, the twitter of birds above, drinking in the beauty of riotous autumn colors. This excursion sent him back to his studies renewed in mind.

I must do this often, he thought.

Yet in time he came to appreciate the spots of beauty within the town walls. The spire of St. Frideswide's Church lifted his heart even as it lifted his eyes heavenward. He thought of his own little church at Wycliffe. Sometimes in the morning, as he entered the town, he paused beside the square Saxon tower of the Church of St. Michael at the North Gate. This rough stone structure stood as a bastion of strength and seemed to fortify him for the day's labors.

3. November 1346-June 1347—The First Year

Wycliffe's first goal, the bachelor of arts degree, required study of the Trivium, composed of courses in grammar, dialectics, and rhetoric. Instruction was in Latin. The teacher dictated the text, a Latin translation from Aristotle, then expounded it.

Watching Wycliffe work, one of his classmates asked, "How do you manage to get it all down? By the time I stumble through the writing of one unfamiliar Latin term, you have moved on beyond."

"I am fortunate to have a good foundation in Latin," he replied. "That makes it easier. If I miss a word or two as he dictates, I can usually remember it and fill it in. Could I perhaps help you a bit from time to time?"

"Oh, if you would!" cried his friend. "He expects us to memorize it, once it it written down. I find that almost impossible."

"Keep working at it," said Wycliffe. "Repetition is the secret. Constant practice will help you form a habit of remembering."

"You make it sound simple. I'll do my best, and if you help me, maybe I'll learn."

Wycliffe found all phases of learning exciting. A feature popular with the students was disputation. A teacher or senior pupil would uphold a thesis against another in public argument. Wycliffe delighted in following the arguments. He would think ahead of the speaker as to how he would handle the question.

"I can scarcely wait for the time when I am allowed to take part," he said. "But alas! That time is at least three years ahead."

Of Aristotle he could never get enough. Not content with what his teacher dictated, he borrowed the book and committed to memory even the most difficult portions.

His classmates marveled. "How does he do it?" they asked. "He moves along without apparent stress or struggle. We spend hours and hours at study, yet he easily outstrips us all."

One day he overheard a group of students discussing the writings of Grosseteste. He joined the group and heard them also speaking of Thomas Bradwardine, who had been at Oxford until called by the king to military chaplaincy in France.

"I must hear the lectures on their works and read all they have written," cried Wycliffe. "I can hardly wait!"

"Grosseteste's writings are in the library of the Friars Minor," said one of the men, amused at Wycliffe's enthusiasm.

"Where is that located?"

The student obligingly gave him directions, but with a somewhat derisive smile added, "Of course only members of the order are allowed to use the library."

That night Wycliffe dreamed that he was struggling to get at Grosseteste's writings. The manuscripts seemed just within reach, but before he could grasp them, they were snatched away.

The thing became an obsession. At last he determined to go and ask. *Maybe the rules are not so strict, or perhaps they will make an exception.*

Off he sped down Fish Street and out the South Gate. Turning right on Brewers Street, he found the Franciscan house. His hunger for the books made him bold.

"Please, sir, could I read the manuscripts of Grosseteste?"

The friar in charge gave him a quizzical look, then frowned.

Wycliffe's heart sank. "I would only use them when no one else needed them..." He hesitated, uncertain what more to say.

"This is most unusual," said the friar, still frowning. Wycliffe's uneasiness increased. "Why this enthusiasm about Bishop Grosseteste's works? Why seek to invade this library?"

"St. Robert...I know he was never canonized," stammered Wycliffe in confusion, "but I count him a saint...and because of his holy life and his courage I must become better acquainted with him. If you would give permission for a short time, I could copy out...I could easily memorize what he has written."

The friar's stern expression softened. "Do you know, young man, that your 'St. Robert' was one of the best friends this house ever had? He used to lecture here. Not only do we possess the manuscripts of his works, but he left us his entire library." Wycliffe stood speechless. What could he say?

"My young friend, I will grant your request. Such eagerness, such boldness, should be rewarded. Come as often as you like. Read all the books. You will find not only holiness and courage in your St. Robert but a great deal more."

As he hurried back through the city, he said, "Boldness! Yes, that can open doors. I must remember that." Later in the day he pushed aside other work and returned to the priory. With trembling hands he took up one of the precious manuscripts. Only darkness halted his reading. He assimilated what he read so completely that it became a never-to-be-forgotten part of him. As he continued to read as often as time permitted, Grosseteste became his model of what a bishop should be.

Soon another exciting prospect loomed. Richard Fitzralph, now chancellor of the university, was about to make one of his infrequent visits to Oxford, and he would deliver lectures in theology.

"I must, I must by some means get into his lecture hall!" cried Wycliffe. He could not forget what the monks at Egglestone had told him about this man.

"You are too greedy," replied a classmate. "Bide your time. Attendance at Fitzralph's lectures is restricted to students in theology."

At this disappointing news Wycliffe cried, "He is soon to go to Ireland as archbishop of Armagh and may never return to Oxford. If only by some means I could hear him now!"

Almost in despair he cast about in his mind for some possible plan. Could he afford to miss lectures in his own courses? Surely this opportunity, if he could seize it, was of greater importance. On the day of the first lecture he approached the hall where the lecture was to be held.

He searched the faces of the throng crowding the entryway. He felt sure he could squeeze through, being smaller in size than the others. Pushing his way along as gently as possible, he entered the hall. Once inside, he found himself forced to the rear against the wall. He could hardly breathe, he could not see the speaker, but he could hear. And what he heard was permanently inscribed upon his eager mind.

Jubilant, he thought, *Dare I try it again?* He dared. He followed the same procedure for the next lecture, and the next. Fitzralph became his hero. Years later he would quote from those lectures.

Before the end of October he received a letter from his father containing dreaded news. The Scots were moving across the border. His father had responded to the call of duty and gone to join the forces in the north.

On the heels of this letter came official news. On October 17 in a fierce battle at Neville's Cross the Scots were defeated and their young king, David, taken prisoner. Anxious days passed before Wycliffe could discover that his father had survived, uninjured.

His first reaction was relief at his father's safety. He could not deny a deep pride in knowing that his father and his fellows had won a stirring victory. Yet questions came to his mind. *War with Scotland, war with France. Could bloodshed and killing be the only means of settling disputes?*

4. 1347-1349—Deadly Interruption

With the coming of the summer vacation, John considered, but quickly discarded, attempting the difficult journey home. He had faced that issue when he left home and had recognized that he might never be able to return. Instead he would pursue his studies with all vigor during the weeks of vacation.

He had begun to feel more at home at Oxford. The intense longing for the hills and dales and familiar paths along the Tees had subsided somewhat.

During the summer Fitzralph's consecration as archbishop of Armagh took him away to Ireland, much to Wycliffe's regret. "My illegal entry into his lectures profited me much," he said. "Had I waited, I would have missed him."

The second year at Oxford sped by even more quickly than the first. Before he knew it, the long vacation of 1348 arrived. "Another year will see my first degree in hand," he said.

But in those early summer days frightful news began to come across from the Continent. A terrible plague from the East had entered the Mediterranean seaports and was sweeping northward through Italy, wiping out thousands. It was known as the Great Mortality, because scarcely a person, once stricken, survived.

In August a ship carrying infected sailors landed on the Dorset coast of England, and the disease came ashore. It advanced steadily and, within a few weeks, reached Oxford. Studies came to a halt, and many fled to the north. Wycliffe remained in his room.

The pestilence played no favorites. Those from town and gown fell before it, young and old. A stricken person might live two or three days, but quite commonly he died within half a day. As the number of dead increased, mass ceremonies replaced individual funeral services.

Few followed the dead to the cemeteries. When no space remained in churchyards, new ground had to be set aside and consecrated. Burying more than one body in a grave became accepted practice.

A neighbor of Wycliffe's at Balliol staggered wild-eyed into his room, displaying a large lump in his armpit. Wycliffe overcame a feeling of panic, realizing he must try to help. He led the man back to his room and urged him to lie down. "Would you like me to go for a doctor?" he asked, knowing as he spoke that the quest would be fruitless. Doctors were too few and patients too many. Besides, no treatment appeared to help.

In agony of soul Wycliffe sat with him through the night, able to offer only the comfort of his presence. As he watched, small black pustules broke out all over the body, and fever developed, accompanied by vomiting of blood. Then came death. Wycliffe stumbled out for help and arranged a decent burial.

Cases multiplied. The healthy cared for the stricken, but the number of healthy diminished daily. With each death Wycliffe shuddered. Would he be the next victim? Footsteps echoed strangely through the empty hall. No one ventured out into the vacant streets except of necessity. The smell of death permeated the air.

Face to face with death, Wycliffe became aware that God was a stranger. *All my life I've talked about God, professed to worship him, learned much about him. But to know about God is not to know him.* Words from a psalm came unbidden to his lips: "My heart is sore pained within me, and the terrors of death are fallen upon me. Fearfulness and trembling are come upon me, and horror hath over-whelmed me." *Oh, God! I am desperately afraid. What must I do?*

The library at the Church of St. Mary the Virgin! Manuscripts of the New Testament lay there in a huge chest. *Might I find help there?* He sprang up and hurried to the church. As he climbed the stairs to the room where the books were kept, a feeling of futility slowed his steps. He stood staring down at the top of the closed chest. He had forgotten that it would be locked!

Some impulse prompted him to lay his hand on the lid and give it a tug. It moved! Someone had neglected to lock it! He threw open the lid, and, without stopping to remember that the books were never to be taken from the building, he gathered up the manuscripts he wanted and hurried back to his room.

From that moment, unless needed by some sufferer, he devoured the manuscripts. He read not just with his mind, but with his heart. He read devotionally, an entirely new experience for him. He read prayerfully in a frantic search for God. Each morning he rejoiced to find himself still alive. One more day to continue his search!

Day after day he persevered. Then one glorious morning the light broke. The written words, the words whose beauty and truth he had admired, took on warmth, color, vitality. Through the written Word came the revelation of the living Word. The love of God encompassed him. That manifestation of holiness made him starkly aware of the blackness of sin, even his own sin. He began to comprehend the message of forgiveness so eloquently expressed in the cross of Christ. Something of the grace of God, made known in the gift of his Son, came through.

The Great Mortality raged on, but John Wycliffe was no longer afraid. He faced life with a new vigor. *Aristotle may teach me many truths, but for ultimate Truth I must turn to the One who said, 'I am...the Truth.' To this Book I must give my best efforts, testing all other truth by it.*

5. 1349-1353—Desolating Aftermath

"Nearly a year now of this horror," sighed Wycliffe. "How much longer?" The summer of 1349 dragged on. Then a definite shift occurred. Days passed with no new cases. Deaths diminished, came to a halt. The pestilence had done its worst at Oxford. With the end of summer, it was over.

Those remaining alive looked about in a dazed manner, as if waking from a nightmare. Wycliffe thought this experience might be akin to that of Noah as he emerged from the ark to find a world swept bare of human beings except for the few with him.

"We who escaped the Great Mortality," he said, "face a world not so empty as Noah's, but different from what we knew before."

As the pestilence came to a halt, students who had fled began to make their way back, joined by a few new brave souls. Wycliffe listened with growing concern to reports of conditions outside Oxford. "At harvest time," said one, "crops rotted in the fields. Laborers are too few to meet the need."

"Worse still," said one of Wycliffe's roommates, now returned, "many serfs have found themselves free to wander where they will. With their masters dead there is no one to restrain or direct them."

"Nor have animals escaped," cried a lad from Yorkshire. "Whole flocks and herds have been wiped out. Carcasses lie rotting, polluting the air for miles around."

In all the bad news came one piece of good news. Wycliffe rejoiced to learn that Thomas Bradwardine had been consecrated archbishop of Canterbury after that post had remained vacant for a year. Another of his heroes! Now he might be able to meet him in person. His joy was shortlived. Before the end of September the new archbishop died of the pestilence at Lambeth Palace only days after his arrival.

"What will happen to the people in their need for pastoral care?" asked Wycliffe. Many priests had died. In trying to meet the need, bishops made frantic attempts to fill the vacancies. In desperation they ordained and installed men who had lost their wives and were at loose ends, most of them totally unqualified, some scarcely literate. If the people had ever needed spiritual leadership, surely it was now. Where would they find it?

Wycliffe chafed at the slowness in returning to formal studies. At length masters, teachers, and students banded together in a determined effort to restore a regular schedule. They would not waste any more time surveying the wreckage.

6. October 1353-February 1355—First Milestone

Nothing moved smoothly in October of 1353 when work was resumed. Eventually Wycliffe struck his pace and pursued his studies in the former pattern. Then came a day he had eagerly awaited. "At last," he exulted, "I can join the bachelors in public disputation!"

This form of the arts had held a special attraction for him from the start. As he entered into it with enthusiasm, the temptation came to spend too much time in this activity. With difficulty he resisted.

"I must remember," he cried, "that I am still only at the beginning of learning. What lies ahead may prove of even greater importance than this lovely art of disputation!"

A little more time and he was ready to submit himself to the viva voce, the oral examination to determine his fitness for admission to the baccalaureate. Four masters examined him. They required him to furnish evidence not only of his learning, but of his morals and his regularity in attendance at lectures. It was a grueling experience, but not once did he stumble. The masters appeared eminently satisfied.

"At last," he breathed, "the first milestone reached!"

His zeal allowed no time for resting. He plunged into the Quadrivium, in which the disciplines were the natural sciences: arithmetic, geometry, astronomy, and theory of music. These studies would lead to the master of arts degree. His teachers soon saw the astuteness of this scholar and encouraged him.

"How do you do it?" cried a fellow student. "Even while you absorb with apparent ease the floods of new knowledge required of us, you retain all the previously learned material without loss. Do you never forget anything?"

"Once I get hold of something," he replied in a puzzled tone, "I seem to retain it. I can't explain how." Sometimes he amazed himself.

The beauty and precision of mathematics delighted him. Roger Bacon of the previous century had described mathematics as the only discipline without fear of error. The laws of physics learned in astronomy intrigued him. He copied out material on optics and the properties of light, adding it to his growing collection. Here was beauty! Here was truth!

He found other students with a like enthusiasm for mathematical and physical studies. Further study of Roger Bacon led to an understanding of the possibilities of the experimental method of science.

"Did you know," asked a classmate, "that Bacon predicted that man would one day produce machines capable of travel under the sea and others able to fly through the air?"

"How could such things ever be!" cried Wycliffe. "And still..." He found his imagination stretching immeasurably.

Buried deep in the world of his studies, he knew little of the recurring controversy between "town" and "gown" at Oxford. Thus he was completely unprepared for the shocking series of events that burst upon the university early in 1355.

7. February-June 1355—Another Interruption

Wycliffe entered the North Gate on February 14 and stumbled through smoke-filled air down Cornmarket. The stench of still-burning buildings made breathing difficult. A debris of stones and other litter filled the streets. An unnatural quiet reigned.

Stunned by the unbelievable destruction he saw, Wycliffe turned into the High Street and stopped just outside St. Mary's, the university church. Scuffles between "town" and "gown" were frequent, but who could have imagined anything like what had taken place in the last three days?

On Tuesday, February 10, a group of clerks had entered a tavern at Carfax called Swydlestock. The vintner served the wine they ordered. An argument with the vintner followed as to the quality of the wine. After several increasingly angry exchanges one of the men hurled the wine vessel at the vintner's head, and the group stormed out of the tavern.

This led to the ringing of the bell of St. Martin's, calling "town" to the defense. Soon after, the bell of St. Mary's summoned "gown" to the fray. Groups from both sides joined in.

Two days of increasingly violent fighting followed. "Town" gained the upper hand, but men were killed on both sides. Pillaging and burning destroyed fourteen college halls.

Wycliffe now stared in horror at the smoking remains of the hall at Oriel College. *Burning! Killing!* All this terrible destruction over a flagon of wine!"

Officials from Westminster had been summoned to restore order. The mayor and bailiff of Oxford were imprisoned, and stern penalties were imposed on the city of Oxford.

"No penalties, no imprisonment," cried Wycliffe, "can replace the property destroyed nor restore health to the wounded nor life to the dead. The Great Slaughter they are calling it." Four months elapsed before classes could be resumed. Wycliffe chafed and fretted at this further interruption. Besides that frustration, he faced another problem for which he must seek a solution.

8. June 1355-June 1356—Enlarged Vista

In establishing Balliol in the previous century, the benefactors had arranged that each student should receive a weekly stipend of eight farthings until he was master of arts. Then he must leave the hall. This meant Wycliffe must begin to consider arrangements for a change.

"Merton!" he said to his friend Walter Brut, a student at Merton. "Could I dare hope to be admitted there?"

"Why not?" asked Brut. "Sounds like the best idea I know."

"Merton is known to be rather exclusive. Only rarely does a northern man gain acceptance. Wouldn't I do better to search in another direction?"

"Go ahead and inquire around," advised Brut. "I'm sure more than one college will show an interest in having you as a member. But don't rule out Merton."

Weeks went by, and he received no response from Merton. Again he discussed the situation with Brut. "I suppose I should give up that dream," he said, "and concentrate on choosing another college, though in my heart I don't feel drawn to any of them. I must make up my mind. Why am I so indecisive? What am I waiting for?"

Brut only smiled. "Perhaps you should wait a bit longer."

The days dragged, and Wycliffe was almost in despair. Then one bright morning the answer arrived. He held in his hands an invitation to come to Merton.

The first to offer congratulations was Walter Brut. "Why did you doubt that Merton would accept you? You underestimate your reputation. I'll help you move."

Down Cornmarket they went, turned left at Carfax into High Street. A right turn into Grope Lane, then the cobblestone street leading to Merton.

"It will seem strange living within the city walls," said Wycliffe. "Even a larger stipend will leave little for books."

Looking about his assigned quarters, he said, "Not much different from the room I left. Perhaps a little larger, but still four of us to occupy it. However, other advantages make that negligible."

Making friends came naturally. He soon developed a special closeness with William Rede and William Barton. The latter, on the same level of studies as Wycliffe, looked forward to theological studies with equal enthusiasm.

Rede was deep into the study of astronomy and optics, subjects that continued to fascinate Wycliffe. These three discussed the need for real libraries. Priories and monasteries had libraries, but they were generally not accessible to those outside the orders.

"Only the hand of God opened the way for me to use the library of the Friars Minor," said Wycliffe. "Outsiders aren't allowed to read there, but my eagerness for Grosseteste led me to march boldly in, ask and receive permission."

"You were fortunate," said Barton. "Every college needs a well-stocked library and adequate space to house it. Naturally each of us would prefer to own all the books he needs. An impossible dream! The alternative should be availability of books for everyone. Merton has a respectable number already."

"The library at St. Mary's offers some outstanding volumes," said Wycliffe.

"Yet books hidden away in an upper room, locked in a chest, hardly constitute a library," said Rede.

"That chest at St. Mary's is one I raided in the year of the pestilence," said Wycliffe. "I felt a desperate need for the New Testament manuscripts. Finding the chest unlocked, I took the books to my room and kept them for some time."

"In those terrible days many sins were overlooked. I doubt anyone else was thinking of books," said Barton.

"Do you know what my dream is?" asked Rede. "I would like to design and construct a building here at Merton which would house an adequate library. In fact, I have a design in mind."

"Dreams do come true," cried Wycliffe with enthusiasm. "Make it spacious, Rede, with shelves and shelves of books!"

"You make it sound almost possible!"

9. December 1356—Disturbing Thoughts

On a sunny December afternoon when the air was not too chill, Wycliffe felt the need of human companionship. He went in search of Walter Brut. "Come, Brut, we need a breath of untainted air."

"Glad you are willing to socialize a bit. Besides, I have news which will interest you."

Crossing the cobblestones, they picked their way toward the South Gate. "I assume we are headed for the path along the Cherwell?" inquired Wycliffe.

"Even on a mild day the ground will not have thawed enough to make it slippery."

As they crunched along through the fallen leaves, Wycliffe asked, "What was that news you had?"

"Knowing your esteem for the archbishop of Armagh—or Armachanus as he is now called—I thought you would be interested in knowing he's in London."

"Esteem? I should think so! But as for getting to see him, London is no better than Ireland. Fitzralph! Armachanus! What is he doing in London?"

"Getting into trouble."

"How so?"

"Roger Conway, a Franciscan friar, preached a sermon in London at Paul's Cross on the familiar theme of the Spiritual Franciscans: the poverty of Christ and the apostles. They had all things in common, and Christ begged for a livelihood."

"I've heard of Conway. I'm sure he would have been extreme in his statements. What does that have to do with Armachanus?"

"He was persuaded to preach in reply. You know the powerful manner in which he would contend that mendicancy has no warrant in Scripture. He further upset the friars by claiming they should be denied the right to hear confessions. They are filing a complaint against him with the pope."

"Regrettable! I'll doubtless hear about it from the local Franciscans. On this subject I can go along with Fitzralph. However, much can be said for the mendicant orders. Their ideals are chiefly those of Scripture. They recognize, as I do, the error into which the monastic orders have fallen—that of piling up wealth and living sumptuously. Too, the friars preach to the people, which most of the secular priests neglect to do."

"What if the pope summons Fitzralph to Avignon?"

"Armachanus will defend himself well. Innocent VI will reprimand and correct, but he'll be fair. I only wish he'd see fit to return the papal seat to Rome where it belongs. Even so, he's a decided improvement over his predecessors."

"Still, little attention is paid to the statutes of Provisors and Praemunire, laws intended to limit the pope's highhandedness in making appointments."

In hot anger Wycliffe said, "The pope goes over the head of the king and of the chapters of the dioceses in appointing his favorites. Those appointed seldom even visit our fair land, but send their servants to garner the harvest of silver and gold."

"If we don't turn back," said Brut, glancing at the western sky, "darkness will find us on the wrong side of the locked city gate. We may already have missed supper."

"Worse things could happen."

Wycliffe remained disturbed that evening over the matters he and Brut had discussed. On every side error stared him in the face. The more he read Scripture, the more he realized how wrong things were.

When he returned to his room at bedtime, he found a letter waiting. Instead of his father's familiar handwriting, he recognized that of his mother. Even before he broke the seal, he had a strong premonition that terrible tidings awaited him.

10. December 1356—Grief

The hour was late. Wycliffe needed desperately to escape to the open spaces, but the city gates were locked. The letter still in his hand, he felt his way down the stairway into the courtyard. The magic mildness of the daylight hours had given way to bitter cold. He scarcely noticed the icy blast which whipped him as he crossed the quadrangle.

By the light of the frozen rays from the waning moon he stumbled across to the chapel entrance. The same dim rays, entering through the great window behind the altar, lighted the interior. He stepped into a choir stall and fell to his knees. Folding his arms on the rail, he pillowed his head there.

Father is dead. His thoughts went back to a day ten years earlier. Riding off to Oxford, he had turned to look once more at the tall figure standing, watching. *Am I never to see that dear face again? Never to feel that strong arm about my shoulder? Never to hear that voice again? Can it be?* How could he sustain such a blow?

Sustain it he must. For the loss of his father meant that he, John Wycliffe, was lord of the Wycliffe manor. This was a responsibility he had not expected to have to shoulder so soon.

Yet the heaviest blow was to his mother. His heart ached for her. He thought tenderly of her courage and strength. She had sought to comfort him, and had spoken little of her own bleeding heart.

He longed to go to her. Her need of him must be great, but she insisted that she could manage the affairs of the manor until he could come. He saw no way he could go before the long summer vacation.

After a time he raised his head and found the chapel engulfed in almost total darkness. As his eyes sought the faint outline of the great window, the moon suddenly broke through the clouds that had obscured it. A flood of silver entered the window, bringing the crucifix behind the altar into sharp relief.

Wycliffe caught his breath. The tightness about his heart loosened a bit, and he whispered, "I do not stand alone! The One who knew incredible suffering and loneliness and loss, and who bore it for me, will surely uphold me in what I now face." He bowed his head again upon his arms and released the tears he had been unable to shed before. At last he could pray.

Friends offered expressions of sympathy which touched him deeply. He spoke little of his loss, for his grief was a private thing. He soon tucked it away within his heart and took up his labors with the old vigor. The pain dulled but did not go away.

11. July-December 1357—Lord of the Manor

Wycliffe made the trip home that summer, but returned before the opening of the Michaelmas term in October. He must continue his labors toward the master of arts degree, still in the future. But the weeks spent in the north made it difficult to settle into the old routine.

The visit home had stirred deep emotions. He found his mother aged more than the years warranted, but her courage never flagged. With an able manager, she handled the affairs of the estate well. His father, with perhaps a premonition that the end was near, had left things in excellent shape.

Leaving had been painful, yet the pull back to Oxford was strong. Now the thought uppermost in his mind was the prospect of being able to teach as soon as the master's degree was his. Already he was at work preparing the lectures he would give in philosophy when he became a regent master.

In December Brut again brought news. "Fitzralph received his summons to appear at Avignon. On November 8 he preached a most notable sermon, so they say."

"I suppose," said Wycliffe, "he expected to convince the pope of the rightness of his position with regard to Christ and mendicancy as opposed to that of the friars."

"Sad to say, his pleading left the Holy Father unimpressed. The matter was turned over to four cardinals for study. Meanwhile, the pope has ordered the English bishops not to hinder the friars from hearing confession or burying the dead."

"Not a very good sign," said Wycliffe. "I understand the English bishops are supporting Fitzralph, even levying a tax for his expenses. This matter could drag on for years."

"Fitzralph is evidently optimistic. He has remained at Avignon to await the outcome."

12. 1358—Master of Balliol

When Balliol Hall found it necessary to elect a new master, speculation ran rife as to who might be chosen. Wycliffe's friends suggested he was a likely candidate, but he scoffed at the idea.

Tension was in the air on the day of the election. Late in the afternoon a messenger informed Wycliffe that his presence was required immediately at Balliol. With quickened heartbeat he walked the still-familiar way past St. Michael's, out the North Gate, and across the Ditch toward the chapel.

The procedure for such an election followed a set pattern. The principal sat to record the votes. Beside him two scrutators took pains to verify the accuracy of the recording. Each of the fellows entered alone to cast his vote.

As Wycliffe made his way to the front, all eyes were upon him. After a pause the principal looked up with a serious expression. "John Wycliffe, it is my privilege to announce to you that you have been elected master of Balliol."

The solemnity of the occasion called for restraint, yet Wycliffe could scarcely hide his immense pleasure. Each fellow approached him in turn to offer congratulations.

"Plans will be made," the principal informed him,

"for your formal installation. Such an event will, of course, be attended by considerable ceremony."

Clearing his throat, he continued, "Because of certain endowments that have been made, you must, before installation, be approved by Uhtred Boldon, the Benedictine monk who is warden of Durham college. We will arrange for that formality."

Wycliffe could see that becoming master of Balliol was no light matter. Upon leaving, he proceeded at what he hoped was a dignified pace back to Merton in search of Brut. Again he would have to readjust his plans.

"Congratulations, my friend!" Brut cried, upon hearing the news. "Only," he continued, in a tone of mock exasperation, "now I'll have to help you move back. Couldn't you have stayed a bit longer at Merton? This frequent moving could get to be a habit."

Still filled with a sense of wonder, Wycliffe said, "It's not much of an advancement financially, but it is quite an honor. How happy my mother will be! I wish my father could know."

"Perhaps he does," said Brut softly.

Wycliffe gave him a grateful smile. "Just think, Brut, I'll have a room to myself and a servant to care for my needs. Think how much more I can accomplish with my studies!"

"Probably a larger room than you have had before as well. Not all your time will be your own, however. Being master is not totally an honorary position. There are duties."

"There's that, of course," said Wycliffe with a sigh. "One can't have everything. Provided with a bed, a chair, a trestle-table, and a bookshelf, I should be quite comfortable."

"Don't forget the mazer," said Brut. "Every master must have that large goblet for pledging toasts."

"Oh, Brut! The utter luxury of a room alone, a place for my books, privacy for study and writing! I feel like singing!"

"In light of your prejudice against the use of vocal music in worship, that last statement says much about the depth of your feeling over this. Singing may not be necessary, but some sort of vocal praise is in order. Suppose we go down to the chapel and offer thanks to God for this event."

13. 1360—Armachanus!

The months that followed proved the most demanding Wycliffe had known. A legal case concerning the college came up. He made an eloquent plea for Balliol and won the case. He rejoiced secretly over such victories. Success gave him a needed lift.

As time passed, Wycliffe became aware of changes in his own personality, in his thinking. The responsibilities of his position matured him. Yet demands made upon him cut increasingly into time for study, which frustrated him. December 1360 proved a dreary month. He slipped into a spell of discouragement when all looked black.

"Fourteen years," he muttered. "What have I accomplished? With what high hopes I came, thinking by now to have a theological degree. Yet I've not even completed the arts course." Who could have foreseen the Great Mortality and all that followed? Though he no longer feared death, its grasping presence never seemed far away. His heart still ached at the loss of his father. In face of so many obstacles, interruptions, and sorrows, it took all his powers to persevere.

While he was in this state of mind, the news came of Richard of Armagh's death at Avignon. This loss of one who had been his early hero and to whom he owed so much was a heavy blow.

Armachanus! I long ago canonized you in my own heart, and you will always be my St. Richard. Now the opportunity to know you face to face, to experience the warmth of your personal presence, the glow of your personality is gone forever.

His mind flew back in gratitude to the lectures he had forced his way into. *That and your writings are all I have now.*

As he sat thus with heavy heart, he forced himself to turn his thoughts to the future. Surely it would be different from the past. Once the master of arts degree was in hand he could look forward to a new beginning. A latent joy stirred, its full flowering hindered by an anxiety he could not explain.

PART 2

Enlarged Views and Beginning of Controversy
(1361–1373)
"The system must change!"

1. January-March 1361—Second Milestone

Circumstances required Wycliffe to return quickly to a more normal outlook. "At last! At last!" he cried. "I can hardly believe my inception as *magister artium* is at hand."

Strenuous weeks of preparation were behind him. As he was making last minute plans for the feast which must follow, young Nicholas Hereford, a student at Queens, happened by. He was among those who had developed a great admiration for Wycliffe.

"I suppose the feast will be a time of relaxation," said Hereford, "with difficulties behind and the degree awarded."

The vehemence of Wycliffe's reply took him by surprise. "Time of relaxation? No! What should be a happy occasion becomes for many a weighty burden. This is no social event, but a rigid requirement involving unnecessary and heavy expense which few can afford."

"Doubtless," said Hereford, "the rank of master of Balliol demands a more substantial outlay than for others."

"So it does. The stationers, who provide all the necessary documents, certificates, and required copies of the speeches, must receive suits of clothes. In my case these must be of some elegance. The bedels, who walk with their silver maces before the dignitaries, expect buckskin gloves for their services, with twenty shillings in addition. That is only the beginning."

Hereford appeared shocked. "Many students are always short of funds. How will they manage?"

"Most will find a way. I hoarded for this purpose a sum obtained on my trip home three years ago. Some will go heavily into debt. Others will request provision of benefices from the pope. With such income they can meet the need."

"But that means they must hold their benefices in abstentia, if they are to continue their studies!"

Wycliffe sighed. "It's a practice of which I disapprove. Such maneuvers are looked upon as almost necessary evils."

Closing activities followed a set schedule. On the evening before the final event Wycliffe took part in a disputation known as Vespers at the Austin friars. The next day he appeared at St. Mary's and delivered a formal lecture before all the masters. At its conclusion, with heart beating rapidly, he received the book, ring, and biretta, emblems of fellowship of a regent master. He then withdrew to a crucifix in the choir to await the congratulations of his new brethren. The feast seemed almost an anticlimax.

Wycliffe breathed a sigh of relief when the day ended. Alone in his room he could freely rejoice at the attainment of one more goal. *I am now not only magister artium but a regent master, a teacher in the university of Oxford.* How sweet the words tasted on his tongue! He was free to give formal lectures in his own lecture hall.

As these pleasant thoughts played through his mind, a knock came and Rede entered. "Still up, despite the late hour! I just want to reiterate my congratulations."

"How good of you, Rede," cried Wycliffe. "I need to relax with a friend."

Relax they did, talking at length of the future each faced. "You really do look forward to teaching, don't you?" asked Rede.

"With the keenest anticipation," replied Wycliffe. "It will be a delight. Only one thought mars the joy."

"What's that?"

"Planning and delivering lectures could be so time-consuming as to hinder the progress of my theological studies."

Rede laughed and clapped him on the back. "Fear not, my dear old friend! You have yet to demonstrate the full extent of your capabilities. You will move along with no difficulty."

"Thank you for the vote of confidence. I hope you're right. I'd like to do some preaching, too. I won't be eligible to teach in the field of theology yet, but nothing hinders me from preaching, except the time to prepare sermons!"

"That you must make time for, Wycliffe." Rede's tone was serious. "Many parish priests do little or no preaching. What they do leaves much to be desired. People aren't being fed spiritually. Preaching is vitally important."

"Spiritual ignorance is appalling. Many find it easy to call God master and profess to honor his Son from heaven, but I daresay a multitude of people live out their lifetimes ignorant even of the Ten Commandments. I can overlook some of the shortcomings of the mendicant friars, because they do preach."

Suppressing a yawn, Rede rose to leave. "I guess you're right. The stories some friars weave into their sermons to hold the crowd's attention get pretty fanciful, but they do preach."

2. April 1361—A Benefice Offered

Wycliffe examined the official seal on the document with mild curiosity, pondering what its contents might be. "The best way to find out is to break the seal," he muttered to himself. He had no premonition that what he was about to read would completely upset his carefully laid plans.

The living of the parish church at Fillingham in Lincolnshire, he read, *is at the disposal of Balliol College. The present priest, John Reynor, is dying. The college wishes to name a successor now, to avoid a delay at the time of his death. With the pope's consent, we name John Wycliffe.*

"No!" he cried. "This can't happen now." He read the paper a second time, then bolted out the door in search of Brut.

Brut scanned the paper Wycliffe thrust into his hand. "Had you no idea," he asked, "that this was in the offing?"

"I knew something of the situation. The old priest has been there a long time. I just assumed he would live on for at least a few more years. Now he is likely to die any day."

"I can't see that it presents any great problem. When the man dies, go and get yourself installed, take a look around, appoint a curate, and come on back. A matter of days, perhaps a fortnight. It's the expected procedure."

"For me," said Wycliffe, "it's not that simple. I desire so desperately to get into theological studies..."

"I know, too, how keenly you have looked forward to teaching. You have quite a following of young students eager for your lectures. It would be a shame to disappoint them."

Wycliffe sat with his head in his hands for some moments. "If I leave now," he said, "to serve a parish in person, will I ever get back to work here? Even were I certain of returning, it appalls me to consider another long interruption."

"You've suffered your share of interruptions. Why let that happen again? Follow the usual pattern: appoint a curate."

"You make it so easy. I wish it were. You know my feelings on absenteeism of priests from their parishes."

"You could spend the long vacations there, with short visits in between. Bishops seem quite ready to grant permission for lengthy periods away from parishes for study at the university."

"Whatever decision I make, I must first be ordained to the priesthood. That means a journey to my home diocese of York."

"Time away from Oxford may be just what you need. Different surroundings may help you think more clearly. The archbishop of York is a good man. Perhaps he may have some advice for you."

"I look forward to meeting John Thoresby. He is, by the way, a Yorkshireman, so we should feel a certain kinship."

"Considering the gifts God has given you, I can't believe he means you to cut short a promising career and spend the rest of your life in a remote rural parish."

"You encourage me to do what I really want to do. One way out, of course, would be to refuse the benefice, which I can hardly afford to do. Quite honestly, I need the money."

Brut looked thoughtful. As they parted, he said, "Of course you would not accept the benefice solely for the money."

Wycliffe knew that his friend expected no response, but the statement troubled him.

3. April 1361—York

Wycliffe drew his cloak more closely against the chill of early April. A moon just past full would provide visibility until the sun rose. A journey of eight or ten days lay ahead of him. York was some two hundred miles to the north. A recent thaw meant muddy roads and slow travel.

Far more difficult to endure than the journey was his inner turmoil. By afternoon of the tenth day as he passed within the walls of York at Micklegate, his mind was made up. *I can't give up my plans. I mean to preach, but not to spend my life as a parish priest. I'll follow the usual pattern of appointing a curate.*

York was an ancient city and the largest Wycliffe had visited. He continued on to the river Ouse, which flowed through the center of the city. Crossing the bridge, he entered the inner city by the Ousegate. His first concern was to find an inn. *After a night's sleep and a chance to repair the ravages of travel,* he thought, *I'll be in a better frame of mind to face the archbishop.*

He was unprepared for the crowded streets at the early hour at which he set forth in search of St. Peter's Cathedral, known as the Minster. Jostled on all sides, he found it difficult to keep his footing. Suddenly he looked up and beheld the magnificent twin towers ahead of him. So struck was he by the majesty that he stood still, ignoring the complaints of those whose progress he hampered.

He pushed his way gently but firmly through the throng. As he entered the nave, he was staggered by its wide expanse. Lifting his eyes upward, he gazed in awe at the wonders surrounding him. Breathless, not realizing that he spoke aloud, he cried, "I feel so small!"

A voice behind him said, "I understand. Even after several years I still experience the same sensation when I stand here."

Wycliffe turned to find one of the young canons at his elbow. "If you are a stranger, could I help you?" the man asked.

"Your help will be most welcome," cried Wycliffe. He stated his name and his purpose. "I have letters of introduction to the archbishop. Could you tell me where I might find him?"

The canon smiled. "He is probably not available at the moment. The archbishop spends much time at the construction site of the choir. By noon he generally descends to the world of ordinary men. Until then, could I show you around?"

Wycliffe followed his new friend down the expanse of the nave. Gazing at the carving over the doors as they moved along, he said, "This part must be quite old."

"You're right. The transepts and chapter house are the earliest parts. Work there began nearly a century and a half ago. Completing what the archbishop proposes may take another century, but he plunges ahead as if he expected to see it done in his lifetime."

The tour ended with Wycliffe's head in a whirl. He was glad to share a simple meal with the canons at noon.

4. April 1361—Perplexity

John Thoresby had been archbishop of York since 1352 and was known as one who performed his episcopal duties with uncompromising zeal. He received Wycliffe cordially and gave him the greater part of the afternoon. He expounded first upon the building project, showing Wycliffe the plans and making detailed explanations.

As he talked, the archbishop's eyes took on a faraway look, as if seeing the finished sanctuary and the glory of the east window in place. In a moment he returned his attention to Wycliffe. "I cannot expect you to have the same interest in this that I do. Let us talk now of the work of the Lord as it goes on at present."

"I have heard," said Wycliffe, "of the personal interest you take in the parish priests and vicars under your care."

"They need help and encouragement. I do my best to supply it. I've prepared a catechism for their use, simple enough for all to read and understand, written in both Latin and English."

Wycliffe sat up straight. "What does it contain, and how is it used?" he asked eagerly.

"My deep concern is for the people, who are poorly taught, in general. This roots back partly to the Great Mortality, which claimed so many priests. We've had to replace them with men hardly qualified. The people must not learn just by rote memory with no understanding."

"But where do you begin?" asked Wycliffe.

"The Lord's Prayer, the Creed, and the Commandments are enough to start on. I insist that my priests expound these at least on the Lord's Day, along with the Seven Deadly Sins and the Seven Virtues."

"Such repetition should be effective," said Wycliffe.

"As you enter the priesthood, be sure to do this bit of teaching as an absolute minimum. Of course, you'll do more. For the people to hear God's Word taught regularly in their mother tongue is of greater importance than to hear many masses."

Wycliffe shifted uneasily. "I'm not sure I'll be serving my parish in person, Sir. You see, I have just become *magister artium* and I expect to take up theological studies. Too, as regent master I'm required to teach for at least two years."

"Of course," said the archbishop quietly, "it is a matter of setting your priorities."

"Are theological studies not a priority? I could spend the long vacations in my parish. A curate could carry on the work."

"From whose hand does this benefice come? The pope? The authorities of Balliol college?"

After some hesitation, Wycliffe replied, "From God's hand. The pope and the college are channels through which he works."

"Since that is the case, perhaps God means you to serve the people of Fillingham parish. There may be souls wandering in darkness to whom you could bring the light of the Gospel."

"It's perplexing, Sir. I'm torn apart. God's ways are hard to understand. I felt so sure he meant me to follow this program of studies and teaching. Is he now asking me to give that up? I do, with all my heart, want to do his will."

"Did the call come to you or to some unnamed curate?"

After another long silence Wycliffe spoke in a low tone. "Could we talk again tomorrow? I need more time."

"Take what time you need. You must be certain."

The conversation proceeded along other lines. "How could I obtain a copy of your catechism?" asked Wycliffe.

Thoresby smiled. "I intend giving you one. Most have taken to calling it The Lay Folks Catechism. That's a good enough title. While primarily intended for the priest, it should also be used by lay people who can read. They should teach it to their households and thus undergird the priest's teaching."

Wycliffe learned that the archbishop had a concern not only for helping his clergy with teaching material but with needs as well. Many vicars charged with the cure of souls did not have adequate living quarters. Thoresby had seen to it that vicarages were erected in some of the poorer parishes. When he found endowments too small, he quietly augmented them himself.

The archbishop agreed to arrange for ordination to take place two days later on a Saturday, as was usual. He would have other conferences with Wycliffe before then.

5. April 1361—Struggle

Wycliffe returned to his inn heavy in mind and spirit. After striving hopelessly to reach a reasoned conclusion, he burst forth at last with, "I won't do it! It makes no sense at all. I've labored too desperately to reach this point. How can God expect me to throw it all away for a country parish?"

Sleep was out of the question. Things Thoresby had said kept coming back. The catechism, the need of the people to hear the Gospel, the opportunity for teaching that could lay a foundation for changed lives. The slight stir of excitement he had felt as he listened to the archbishop surfaced again.

At last, with a weariness as deep as if he had undergone a physical struggle, he lay down. "I know how Jacob felt after he had wrestled all night with the angel," he said. He slept for the brief time that remained until dawn.

When he came into the archbishop's presence, he looked at him for a moment without speaking. Then he said quietly, "I will go to Fillingham. I cannot struggle against God."

"I prayed for you through the night, my son," said the archbishop. "God has surely guided you to the right decision."

They discussed the meaning of ordination and talked of Wycliffe's ministry, and he knew he was truly committed. As he sought words with which to express this, the touch of the archbishop's hand on his arm told him no words were needed.

"Throw yourself into your work at Fillingham," said Thoresby. "Get to know and love your people. Preach the Word. Guide your people by precept and example in living the Christian life. You will be a blessing to them and they to you." With a twinkle in his eye he added, "You may learn as much or more than you teach."

"I no longer doubt that this is God's will, sir. It is what our Lord himself did...what he commissioned his disciples to do."

"After a couple of years, see how things are going. Perhaps then you might ask your bishop's permission to return to your studies. You will have trained a curate to carry on as you have begun. God does not mean to deprive you of further studies, but only to prepare you more fully for them."

Wycliffe spent the hours before his ordination in quiet prayer. He took his vows with a submissive heart, deeply committed to doing the will of God, wherever it might lead.

He felt an exhilaration of spirit as he journeyed back. *The road seems smoother*, he thought, *and the miles go more swiftly*. Before it seemed possible, he glimpsed the spires of St. Mary's and St. Frideswide's. Outside the North Gate he passed within the walls of Balliol.

6. April-July 1361—Preparation

His friends were astounded at his decision. He made no effort to defend his action, but quietly stated that this was what he must do. Only Brut and Rede seemed to understand the choice he had made.

Almost immediately orders from the bishop of Lincoln came summoning Wycliffe to Holbeach to await institution to Fillingham parish.

"Why Holbeach?" asked Brut.

"Apparently it suits Bishop Gynwell's convenience. You have to admit, it would be awkward for me to go to Fillingham for the installation while the priest is still alive."

"I'm not sure of the exact location of Holbeach."

"It's three or four days' journey from here," said Wycliffe. "I follow the route I took to York as far as Stamford, then turn off to find Holbeach. This is certainly more convenient for me."

He made his arrangements and departed. Ten days later, to Brut's astonishment, he was back.

"You are looking at the newly instituted parish priest of Fillingham," Wycliffe said. "On the 13th of May word came that John Reynor had died. All was in order, so my installation took place next day. There was nothing to hold me, so I turned my steps toward home."

"When will you leave for Fillingham?"

"The bishop agreed to a delay of several weeks, since I have matters to clear up here. I think late June or early July would be a fair estimate of my departure time."

"Well, I regret that I won't be able to help you move this time," said Brut, with a smile. "Fillingham is out of bounds."

Wycliffe gave him an affectionate clap on the back.

One thing and another delayed his departure for Fillingham. Finally, the last week in June saw the final act in which he would sign his name as master of Balliol.

Brut and Rede had remained at Oxford during the long vacation and were on hand to see him off. The morning of his departure arrived, dreary and overcast.

"I could have hoped for sunshine," Wycliffe said. "At least that would have made things seem brighter."

"Be thankful for small favors," said Brut. "The July sunshine can make for uncomfortable travel."

"Don't be downhearted, Wycliffe," said Rede. "You must not take a heavy heart to your new field of labor."

"I'm in a peculiar situation," said Wycliffe. "I don't want to go, yet I don't want to stay. It reminds me of the first time I left home for Oxford." With difficulty in controlling his emotions, he added, "I'm going to miss you two. Nobody to talk to, nobody to argue with."

They fell silent. Just then his man came up with the horses. With a tender touch on the shoulder for each of them and a smile that was rather too close to tears, Wycliffe swung into the saddle and turned his back on Oxford. It was a low moment.

7. July 1361—Fillingham

Rain fell every day. The inns at which he found lodging were depressing. Several beds to a room, two men to a bed. A general lack of cleanliness prevailed, accompanied with infestations of fleas or other vermin.

"If, by God's grace, I arrive at the end of this journey," he said to his servant, "I shall remain there for the rest of my days. I am dirty, I am hungry, I am unbelievably weary. I shall travel about my parish on foot and never mount another horse."

He soon felt ashamed of this outburst. *Surely*, he thought, *we must be nearing Lincoln.* As he scanned the horizon, the majestic spire of the Lincoln cathedral appeared, piercing the clouds.

Hastening his pace, he entered the lower town and made his way toward the steep incline which led up to the cathedral. He had a special purpose in making this detour from the direct path to Fillingham. Leaving his weary horse with the servant, he climbed the precipitous way on foot.

He entered through the Norman doorway and paused for a moment before passing down the nave through the forest of Purbeck marble and limestone pillars. At the eastern transept he turned right and halted again. Then with reverent steps he approached the magnificent marble monument marking the tomb of Robert Grosseteste.

More than a century had passed since Bishop Grosseteste laid down his crozier and entered into his eternal rest. His tomb had become a shrine, though more than one pope had ignored the request for his canonization.

Wycliffe stood with bowed head. "He feared no man, not even the pope," he murmured, "but only God. His courage stands as a beacon to all who would follow Truth. I owe him much." He knelt in prayer.

Ten more miles to Fillingham. He should reach journey's end before sunset. Not so many sheep as in Yorkshire, he noticed, but now and then a sizable flock dotted a wide sweep of pasture. Tiny hamlets lay in secluded hollows and on hillsides, each surrounded by its strips of cultivated land.

He slowed his pace. To this point he had pressed ahead with eagerness to finish the miserable journey. Now, nearing his goal, he wanted to hold back.

What is it? he asked himself. *Certainly not fear. True, I face a new situation. Yet why is this so different from my first journey to Oxford? I faced the unknown then even as I do now. Yet I do not remember experiencing this hesitancy, almost an unwillingness to take the final steps.*

This comes from something more than merely facing the new. At Oxford my chief responsibility was to my studies. My life did not so much affect others. What I do and say here, how I live, may affect for eternity those to whom I minister.

Speaking aloud now through stiff lips, he cried, "Oh, God! How awesome is the task to which you have called me. Give me grace, O my God, else I am quite unable for the task."

"Master," his servant called, "here we turn."

Excitement stirred again as he entered the rough and somewhat overgrown road. Soon three small cottages with weather-worn thatching appeared on the left, then a larger stone cottage on the right, and a bit farther two more thatched cottages. He slowed his pace, looking for the church.

"There it is!" he cried at length. Through the trees the unmistakable stone structure became visible. Dismounting, he handed the reins to his servant. "Remain here," he said. "I shall not be long."

He followed a path between a double row of ancient limes, past scattered tombstones. A gap through overhanging foliage permitted him a clear view of a square tower rising above a small porch with arched openings on three sides.

To the north stretched an open field. To the west he glimpsed a lake. Elms and oaks towered over the church, with a few yew trees beneath.

He entered the little porch and tried the massive door, fearing to find it locked, but it opened readily. The interior was little different from parish churches in other rural areas, but as he stood in the nave, this one became quite special. Here he would meet with God's people. Approaching the altar, he knelt to meet first with God alone.

As he closed the door and turned to leave, he almost collided with a man coming toward him. It was the verger. "Good evening, Father, and welcome," he cried. "Didn't know just when to expect you. Hardly fitting that you should arrive and find no one about."

Wycliffe fixed his eyes on the kindly face. *My first parishioner*, he thought. *What will the others be like?*

"You'll be wanting to see the rectory across the way. It's ready for you, all fresh and clean." He led the way across the road to a small, neat-looking house standing in a grove of oaks.

"Someone will be right along with refreshment. You'll be hot and tired, and in need of rest."

The wearisome journey was over. Night fell and he was alone. He stretched out gratefully on the bed. *Home! I'm home*, he thought. *Tomorrow begins my new life. Rector of St. Andrew's parish church, Fillingham. I rather like the sound of that.*

8. July-December 1361—A Beginning

Wycliffe immediately threw himself into his work. Unexpected difficulties faced him. Uncertainty gripped

St. Andrew's Church at Fillingham, Wycliffe's first benefice, near Lincoln

him as he stood in the pulpit. What should he preach to these people? How could he reach them? They were a diverse lot.

William de Bandolf, a knight, was lord of the manor. He and his wife lived in the manor house set back from the road just past the church. He had a ten-year-old son, Thomas, and several younger children. Sir William spent part of his time at other manors in his possession. Local villagers in his employ worked his land, and a shepherd cared for his sheep.

Remnants of a Neville family still lived in the area, their prominence due to the sturdy crossbowmen they once provided for the king. Except for a few other families with large holdings the greater part of the population consisted of farm workers, laborers, craftsmen, and household servants. There were no serfs. The different groups seemed to get on well. At least Wycliffe found no open quarrels in the early days. None seemed to be very spiritual-minded. He would have to feel his way.

He preached a sermon on prayer. "Prayer stands principally in a good life, and of this prayer Christ speaks when he says in the Gospel that we must always pray. Prayer is worth nothing unless it is done with devotion, cleanness, and holiness of life. The prayer of a layman who shall be saved is better than the prayer of a prelate who shall be damned."

The people seemed to listen, but their acceptance of him was tentative. Some appeared shocked at his suggestion that a prelate could be damned!

Can they be so naive, he wondered, *as not to know that devotion, cleanness, and holiness of life is not characteristic of every prelate? Do they believe that all priests and prelates are bound with certainty for heaven?*

He preached on faith. "Faith, like lenses properly arranged, will enable us to see things far off as if they were near, and to read minute letters like young men."

He pondered upon that sermon. *They don't know what I'm talking about,* he mused. *They are not ready yet for "strong meat." "Milk" it must be for a while.*

He sighed and dug deeper into the Scriptures, first for his own benefit, then for food for his parishioners. *God's Word,* he thought, *is the most important study of all. I must strive so to teach that it will enter their hearts and lives. Repetition is the key. The old prophet says, "Precept upon precept, line upon line, line upon line, here a little, there a little." True, the prophet's hearers scoffed, but he was right.*

To his chagrin, the people assigned greatest importance to ceremonies such as processions around the church building and to reciting endless Pater Nosters and Ave Marias in Latin. His vehemence in speaking to them on this subject offended them. Things should continue as they had always been!

He contented himself for a while with employing almost exclusively the archbishop's "Lay Folks Catechism." He amplified the suggestions for the use of the Lord's Prayer. Slowly they learned to recite it from memory in English. This was a first step. He paused often to explain again the meaning of a phrase. Visiting among them gave opportunity for questioning them on the matters upon which he preached and taught.

As he got to know them, he felt more comfortable, and the feeling seemed mutual. A woman who served as a domestic in the manor house approached him timidly, asking, "Father, when the pardoner comes 'round, he says if we confess our sins and then pay him a penny, the sins are all forgiven. Why, when we confess to you, must we do penance?"

The opening he had hoped for! "It is a false idea to think that money payment can remove sin," he explained. "Neither payment nor penance mean anything. What matters is repentance, being sorry for breaking God's law, resolving to keep it in the future, and asking God's help. Doing penance is to remind the sinner how grievous is his sin in God's sight and to help him avoid repeating it."

This was a difficult idea to get across, because they did not want to believe it. How much simpler just to pay, receive absolution, and forget about it.

9. 1362—Westbury-on-Trym

As the weeks grew into months, he found his hands more than full. *Thoresby was right*, he wrote to Brut. *I seem to be learning more than I teach. I find the slow spiritual growth of my parishioners discouraging. Perhaps this is not the work I am best fitted for, but it is a work to which God has called me. No matter how I feel, he must mean to accomplish something through me—and in me.*

He received frequent invitations to the manor house. Sir William seemed to enjoy his company. Perhaps the fact that the rector, too, was lord of a manor gave his host a closer feeling. As they walked through the fields, Sir William talked freely of crops and political issues. But when Wycliffe suggested that he have prayer with his household and instruct his children and servants, he fell silent or gave an indifferent response.

When the newness had worn off, the villagers welcomed him into their humble homes. He tried to be impartial in visiting his parishioners, but his feet turned often to a cottage near the west end of the village where lived Martin, one of those who farmed the lord's lands.

Martin owned a small plot of land and took pride in keeping his cottage neat and in good repair. Moreover, he was one of the few heads of families who made a real effort to have prayer in his home and train his children as far as he was able.

His wife Beatrice kept a careful eye on her vegetable plot, managing to choose some choice bit for the rector on his visits. She found joy, too, in her flower garden, which produced in glorious profusion, according to the season, violets, roses, daisies, lilies, marigolds, and dainty columbine. Two children, Joan and Thomas, often sat beside the priest in the garden and listened eagerly to the Bible stories he related.

When the old urge to be in the great outdoors asserted itself, he took the path to the lake. It was a small body, perhaps a mile in length and three miles around. While it belonged to the lord, it had by long custom been the property of the village. Any who wished might take from its abundant supply of fish. Geese and swans often graced its bosom. Sometimes young Thomas from the manor house, or the other Thomas and his sister, joined him in his walks.

A letter came from Rede. *The return of the pestilence during the last year has caused heavy losses*, he wrote. *Among others, Henry, duke of Lancaster, succumbed. John of Gaunt, third son of the king, and your overlord at Wycliffe, succeeds to that position.*

On a brighter note, we have a new pope. Urban V may be a different sort from his predecessors. He was not of the college of cardinals, but abbot of the Benedictine convent of St. Victor at Marseilles. He is reported to have said, when he had no inkling that he would ever be pope, that if a pope were elected who would restore the papacy to Rome, he would die content. We shall see whether he decides to die content.

Wycliffe paused in his reading and exclaimed, "A different sort of pope! Perhaps God has sent us a man who will work to restore the papacy to what it should be."

The letter continued, *The university has forwarded its roll of masters, including your name and mine, to the new pope asking that he exercise the power of provision in their behalf. For you a canonry and prebend of York is requested, 'notwithstanding that he holds the church of Fillingham, value thirty marks.'*

"The scoundrel!" cried Wycliffe. "He has made no mention of what his prospect is! That, naturally, I am eager to know." He gave a sigh of pure delight. "A canonry and prebend of York, with no requirement that I give up Fillingham. York is near enough that I can easily give some time there. Incredible that I should have the opportunity of working with John Thoresby!" He continued to dream happy dreams of what the future held.

The response of the new pope came as a rude shock. He provided for Wycliffe, but not the requested post. In late December of 1362 the news reached Fillingham.

"A canonry in the collegiate church of Westbury-on-Trym as prebendary of Aust!" exclaimed Wycliffe. "I can't believe it. I never heard of Westbury-on-Trym. Where is it?"

The more he learned, the more disgusted he became. Located far to the west, near Bristol, the church was described as "destitute of counsel and ministers."

"I have no doubt of its need," cried Wycliffe, "but I am not the man to meet the need. The pope knew I had Fillingham. How impractical to appoint me to a place as far away as possible."

He knew in his heart that he had no intention of spending much time at either post. "I've been here two years," he said. "It's time to return to my studies. During the long vacations I can serve my parish. A curate can carry on in my absence."

A summons arrived from the dean at Westbury-on-Trym requiring his presence for induction into his new post. He ground his teeth, and complied. Upon reaching Bristol, he learned that Westbury was located three miles farther.

The dean, Richard de Cornwall, inducted him into possession of the canonry and prebendary. He took an oath to observe the statutes of the church. "You are not required to serve in person," said the dean, "but you must provide a vicar to serve in your place."

"A vicar!" he muttered to himself. "Where will I find a vicar? Nearer London I might find someone, but who would come to this remote spot for the pittance I can pay?"

10. August-September 1363—Request Granted

At the end of August Wycliffe presented himself at Lincoln cathedral before the newly consecrated bishop, John Buckingham. His purpose was to request a license for non-residence at Fillingham, that he might return to his studies at the university. This was common practice with respect to theological students. Buckingham delayed only long enough to be sure his scribe extracted the expected fee for the license. *Always a fee for any transaction*, thought Wycliffe. He returned to Fillingham, the document in hand.

"Free!" he cried exultantly. "Free to return to Oxford. I have fulfilled the conditions recommended by Archbishop Thoresby two years ago. Surely he would approve my present action."

He spent the month of September getting things in order and making sure his curate knew what was expected of him. Leaving was not easy. He had become attached to his parishioners, who wept and begged him not to go. With assurances that he would return at the long vacation, he departed, allowing time to reach Oxford before the opening of the new term.

As he rode along, he gave a deep sigh. *I arranged for Fillingham, but I've done nothing about Westbury-on-Trym. Where will I find someone willing to supply that post?*

11. October-November 1363—Oxford Again

Among the most enthusiastic of those welcoming him back was Nicholas Hereford. Brut and Rede received him with open arms, along with a number of old friends, masters as well as students. After investigation as to living arrangements, he engaged rooms at Queen's. This college, due to a perpetual shortage of funds, was always glad to accommodate lodgers.

"You'll be interested to know," said Brut, "that the archbishop of Canterbury is establishing a college to be called Canterbury Hall. He has received a charter from the king, allowing for a warden and three monks from Christ Church at Canterbury and eight needy secular scholars."

"Seculars and regulars studying together!" cried Wycliffe. "I'm amazed and delighted. Tell me more."

"The seculars are to have decidedly lower status than the monks."

"That will cause trouble," said Wycliffe. "The archbishop has made a serious error."

"Not his only mistake," said Brut. "He has made Henry Wodehull warden. Wodehull is a troublemaker of long standing."

Wycliffe sighed. "Such a college is an excellent idea, but he is not going about it in the right way. Too bad."

Wycliffe assumed his teaching duties as regent master. He had long had his lectures in logic and philosophy prepared. To his joy, he found the load not so heavy as to prevent his beginning theological studies.

He must first follow the biblical course. After obtaining a baccalaureate in theology, he could enter the systematic section. Biblical studies consisted of reading and interpreting Old and New Testament. The Scriptures were studied from the Latin Vulgate. Interpretation took the form of glosses or brief comments and explanation inserted between the lines or in the margin.

Rede asked Wycliffe, "What led you to the study of theology?"

"I suppose," he said, "it's been a growing thing. At first it was what my father wanted for me. Always a passion for truth has lured me. In the year of the Great Mortality I discovered that ultimate Truth is found in the Scriptures. In any field, whatever professes to be truth must be tested by the truth of Scripture. Surely that branch known as the queen of sciences deserves my best efforts."

His duties as regent master presented a growing challenge. Eager students crowded his lectures. He attained a high reputation as scholar and teacher. Other masters and teachers treated him with marked respect, in spite of his philosophical position as an ultra-realist. At this time the popular position was that of nominalism. He made enemies over this issue, but even enemies respected his scholarship.

12. 1364—Deep into Theology

That winter was the most severe within memory. A great frost descended in November and lasted until March, affecting the continent as well as England. The Rhone froze at Avignon and the Meuse at Liege. Oxford suffered greatly. Shivering beside his inadequate charcoal burner, Wycliffe longed for the great fireplace in the manor house beside the Tees.

Although his biblical studies at this time were in the Old Testament, he found that the reading and rereading of the New Testament he had done during the Great Mortality cast light upon the Old Testament. Two years of sermon preparation and preaching at Fillingham had deepened his understanding of Scripture.

"This is the most fulfilling experience I have known," he cried to Brut. "It is not just a matter of reading the words, but of tasting, savoring, digesting them. I write my own notes and record my own thoughts as I read of God's dealings with men."

"You really are excited over this study of Scripture," said Brut. "It seems to make you come alive in a new way."

"I marvel at the beauty of the language, but it is the content of the matter that charms me. The unfolding of Creation is breathtaking. I agonize over the tragedy of the Fall. Then comes Abraham with his strong faith, followed by Joseph, Moses, Joshua—they all come alive."

His friendship with Walter Brut continued to deepen. He also made warm friendships with others in theological studies. Common interests led to the development of strong bonds. Wycliffe soon realized that several of these men were beginning to attach themselves to him as disciples. This pleased him, but it also placed a heavy responsibility on him.

Early one April evening Brut pulled Wycliffe away from his desk. "We thought spring would never happen again, but it has arrived. Breathing a a bit of it should clear your brain."

They followed the Thames along a path carpeted with soft green grass. New leaves on the trees and the gold of daffodils announced unmistakably the miracle of the escape of earth from winter's icy grip. They strode along in companionable silence.

Wycliffe broke the spell. "In studying the Scriptures I must be free to hear what they say to me. Why are we restricted to what the Fathers thought they said?"

"Perhaps the Fathers were wiser than you or I," said Brut.

"I don't discount their wisdom. Much in their writings is valuable, even essential. But I refuse to be bound, even by Augustine, as greatly as I admire him. I must do some thinking on my own."

"Isn't it possible you might get off the track and head in a wrong direction?"

"What if I do take some wrong turns, as I undoubtedly will? Does not learning come by that path? An increase of knowledge should lead to correction of errors. I may find myself coming back to accept what I previously doubted or rejected."

Brut pondered this. "That course may prove right for you. Your mind outreaches what most of us are capable of. I have no special confidence in my own powers of independent thinking as yet. I need someone to follow, a guide."

"Someone to follow, yes, but not slavishly. Another thing disturbs me: the attitude of advanced theological students toward biblical studies and biblical students."

"They do seem to look down upon the study of the Scriptures as somehow inferior."

"Scripture is the necessary foundation of all theological study. Why do they consider it merely preparatory for what they call theology proper? They apparently have little use for the Scriptures, once they move on to advanced courses."

"From what you've said about the lectures of Fitzralph, he didn't follow that line."

"Indeed he did not. In teaching against error in any form, he consistently appealed to scriptural rather than scholastic proofs. However, there are few of Fitzralph's stature among us."

Such outings, though infrequent, did much to keep Wycliffe's spirits up. He appreciated the opportunity to exchange ideas with Brut. In some ways Brut was a puzzle. He had entered wholeheartedly into theological studies, but had no interest in pursuing a career in the church. He came from Wales and called himself a Briton, fiercely proud of his ancient heritage. Because of his distinguished background, he found acceptance in circles which he might not have otherwise. Yet this seemed unimportant to him.

With the October term Wycliffe entered his second year of theology. His notes on the Scriptures were growing into a sizable commentary, incorporating much of what he found excellent from the teaching of others, as well as his own thoughts.

"If only I could speed things up," he cried impatiently. "Once I attain the status of bachelor of theology, I'll be permitted to expound the Scriptures in my own lectures. That goal seems so far away."

The passing months brought him to the historical books of the Bible, where he walked alongside the participants in the drama. The Psalms and wisdom literature charmed him.

Then came the prophets! His own voice thundered out the denunciations against the sins of the people. He joined Isaiah's call to repentance. His sobs blended with those of Jeremiah over Jerusalem. He trod the weary miles to Babylon with the exiles. He exulted over the Messianic prophecies describing future glory.

13. 1365—Pope's Demands

Parliament sought to halt certain ecclesiastical abuses, especially the pope's arbitrary provisions of rich benefices for his favorites overseas. English gold was still being drained off into the papal coffers. In a final move Parliament decided to withhold the grant of

Peter's Pence, that annual tax due the pope from every person who owned property.

Wycliffe discussed this news with John Aston, a fellow of Merton who had become an admirer of his. "The action taken is proper, but trouble will follow. We may find our Holy Father not so holy as we have been led to believe."

"I can hardly imagine him remaining calm when he hears of Peter's Pence being withheld," replied Aston. "He's probably unhappy already over the search constantly being made at Calais to discover persons carrying gold and silver."

They were not wrong, as Aston confirmed as he burst in a few days later. "Can you believe that the pope has retaliated by demanding that the king pay the annual tribute of 1,000 marks agreed to by King John in the last century?"

"Ridiculous!" cried Wycliffe. "Surely he can't be serious."

"Oh, but he is," Aston said. "He also demands the arrears since the last payment. That, he reminds us, was in 1333."

"Does he really think England will pay?"

"He means to assure it. He threatens to take proceedings in his own courts, should Edward III default. Now that peace is restored and England is rich, she can meet her obligations."

"The king will have to lay it before Parliament. Of course they cannot agree to such an outlandish demand."

"These things drag along. No action will be taken before next year."

"By the way," said Wycliffe as Aston turned to leave, "the archbishop's Canterbury Hall has problems. Wodehull is unreasonable, and the secular scholars are dissatisfied."

"Joint education of monks and priests has long been a dream of many. It's a good idea, but apparently one that's not going to work in this case."

"I think one problem is that the archbishop is sick and unable to keep in close touch. Wodehull has taken too much upon himself," said Wycliffe. "Maybe it can be salvaged."

The matter continued to trouble Wycliffe. He had hoped that such a plan could succeed, that even on this small scale regulars and seculars could live and study together harmoniously.

As he entered his third year of biblical studies, he was now into the New Testament. This was perhaps the happiest time he had yet experienced. God's presence became very real. The Scriptures opened up more and more. "*Truth!*" he would whisper. "*This is truth that is not found in its entirety elsewhere.*"

Late in November he received a summons from the archbishop. Islip wished to see him at his earliest convenience. He was residing in his palace at Mayfield, struggling to recover from a stroke suffered some months earlier. His business was urgent.

"At my earliest convenience!" exclaimed Wycliffe to Brut. "It's not convenient at all."

"But," Brut pointed out, "one does not take lightly a summons from the archbishop."

"True. I must arrange for a brief absence and be on my way to Sussex. My curiosity is aroused."

"Mine as well. I shall await your return with impatience."

14. November 1365-May 1366
Canterbury Hall

The archbishop took his time with the interview. Wycliffe returned to Oxford perplexed in mind. He sent immediately for Brut. Upon reflection he called John Aston as well.

"I called you two because of your special interest in the matter. I need your thinking on a strange situation."

"Don't keep us waiting," said Brut. "It's bound to have something to do with Canterbury Hall."

"The archbishop has decided that the project is a failure. He wants to give up the attempt to include regulars and seculars in the same institution. He has determined to remove Wodehull and the other monks. It will remain an institution for seculars alone."

"How can he do that?" asked Brut. "He doubtless has power to remove the warden, but to change the purpose for which the college was initiated will go against the terms of his charter."

"He plans to revise the statutes. This will cause trouble in the chapter at Christ Church, but he feels sure he can manage."

"Why give up the plan?" asked Aston. "Wodehall was a bad choice as warden. Why not replace him with another monk?"

"His mind is made up," continued Wycliffe. "Now, as to why he sent for me..."

"Yes, what does it have to do with you?" asked Aston.

"I could guess," said Brut, "but tell us plainly."

Wycliffe sighed. "It's a real puzzler. He wants to appoint me warden of Canterbury Hall and replace the three monks with three seculars. I hardly know what to think."

"I know what to think," cried Brut. "The archbishop offers you an opportunity to take over and build up this college."

"His particular interest," said Aston, "was to provide poor scholars with an opportunity to complete their studies in theology. You recognize the importance of that."

"How did he happen to select you?" asked Brut. "He has little personal acquaintance with you."

"Largely my reputation, such as it is. He was overly generous in his assessment of my character and abilities."

"Word about you does get around," exclaimed Brut. "Tell us what he said."

"I'll tell you, but do not repeat it. The choice fell upon me because of his confidence in my fidelity, circumspection, and industry. He found my conversation laudable, my life honest and above reproach, and my knowledge of letters outstanding."

Brut whistled. "Quite a commendation!"

"What did you tell him?" asked Aston.

"That I would consider the matter seriously and be in prayer about it. I'm to give him my answer within a fortnight."

"You feel some uncertainty as to your answer?" asked Brut.

"It's too important a matter to give a spur-of-the-moment reply. In the light of what you two have said, I'm fairly certain what my answer should be, but I must be sure. You do understand that this is a confidential matter. Neither of you must discuss it with others. Islip has yet to take action."

The outcome was that an irate Wodehull and the monks, ousted by the archbishop, were forced into an unwilling retreat to Canterbury. On December 9, 1365, the archbishop signed at Mayfield a deed naming John Wycliffe warden of Canterbury Hall. He replaced the three monks with three seculars: William Selby, William Middleworth, and Richard Benger, all from Merton.

The new statutes altered the character of the college, making it chiefly for seculars, though in theory monks from Christ Church might still be received. Islip made these changes without consulting his chapter, deeming it unnecessary.

"Does the college own any books?" Rede wanted to know.

"A few. Islip intends to donate his personal library."

Brut, with a look of amusement, asked, "When are you moving? I suppose I'm still in charge of that department."

Wycliffe laughed. "Good of you to remain on call!"

As they busied themselves with this task, Brut laughed at Wycliffe's bubbling excitement. "I do realize, my friend," he said, "that you are entering upon a work you had not anticipated, but one which gives you a marvelous opportunity. Who knows better than you the need for more parish priests?"

"One matter keeps creeping in to disturb my joy," said Wycliffe. "The need to supply a vicar for Westbury gnaws at my conscience. Yet my hands are too full just now to give it much thought. I keep saying, 'I'll attend to it later.'"

"You had better settle that matter," said Brut. "It's not right to leave the spot unfilled."

With a sigh, Wycliffe agreed. Within a week he had found a man who was willing to go. One less thing on his mind.

Then came a stunning blow: Simon Islip, archbishop of Canterbury, died. "What will happen with regard to Canterbury Hall?" asked Wycliffe in alarm. "The chapter at Christ Church has not adopted the changed statutes, nor has the king given his approval."

"Furthermore," reported Aston, "Wodehull and the monks are waiting about hoping a new archbishop may reinstate them."

"Islip appointed me warden," insisted Wycliffe, "and I intend to remain. I must see his purpose carried out, his dream fulfilled."

Days later Parliament opened, and Wycliffe's mind became occupied with the subject to be dealt with there. The king, as expected, laid the matter of the pope's demand for the tribute money before Parliament.

The unanimous response was that neither King John in the previous century nor any other king could bring this realm into such subjection to the pope, except by consent of Parliament. Should the pope attempt such action as threatened, the king with all his subjects would resist with force and power.

"Will this end the matter?" fumed Wycliffe. "I doubt it."

15. July 1366-February 1368—Complications

"Simon Langham has been appointed archbishop of Canterbury in Islip's place," cried Wycliffe in dismay.

"Bad news, that," said Aston.

"Bad news! It's the worst news possible. The monks of Canterbury will lose no time lodging an appeal with a Benedictine archbishop."

With three years of biblical studies behind him, he now entered upon the study of the Sentences of Peter Lombard. Yet worries concerning the future of Canterbury Hall plagued him.

On March 25, 1367, Simon Langham was enthroned as archbishop of Canterbury. He immediately acted to deprive Wycliffe of his wardenship and reinstated Wodehall.

Wycliffe raged. He called in Selby, Middleworth, and Benger. "You replaced the three monks at Islip's order, so you may be sure the archbishop aims at you as well as at me. We do not give in to him. Here Islip placed us, and here we remain." He stubbornly refused to admit Wodehull and the monks. The impasse continued.

When the archbishop saw that Wycliffe was not going to give up, he sequestrated the revenues and confiscated the books which Islip had left to Wycliffe for the college.

"I have too many things on my mind to be forced to fight the archbishop," cried Wycliffe. "Now he's trying to starve us out. Without income we shall be hard pressed to continue."

"Shouldn't we perhaps give up now?" asked Selby. "Without financial resources, how can we live? We could still make other arrangements."

Wycliffe glared at him. "Give up? Certainly not! We'll hold on until justice is rendered. The archbishop is a thief. Islip left the books to the college, but in my hands."

When Langham saw that previous measures had failed, he ordered the expulsion of Wycliffe and his three associates.

At this Wycliffe exploded with rage. "He orders me expelled? Well, let him come and remove me bodily. I shall appeal to the pope. Surely he will see that justice is done." The university, to his disappointment, did not come to his aid.

Aston was concerned over his friend's predicament. He found him edgy and distraught. "You should give up, Wycliffe. You fight against opponents who are too powerful."

"No!" cried Wycliffe. "I'll fight to the end. If I'm defeated, I shall at least know I did not act the weakling, but stood for justice. Let them be the ones at fault. I am not."

"Your appeal was not overly strong. You justified Islip's action only on the basis that it was an archbishop's mandate."

"That should carry enough weight," exploded Wycliffe. "What more is needed?"

In the end the pope heard the case, but delayed action. He referred the matter to a cardinal and empowered him to act. The cardinal was in no hurry to do so.

16. March-October 1368
Change Contemplated

One morning as Wycliffe sat deep in study, a startling thought intruded. Leaping up, he exclaimed, "My license to be absent from my parish is about to expire. I dare not let that happen. Have five years passed since I got that first license? Seven years since I entered my work at Fillingham?"

His application to the bishop received favorable action. A new license permitted him another two years in which to study.

"I'll go to Fillingham," he said. "I have neglected my people. Spending time with them will be a pleasant change from the strife here at Oxford. Preaching will be a joy now that I understand their needs better." He found his curate doing a good job.

Before heading back to Oxford, he arranged a conference with Bishop Buckingham at Lincoln. Early in the year he had encountered a man who served a parish near Oxford. This man had a strong desire to move to another parish and showed interest in the possibility of exchanging with Wycliffe.

Wycliffe had agreed to consider the matter. Such a change had advantages, but one outstanding disadvantage. Before meeting with the bishop he had made a decision.

"Are you certain you would like to exchange Fillingham for Ludgershall?" asked the bishop.

"The chief advantage is its nearness to Oxford. I could keep a closer eye on my flock."

"You realize that it is worth only ten marks, whereas you receive thirty at Fillingham. That is a big difference."

"That seemed a serious drawback until I thought of the time and money spent traveling back and forth to Fillingham. I am convinced the change would be beneficial to all concerned."

Buckingham agreed to the exchange. *Plus payment of the ever-present fee!* Wycliffe thought. *Nothing without a fee.* He left Fillingham without telling his people he would not be back. It would have made for too painful a departure. Only when he was settled again at Canterbury Hall, did he mention it to anyone.

In mid-September came news of the death of the Duchess Blanche, wife of John of Gaunt. Wycliffe sent his condolences, since the duke was his overlord. "I understand," he said, "that much of his life was wrapped up in his beautiful wife. Three children left motherless—the son, Henry of Bolingbroke, and two small daughters. Sad indeed!"

Aston dropped by. "The pope has made our archbishop a cardinal, an action which has filled our king with wrath."

"Langham with a cardinal's hat! Amazing! I suppose the king's wrath is due to his not being consulted on the matter."

"It's no light matter to stir up the anger of a king. He has confiscated the archbishop's temporalities."

"Langham gets a taste of his own medicine, then. I doubt his resources are anything like as slim as ours, by his withholding the income of Canterbury Hall from us."

"They must be pretty slim. The word is that he has been driven by lack of money to sell his cross."

"What will this do to my case? Anything?"

"Probably not. That's in the hands of Cardinal Androin and will remain there until he sees fit to come to a conclusion."

"With Langham in disgrace, should I be able to count on the king's support? His opinion will count in the final decision as to Canterbury Hall. Who now succeeds Langham as archbishop?"

"I've heard that your bishop in Worcester is pulling all strings to obtain it."

"Wittlesey? I can't say I think much of his abilities. Still, if one has the right sort of pull, that doesn't seem to matter."

Within the month Wittlesey received his desired prize. He was translated in October to Canterbury, soon after Langham formally resigned the archbishopric. Wycliffe's income from Westbury-on-Trym continued to arrive, but little remained after paying the vicar. Besides his usual expenses, he had a special need for money at this time. His friends, though surprised, agreed that opting for Ludgershall was a good move.

"It pays less," said Wycliffe, "but I can spend more time there. It means an end to those long, bone-wearying journeys."

"Fifteen miles to Ludgershall, I believe," said Hereford. "A half-day's journey."

"As to my labors in the parish, not only will I be able to spend vacation time there, but I can count on frequent weekend visits."

In a half-mocking tone Aston asked, "Does that make you less of an absentee pluralist? There's still Westbury-on-Trym."

"I should have the grace to blush," said Wycliffe, "considering my outspokenness as to absentee pluralism."

"You are, after all, only a minor offender," said Aston. "Think of the multiple benefices so many of our ecclesiastical brethren hold. Even your Bishop Buckingham is not above blame."

"As to Westbury-on-Trym," said Wycliffe, "nobody ever expected me to reside there. My long-continued sin was inability to supply a vicar, a fault belatedly remedied. I can only solace myself in the knowledge that, if I surrendered the position, the person who followed me would do exactly as I have done."

"As is often the case," said Aston, "one must choose the lesser evil. It seems not possible to always choose the good!"

"It's the system," said Hereford. "The accepted arrangement by which a priest obtains an education."

"By the way, Wycliffe," said Aston, "you remain resident and warden at Canterbury Hall. No word from Cardinal Androin? Will he rule in Langham's favor, since he is a brother cardinal?"

"No word. Wodehull keeps trying to edge me out. I've used up all my hard words. He and the monks will not give up."

"And neither will you," said Hereford with a laugh.

"The outcome rests with Androin," said Aston. "One day he'll stir himself to act, but who knows when?"

With a meaningful glance at Wycliffe, Aston continued, "I've saved until now a bit of news which I have hardly been able to keep to myself. William Rede has been provided to the See of Chichester."

"Rede a bishop!" Wycliffe cried. "Actually I had lost track of him since he left Oxford. He has doubtless been doing the same superior job wherever he has gone as he did here. Always an outstanding mind, he excelled in several branches of learning. I can't say I'm surprised to see him advanced to a bishopric."

He sat back in his chair. His thoughts wandered back through the years. "Rede was one of my best friends at Merton," he said. "What discussions we used to have. He taught me much. With what delight I used to listen to him and read his scientific treatises. He knows the Scriptures well, and he recognizes the importance of preaching. If only he holds to his old ideals, God can use him. I must write to congratulate him. Dear Rede!"

Aston and Hereford smiled at each other. Wycliffe, still deep in his musings about Rede, hardly knew when they left the room.

17. November 1368-February 1369 Ludgershall

Something more than the briskness of the morning stirred Wycliffe to unusual excitement on that 11th day of November. He was on his way to Ludgershall for his institution as parish priest. His journey led him through low hills and along wooded paths, where acorns and dry leaves crunched beneath his horse's hoofs. He breathed deeply, savoring the delicious autumn odors. While he was still some distance from his destination, a higher hill crowned with a village came into view.

"Ah," he cried, "Brill-on-the-Hill! Quite as described to me. An unmistakable landmark."

He reached Ludgershall and found the ancient church to the south just outside the village. The verger, on the lookout for him, took charge and introduced him to his new occupancy. The church had no rectory. A heavy-lidded chest in the vestry would supply storage-space for his vestments. The verger led him up a narrow stone stairway inside the church and through a doorway into a small room known as a parvis.

"This will be your living quarters," he said.

Parish Church of St. Mary the Virgin, Ladgershall, Buckinghamshire

Wycliffe saw that the room contained a narrow bed, table, and chair. A candle stood upon the table. Hooks on the wall would hold his clothing. One small window afforded a view down the sloping green upon which the building stood.

"Adequate!" said Wycliffe. "It rather reminds me of my first room at Oxford, except that four of us occupied that room, leaving no space for table or chair. Sufficient for the time I shall spend here. It resembles Elisha's room upon the roof of the Shunamite woman's house."

The next day a number of parishioners, including local lords, gathered in the parish church for the institution of their new priest. Wycliffe thought how different this was from his institution to the Fillingham benefice at Holbeach nearly eight years earlier. He was uncertain as to the status of the several lords. Doubtless in time he would find out all he needed to know.

He discovered that a road about a mile in length encircled the village. The houses occupied little plots of ground within the circle. Fields stretched out from the village like spokes of a wheel.

Some of the houses were very poor indeed, little more than hovels. Wycliffe found living conditions shocking. At his own manor at Wycliffe there were few serfs. Each man owned or rented the fields he farmed. At Ludgershall the land belonged to the lord. The people were bound to the land and were required to deliver a portion of the produce to the lord. They worked the lord's personal fields as well.

Heavy flooding, common about Ludgershall in the winter months, prevented him from visiting his parish again as soon as he would have liked. Pressure of affairs at Oxford caused further delay. A few weeks into 1369 he managed to spend a number of weekends at Ludgershall.

He slowly gained information about his new parish and his people.

The situation with regard to lords and manors remained confusing. Theoretically the manor was co-extensive with the parish. But several smaller manors within the parish had been released to lesser lords.

At present the local estate was in the hands of Sir Gilbert de Chastelleye, who had received the grant ten years earlier and lived in a manor house northeast of the church. He made a show of friendship to the new priest, but Wycliffe could feel little warmth toward him after observing the living conditions of his serfs. *I shall have much to say to him later,* he thought.

18. March-June 1369—Another Milestone

In the early spring of 1369 Wycliffe attained the status of bachelor of theology. Now designated a cursor, he entered upon his "opponency" by a lecture called the principium. Two years or more must pass before he could qualify for his doctorate.

After the ceremonies and formalities, a few close friends gathered in the warden's quarters at Canterbury Hall.

"What now?" asked Hereford.

"You should know the answer to that," said Aston.

Wycliffe smiled. "A full year of lecturing on a book of the Old Testament and one of the New, a chapter at the time."

"Of course," said Hereford. "When will you begin?"

"Not until some time after the long vacation," replied Wycliffe. "In October I must begin lecturing on the Sentences."

"That will offer opportunities for 'opposing' the arguments of others who are involved in the same task," said Brut.

With a laugh, Wycliffe replied, "You know how I revel in that kind of thing. Part of the beauty of study here at the university is that one can voice one's opinions, no matter how radical, and find someone who will fight for the opposite view."

"A means of making enemies at times," said Hereford.

"Not necessarily," said Wycliffe. "You can disagree with a person and still remain on friendly terms."

"I take it you plan to spend time in your parish during the summer," said Brut.

"The permitted two months absence from my studies," said Wycliffe. "This Canterbury Hall affair hangs unfinished. Much is to be done here. With the future uncertain, it's difficult."

"I notice Wodehull is still about," said Aston. "Does he trouble you much?"

"From time to time he appears and renews his demand that I surrender the wardenship. I respond in the same way each time."

Aston chuckled. "What that manner of response is, we well know. I should hate to be on the receiving end of it."

"In the weeks before the long vacation I mean to concentrate on preparing the biblical lectures."

"Some who give such lectures don't take a very high view of the importance of Scripture," said Brut. "Your approach will be quite different, with your zeal and enthusiasm."

"I've finally settled upon the book of Nehemiah for the Old Testament lectures. One day I'll be free to lecture from every book in the Bible. Students and others shall hear truth expounded, recognize it, and learn to live by it."

A letter from Rede reached him about this time. *I have received the temporalities*, he wrote, *and my consecration*

*should take place in late summer. It would mean much to me if
you could be present.*

Wycliffe smiled. "How like Rede! He hasn't
changed. He must know I can't come, but it is kind of
him to think of me."

His smile was quickly erased by the next news that
came. Only days earlier King Edward III had announced
that he was again assuming the crown of France, which
he had earlier claimed but been unable to hold. He had
new seals prepared, one engraved *Rex Angliae et Franciae*,
the other *Rex Franciae et Angliae*. An order had gone out
for the muster of "all fencible men between the ages of
16 and 60."

Wycliffe was horrified. "Again at war! Why does the
king want to open hostilities again? Why can't he leave
the crown of France alone and concentrate on England
without troubling the kingdom to support this venture?"

19. July-August 1369—Parish Problems

It was with troubled heart that Wycliffe made plans
to go to Ludgershall in July. Besides the war threat, the
pestilence had again broken out. It reached Oxford just
as he left for Ludgershall. Would he find it in his
parish?

The pestilence seemed at first to bypass the parish,
but then it struck. A number of people and much live-
stock perished. As an added calamity, excessive rainfall
came just at harvest time. Wycliffe slogged through the
muddy road around the village and looked over the
fields. The crops would be an almost total loss. What
would the people eat during the winter? Any available
food would be extremely high in price, out of reach of
these humble workers.

On top of what seemed like insuperable problems
came the command from the king that not only were the

"fencible men" to be kept at the ready, but the shire was to provide several thousand arrows, of which the parish of Ludgershall was assigned its share. A strict order warned that no one must depart from the village.

"Surely such an order is hardly necessary," cried Wycliffe. "Where would they go? To live at all they must have help from the lord of the manor."

He was increasingly appalled by the conditions in the village. One man lay just outside the doorway of his hut in a drunken stupor. Finding it impossible to get any coherent information from him, he looked for the man's wife.

"What is the meaning of this, Susan?"

She hung her head and replied, "We are in such need that he borrowed money from the lord, but before he got home, he spent it all on drink." Wringing her hands, she asked, "What will we do, Father? We have nothing to eat."

He put a few small coins into her hand to ease her immediate pain. *I can understand the temptation to get drunk and forget his troubles,* thought Wycliffe, *but his family remains hungry, and nothing is bettered. He is still in debt to his master, and must doubtless incur larger debts.*

Conditions seemed somewhat better in several houses. Then he came to a miserable hut in such a state of dilapidation that he felt sure no one could inhabit it. Out of curiosity he poked his head inside and was met by a nauseating stench. In the darkness he could see nothing except the floor, which recent rains had reduced to a miry bog. As he was about to withdraw, a sound came from the darkest corner.

The hut was indeed occupied! As his eyes grew accustomed to the darkness, he stepped cautiously toward the sound. On a mat in the mud of the floor he found an old man. Profoundly shocked, he spoke a few comforting words to the old fellow, then went in search of aid. He gave instructions to one of the neighbors for some relief to be afforded by seeing that the bed was raised out of the mud and the old man cleansed of at least some of his filth.

In hot anger he went to the manor house. Sir Gilbert's smile gave place to a look of alarm. He had not yet seen the rector in one of his rages. "You sit in a warm, dry house and feast on fine foods, while an old man lies starving in mud and filth in a place unfit for human habitation. Did you never hear of Christian charity? Your beasts fare better than your serfs."

Sir Gilbert made stammering excuses. "I'll do what I can...I didn't know. But this man has never been worth much, always lazy. You know the damage done by the rains. This loss of crops and animals of recent days means loss of money to me. I can't afford to build fine houses for my serfs or furnish medical aid for their illnesses. They could better themselves, if they would. It's not my responsibility to do more than I am doing."

He reluctantly agreed to send help. Wycliffe left with his anger unabated. Hours later, in a calmer mood, he observed with amazement, "I have never seen real poverty before. I had no idea people could live like this. A system in which some have so much and others have nothing is wrong. Is this an isolated situation or a common condition?" He could eat no supper that evening.

20. September 1369-August 1370—Troubles

His return to Oxford after the two-month stay in his parish offered no respite, only a different set of frustrations. In his absence a letter had come from Rede, saying that his consecration as bishop of Chichester was set for September 2. His insistence that Wycliffe be there touched him, but he saw no way he could attend.

At the end of October came news of Cardinal Androin's death. Just prior to his death he had given the decision on Wycliffe's case in favor of Langham. Wycliffe's appeal had been dismissed. The matter had not been attested, but was left in the hands of Cardinal Bernard, who seemed in no hurry to conclude the matter.

Wycliffe fell into a spell of dark depression. Hereford spent much time with him, seeking to encourage him.

"I felt all along that the decision would somehow go in my favor," Wycliffe said. "Doubts sometimes gnawed at my mind, but since I knew I was in the right, I managed to push them away."

"Surely you'll give up now, and not wait until they remove you by force," said Hereford.

Wycliffe's temper flared in a characteristic manner. "No! By all the saints, no! Wodehull and his friends lurk about like hungry vultures, waiting to pounce upon me and drag me away. Here I stay until the business is finished. I have fought this long; I will fight to the end, even knowing that I face defeat."

Tension mounted as the last weeks of 1369 dragged by. Wycliffe was on edge, short-tempered. He complained to Aston at how little time bishops and others in ecclesiastical positions spent on spiritual care of their offices. "Caesarean clergy" he called them, devoted to the service of state rather than of God.

"Prelates and doctors have no business holding secular offices, nor have priests and deacons and lesser clergy. Who hold offices of Chancery, Treasury, Privy Seal? Bishops all!"

"I doubt that's going to change," said Aston. "How did these men get to be bishops? They were capable men, able to assist the king in secular offices. He rewarded them with bishoprics. They're obligated to continue to put his business first. It's a part of the system."

"Then the system must change. It's not only bishops. Who are stewards of the king's lands, of the hall, of the wardrobe, of the kitchen, of accounts? Those in some sort of holy orders. Couldn't others be found to keep count of the king's silver plate and care for his clothing without priests being thus employed?"

"As difficult as it may be to bring about any change," said Aston, "you are not alone in your concern. Among the nobility are those convinced that high offices should not be in the hands of the clergy. Many of the knights of the shires who sit in the Commons when Parliament meets are of the same opinion, though perhaps for different reasons. The motives of most of these for wanting change are quite different from your own."

"Whatever the motive, some change would do a world of good. William of Wykeham, bishop of Winchester, should not be chancellor of England. He has a spiritual office to fulfill of more importance than building castles at Windsor for the king."

"Still," continued Aston, "when he is indebted to the king for that bishopric, it would be difficult to refuse to do his bidding. Wykeham has marvelous talents along the building line."

This theme became almost an obsession with Wycliffe. Winter flooding prevented visits to Ludgershall. He worried about his people. He reached the depths and could not find his way out.

What finally saved him in these dark days was his lectures on the Sentences. Concentrating on his own lectures might not have been enough, but the challenge of disputing with a worthy opponent did the trick. He came into association with William Woodford, a Franciscan friar, in the same course of lectures.

Woodford, aware of Wycliffe's high standing and impressed by his arguments, proposed an arrangement. "After I have written out my arguments," he said, "I will send you the notebook. When you have considered my logic, write your comments and counter-arguments beside them and return the notebook."

Wycliffe found this procedure to his liking. They followed the practice throughout the term. That they disagreed on some points did not diminish mutual admiration and respect.

Cardinal Bernard published his decree concerning Canterbury Hall in May 1370, finally forcing Wycliffe out. He had the doubtful satisfaction of knowing he had inconvenienced and frustrated Wodehull as long as possible and that he had drawn his pay as master up to the final moment. There was no amusement this time when Brut helped him move back to rooms at Queen's.

Weary and dejected, Wycliffe turned to Brut late that evening. "You are probably the only one who understands why I fought so desperately over Canterbury Hall. At the beginning you pointed out to me what I could hope to accomplish as warden."

"It did seem an opportunity God was offering you," said Brut."I had high hopes for what might be accomplished."

"Yet, in the end, it comes to nothing. Why did it turn out like this?"

"I grieve with you and for you, my friend. I wish I could give you an answer."

"Is there really an answer?"

"I know in my heart that there is an answer. Sometimes God shelters us from the stormy blast; again he leaves us exposed to the tempest. He can use frustration and disappointment to teach some lesson, to make us stronger, to press us more closely to himself. I don't need to tell you this. You know it from the Scriptures you love so well. Christ never promised his disciples an easy path. He only promised to be with them."

Wycliffe, too moved for speech, could only lay his hand upon his friend's arm and murmur, "Thank you, Brut."

In early summer Wycliffe's mother died. This was a heavy blow, though he knew she had grown feeble. He made the journey home depressed in spirit and deeply grieved.

The heavy door of the church opened with its familiar creak. He proceeded slowly to the chancel rail. In the floor just before the stone altar was a newly-made grave. His mother now lay beside his father. In a strange way it comforted him. At least in death they had each other. He had no one.

There was still something of the tug of places he had known and loved. He wandered down the path to "the meeting of the waters," finding the old fascination returning. He stood on the bank, but did not follow his boyhood habit of leaping across the stones to the middle of the stream. "At forty I'm not old," he said, "but I'm too old for that caper."

The efficient overseer who had handled things since his father's death agreed to stay on. Wycliffe remained long enough to assure himself that nothing further demanded his attention.

He wondered whether this would be his last visit to his old home. A strange thought occurred to him. *I have lived longer at Oxford now than I lived here! With the blood-ties severed and with the passing of the years the other ties bind me less firmly. Oxford is now my home.*

21. September 1370-February 1371 Growing Awareness

Wycliffe spent September taking stock before the arrival of the new term in October. Sitting at his desk in his room at Queen's, he eyed the bookcase which held copies of all his works to date. Most of his philosophical works had seen publication, and even some theological treatises from his lectures.

With the help of friends he had made this start at publication. Once the scriveners and binders produced copies of a work, money brought in from sales made possible the publication of other works. The volume of sales and the distances to which copies found their way seemed incredible.

When Wycliffe expressed surprise, Brut exclaimed, "Surely you must know of your standing as a philosopher and theologian! No one in England can compare with you, and quite possibly no one on the Continent. Anything you write and publish will immediately find eager readers."

He seldom wrote out his lectures in full before delivering them. Later, sometimes much later, he went over his notes, made changes and revisions, added new material and put the work in finished form ready for publication. This kept him at his desk.

"I can't afford to dwell on past accomplishments," he said. I must apply myself to the remaining lectures on the Sentences. I hope Woodford will agree to continue our practice of last year. It sharpens my thinking to be forced to confute the arguments produced by so keen a mind."

One morning in his writing he reached a point which had troubled him before. *I keep coming back to the church's teaching on the sacrament of the Eucharist: that the substance of bread and wine are changed at consecration so that only what appears to be bread and wine remain. Philosophically this cannot be.*

In argument with Woodford Wycliffe had asserted, with some hesitation, that when the bread is transubstantiated into the Body of Christ, it is annihilated. They had left the matter hanging, unable to reach a satisfactory conclusion.

Now Wycliffe realized that this explanation failed to satisfy him. *Is it possible for matter to be annihilated? My philosophical training denies it. My theological training confirms it.*

He shook his head in despair at the difficulty of the question. He decided to leave the matter out of further consideration for the present.

In the new term Wycliffe struggled with a heavy work load. Knowing that he advanced rapidly now toward the coveted doctorate gave his efforts added impetus.

When Urban V died on December 19, the cardinals lost no time in choosing his replacement. On December 30 Gregory XI took the papal throne. Wycliffe hoped he would be an improvement over his predecessor, in whom he had long since lost all confidence.

It appeared that such hopes were not misplaced. In January a papal provision promised Wycliffe a canonry at Lincoln, with reservation of a prebend, when one became available. The prebend supplied the revenue from the cathedral which constituted the canon's remuneration. Without it he could not become a canon. "See," said Brut, "what did I tell you? The renown of our outstanding philosopher has reached even the ears of the pope."

Wycliffe had little inclination to waste time glorying in such renown. He knew now that the poverty at

Ludgershall was by no means limited to that area but was widespread. Nor was his concern only for physical need. Spiritual neglect was appalling.

"Bishops have gone far beyond giving license for a rector to be absent from his parish to pursue theological studies at the university," said Wycliffe. "There seems some excuse for that, provided a vicar or curate is left in charge. Now a license to let out the rectory to farm is easily obtained. The cure of souls is recognized, even authorized, as merely a source of income."

"Isn't that rather an exaggeration?" asked Brut.

"Not at all. It is taking place. I know of a number of parsons who have not even left a vicar in charge when they deserted their dull round of duties among an ignorant and unresponsive people."

"What happens to the rectory and church land in such a case?" asked Brut.

"Sometimes the bishop rents it to a man with a family who farms it. Sometimes very irresponsible people move in. I have even known of a rectory serving as a tavern."

Brut sighed. "I suppose the wandering parsons betake themselves to the cities, where they can find employment as chantry priests, spending their time singing masses for the dead. Not enough to live on from that, I imagine."

"Some find employment in the mansions of the nobility. The pay is small, but they still have the paltry amount their benefices pay for work they don't perform. They eke out a better and easier living than if they remained in their parishes."

This led him to do some serious thinking upon the enormous riches piled up in monasteries and ecclesiastical institutions and of the properties under their control.

"I admit," said Wycliffe, "that some of my ill-feeling toward monks may result from the battle over Canterbury Hall."

Brut shook his head. "There is more involved than that. Monks remain sheltered within their monasteries, not touching the world. Few are any longer real scholars. They copy manuscripts and preserve much that is valuable, but their work remains locked within their walls, unavailable for use by others."

"Their feigned life of contemplation is against any teaching of Scripture," cried Wycliffe. "God's law calls a man to preach the Gospel of Christ, not to shut himself away in a monastery. Such teaching comes from the fiend."

Hereford, entering the room, asked, "What's all this about the fiend?"

They explained the topic under discussion. Nodding in agreement, Hereford added, "Besides their general uselessness to church and society, the monasteries continue to receive property and wealth through endowments. You've told us, Wycliffe, that the reason your present benefice pays so little is that a large part of the income goes to a monastery. That's surely not the only case."

"I've heard you say," said Brut, turning to Wycliffe, "that monastic houses were established at Oxford in the first place that they might have the services of lawyers and accountants for managing their income and properties."

"A case can be made as well against quite a few bishops and cardinals," said Wycliffe. "There is a greed about them. Not content with their wealth, they are determined to increase it."

"The labor of serfs on the extensive lands belonging to the monasteries and bishoprics surely brings in yet more wealth," said Brut.

It was a theme Wycliffe never tired of stressing. "Why should all that wealth be piled up, unused, while across the land people live in poverty and near starvation? To say nothing of the neglect of the spiritual care of the common people."

"Even the bishops can't touch the monasteries," said Hereford. "They are accountable only to the pope. That makes them practically a law unto themselves."

"What right has the pope to control the wealth of England?" asked Wycliffe. "The riches of a country should be controlled by those within the country. The king should have authority to take possession of property that is mismanaged. Or when the need is great somewhere else, he should redistribute, put some equalization procedure into effect."

Hereford shook his head. "You propose action that is impossible at present. Your theory of need for redistribution is sound, but I see no possible way of implementing it."

"There has to be a way. The question is, who rules England, the king or the pope?"

Hereford sighed. "The king is in his dotage. He is controlled by Alice Perrers, his mistress. The Black Prince lies ill of an incurable disease. Who, indeed, rules England? The bishops who hold the most important offices in the kingdom!"

Wycliffe had already begun to inject this need for disendowment of the monasteries and the church into his lectures. The idea received mixed reactions. As word of this direction of his teaching spread, opposition manifested itself. The murmurings were low and their sources nameless.

22. February-June 1371—Encouragement

"Sorry to interrupt you," said Aston as he burst into Wycliffe's study one February morning, "but there's news you must hear. It seems the war in France is going badly. Looks like England has undertaken a task beyond her strength."

"I could have predicted that earlier," said Wycliffe. "A quarter of a century ago England could revel in the triumphs of Crecy and Poitiers. Those days are long gone. We live in a different world. Yet the military leaders will make their usual cry for money when Parliament meets."

"Even as we speak Parliament is probably assembling at Westminster. I have an idea the plea for more funds for continuing the war will have to wait. Other concerns will come first."

"You don't mean they intend to debate the question of Caesarean clergy at this meeting?" cried Wycliffe.

"That's exactly what I mean. The 'anti-clerical party' among the Lords intends to bring up the matter of the incompetence of ministers in charge of the government. The very thing you've been ranting about recently."

"Not exactly," said Wycliffe. "My complaint is that they are so bound up in their government jobs, they neglect their spiritual ministries. If what the Lords maintain is true, they are not doing either job well, and some action is due."

"With the king and the Black Prince both ill and unable to function, the bishop-ministers hold the reins with regard to affairs within the realm as well as in making decisions about use of money for the war. The nobles are shut out from any control."

"Then this is assuredly the time to bring pressure upon the king for removal of all clergy from the civil service."

"If what I hear is true, the Commons are no less hostile to the bishop-ministers, but for a different reason. Their concern is the serious mistakes the ministers have made concerning military affairs. At the new call for money, the Commons will want to know how the money previously granted was spent."

"All this sounds encouraging. If the Commons are ready to join the Lords in the demand for the removal of civil servants, there is a good chance of success. They're on the right track. Some might listen to me. I think I should go to Westminster."

Aston was uncertain of the wisdom of this. When Brut heard of Wycliffe's intention, he urged against it. "Lecturing on these subjects at Oxford is one thing. Talking about them at Westminster can only bring the wrath of the bishops upon you."

"Not all the bishops," insisted Wycliffe. "Surely I can count on Rede."

"You will almost certainly put a strain on a valued friendship, if you appear there in person."

"So be it," retorted Wycliffe.

"Let the politicians wrestle with these questions," cried Aston. "They move in the desired direction. Why get involved?"

Arguments were to no avail. Wycliffe was determined to be present when matters so dear to his heart were at stake. Might he not manage also to inject the question of disendowment of church and monasteries by moving quietly among the members of Parliament? Upon arriving he did talk with Rede, but found him preoccupied with other matters and noncommital on this question.

He remained long enough to hear the outcome, then hurried back to Oxford to report. "The king rejected the petition asking for the discharge of all clergy from any type of civil service."

"Then the whole thing came to nothing!" said Aston.

"Not quite that bad," said Wycliffe. "No one supposed the king would make a clean sweep all at once. He arranged for a compromise. Bishop Wykeham gave up his post as chancellor and was succeeded by Sir Robert de Thorpe. Brantingham, bishop of Exeter, resigned as treasurer, replaced by Richard le Scrope. A few other Caesarean clergy lost their places. So a beginning is made."

"What about the money to finance the war?" asked Hereford.

"The nobles eyed the enormous endowments of the church and monasteries and began an attack. Several lords made speeches giving reasons why a substantial part of this wealth should be used toward the expense of the war."

"I'm sure that did not sit well with the clergy," said Brut. "Indeed not," said Wycliffe. "The proposal that the clergy be deprived of its temporalities, which in time of war should be considered property of the kingdom, was voted down. However, the new budget made a heavy demand on ecclesiastical property."

Wycliffe was content for the moment. He must be patient. His voice had been heard through those with whom he had spoken. He determined to redouble his teaching efforts regarding Caesarean clergy and ecclesiastical disendowment.

"You see," he pointed out to his friends, "the reforms I so deeply desire are beginning to come about." Even their reminder that the aims of those who pushed for these actions were not the same as his own did not deflate his high spirits.

One afternoon several weeks later he spied a familiar figure striding toward him. "Rede!" he cried. "The bishop of Chichester is honoring us with a visit!"

Bishop William Rede could hardly restrain his excitement. "I've news for you, old friend. Remarkable news! Exciting news! Where can we find a quiet spot in which I may tell you about it?"

Seizing his arm, Wycliffe led Rede into his study and closed the door. Settling his friend in his best chair, he drew up another. "Out with it! It must be something great to excite you so!"

Rede's warm smile lent a radiance to his whole countenance. He hesitated only a moment. "Do you recall a conversation we had years ago on the subject of the need for a library at Merton?"

"I remember exactly where we were when we spoke of this. You had a dream of some day bringing into being a proper building for a real library."

"And you said that dreams sometimes came true. You were right. The dream is coming true. My plans for building the library have been approved. Work begins within a few weeks."

Before Wycliffe could express his delight and ask the first question, Rede leaped to his feet and pulled Wycliffe to his. "Come! I must show you the location and describe my plans."

Within the walls of Merton near the chapel, Rede pointed out just where the building would stand and how it would be constructed. Wycliffe was reminded of the archbishop of York and his eagerness over the structure he was bringing into existence.

Later when they returned to Wycliffe's rooms and Rede's excitement had subsided, he said, "You, my friend, have dreams, too—dreams of a different kind. You would bring about reforms in institutions which are set in a time-hardened pattern. Your dreams, I fear, will prove harder to bring to reality than mine."

Wycliffe sighed. "So it may be. Yet I must strive for the right as God reveals it to me. The glimmer of hope which recently appeared on the horizon may promise that dawn is near."

23. October 1371-February 1372—King's Man?

"What brings a black look upon your countenance this bright October morning?" asked Hereford as he entered Wycliffe's room.

"I do not care for the news this letter carries," replied Wycliffe. "John of Gaunt, the duke of Lancaster, has entered into marriage with Constance of Castile. I knew he was considering that alliance, but I hoped he would think better of it."

"You have something against the lady, or is it the political implications you fear?"

"I deplore the fact that he made this alliance for purely political reasons. He declared earlier his intention to become king of Castile, but the war on the Continent has gone badly for our forces. The lady is heir to that throne, though with little hope of gaining possession of it. Gaunt intends to renew the battle, hoping to gain the throne through his wife's claim. No good can come of it."

"Rumor has it," said Hereford, "that he has a deep romantic attachment to Lady Katherine Swynford, widow of one of his former retainers. Too bad her social status prevents his marrying her."

"I've seen her," replied Wycliffe. "A beautiful woman, but such an adulterous relationship is an abomination in the sight of God. He should give her up and remain true to the lady he has chosen to make his lawful wife. Perhaps he will."

Hereford said nothing, but his expression indicated doubt.

At this point a communication from London arrived. "Ah!" cried Wycliffe, breaking the seal and reading. "Someone else is interested in property left to religious institutions."

"What now?"

"A papal nuncio, one Arnold Garnier, has crossed over to Dover with a train of servants and a dozen horses. He has secret instructions, obviously no longer secret, to recover all property bequeathed for deliverance of the Holy Land. He is ordered to invoke the aid of the secular arm if necessary."

"It would seem that the Holy Father has heard of the discussions of the recent Parliament. Evidently he anticipates some difficulty in carrying out the orders," remarked Hereford.

"In the light of the king's edicts relating to the removal of wealth from the country, Garnier will find himself unable to fulfill his commission. We shall see what develops."

In his last year of theological studies the requirements were heavy but of a kind which gave him great satisfaction. Having finished the Sentences, he was now termed *baccalarius formatus.* Within the year he must preach at St. Mary's a Latin sermon of one-and-a-half hours, or not to exceed two hours.

In excited tones he reported to Brut, "This year I am to read the works of the early church Fathers and the Schoolmen."

"You can probably already quote all of Augustine from memory."

"Perhaps," said Wycliffe, "but I am happy to deepen my acquaintance with other fathers. I hold Thomas Aquinas' Summa important, and of course the writings of Grosseteste and those of my beloved Richard Fitzralph."

To these he must add the study of canon law, in which he was expected as a theologian to become expert. Besides strictly church law he intended to include Roman law, according to the ancient code, and the canonical law of England, now in effect.

In early February of 1372, while busily engaged in these labors, he received a call to Westminster. The document, issued in the name of the king, bore the duke of Lancaster's signature. With mixed emotions he slipped quietly away from Oxford.

"I don't know what this call will involve," he said. "I feel it is better to say nothing until I know more. My friends would advise strongly against possible political entanglement."

Gaunt was not only his overlord, but the most powerful man in England. They had met upon other occasions, but to be called to a private conference was unusual. After being ushered into the duke's presence and the exchange of normal greetings, a moment of silence followed. The two men seemed to be taking each other's measure.

The duke was a handsome man. Tawny golden hair fell just below his ears. Clear blue eyes relieved the starkness of his narrow Plantagenet face. A closely-trimmed beard echoed the tone of his hair. He bore a marked resemblance to his father, King Edward III, as he had been in earlier years.

Motioning Wycliffe to a chair, he said, "I have heard much about the outstanding philosopher and theologian at Oxford. It pleases me to know you are voicing dissatisfaction at certain ecclesiastical situations which I, too, find disturbing."

They quickly relaxed and discussed the problems of church and state which wore on their hearts. Wycliffe found it easy to talk with the duke about his objection to the Caesarean clergy. "Saddling clergymen with responsibility for state affairs and even military concerns leaves them no time for the spiritual concerns to which they are primarily called. This has brought about a disturbing neglect of proclaiming the

Gospel and caring for the eternal welfare of people's souls."

The duke seemed amused at the term "Caesarean clergy." "I see what you mean and agree with you that a bad system has grown up. You realize that the late Parliament made a beginning at correcting the situation. The king feels it unwise to proceed too rapidly with any sweeping change. We must be patient."

Wycliffe moved fearlessly into his next subject. "No one is more fully aware than your grace of the immense wealth in the hands of the monasteries through generous endowments over the years. The same is true of a number of bishoprics."

Before he could continue, Gaunt broke in. "This, too, I am told came under discussion in Parliament, though I was not present. Those institutions will be required to do their part in support of the war effort."

"The need I speak of is something rather more than that. I am deeply troubled that a disproportionate part of the wealth and property is in the hands of such a small group, while so many people of our land live in wretched conditions of poverty with no hope of bettering themselves."

"And how do you propose remedying the situation?"

Sensing that the duke expressed a real interest and was not merely baiting him, Wycliffe continued fearlessly. "Some system for disendowment of these institutions must be worked out, better use made of the property. In the hands of the king it could be put to use in aiding the poor of the land to ameliorate their condition and to make possible a more rewarding life. Among other things it would involve abolishing serfdom."

"You realize how difficult, some would say impossible, the execution of such a plan would be—how revolutionary and unpopular, especially with the ecclesiastical hierarchy?"

"I believe I have fully considered the difficulty. God does not expect us to hold back from pursuing what is right merely because it is difficult. Your grace, I am a student of the Scriptures, which I consider the Word of God, the prime guide of his people in all matters of faith and practice. I feel that Jesus of Nazareth and his apostles would be shocked at the opulence and luxury of the lifestyle of many who claim to be leaders and teachers of his people today."

The duke appeared thoughtful. "We shall speak of these matters again. For the present I urge a degree of caution in your public expression of such ideas."

The outcome was agreement that they could be of mutual help to each other in pushing for the reforms they sought. Wycliffe was to consider himself attached to the king's service in an informal capacity. His primary commission would be to produce tracts suitable for publication and distribution.

"As an introduction into affairs of state," said the duke, "come with me now to Westminster Hall. Chancellor Thorpe is bringing before him Arnold Garnier, papal nuncio."

Wycliffe took his seat in the Hall in great excitement and leaned forward so as not to miss a word.

Thorpe looked sternly at the man who stood before him. "You are here by order of the crown. You will hear read ten articles which you will swear on oath to abide by."

Garnier swore with reluctance to each article as read. He took oath not in anything to act contrary to the rights and interests of the realm, nor to introduce papal mandates or letters, nor to forward treasure out of the realm in money or bar gold or silver for pope or cardinals. With a stern warning to abide by what he had sworn to, Thorpe dismissed the unhappy man.

"So much for Garnier!" said Wycliffe. He headed for home assured by the duke that they would meet again soon. His head was in a whirl.

As he had expected, his friends were not overjoyed to hear of this meeting and its result. They urged caution in such an association.

Soon after his return he faced conflict with a Carmelite friar. John Kenningham, a doctor of theology, who was highly respected at Oxford and was master of the Carmelite school. In a pamphlet he criticized what he considered Wycliffe's eccentric views of Scripture. The man was courteous in his approach, referring to Wycliffe as *reverendus magister meus*, but he used no gentleness in his attempt to tear Wycliffe's arguments to pieces.

Wycliffe did not hesitate to take up the challenge. He gave particular care in his written reply to answer the criticisms of his position with regard to Scripture. "This is a persistent critic," said Wycliffe. "This pamphlet war will not end soon. I can reply so as to overwhelm most of his arguments, but in places my defense would be weak. I must study those areas more fully."

What stirred Wycliffe to unusual venom in his replies was Kenningham's sneering statement that his opponent had joined "the house of Herod," referring to Wycliffe's union with Lancaster.

24. March-April 1372—Goal Reached

A matter of overwhelmingly greater dimensions brought to a temporary halt the battle with Kenningham. The final events leading up to the awarding of his doctorate were unfolding.

Wycliffe worked long and hard upon his sententiary treatise, which he called *de Benedicta Incarnacione*. It was a long exposition of the Person of Christ. He would be required to give the address without manuscript, but the manuscript must be approved by the chancellor and masters of the theological faculty before it could be handed to the stationers for publication.

He faced fearlessly the officials who would judge the merit of his exposition, hardly aware of the large assembly of disciples, critics, and others interested in hearing what would be an outstanding presentation. The judges held the manuscripts in their hands, watching carefully for any deviation.

"I will begin," he said, "by opposing the current fashion of obscuring the humanity of Christ. The Christ of Aquinas is not our brother, not a man, but only a ghostly image. I consider the humanity of Christ a most precious jewel.

"The miracle of the Incarnation is a greater miracle by far than that of Creation. For at the Incarnation Christ took upon himself the nature not of a man, nor of many men, but the *communis humanitas*, the common human nature, of all men, manhood as it is in the *forma exemplaris*, the ideal form, of the Divine Idea."

He paused briefly and let his glance sweep over the faces of his hearers.

"This likeness he can never lose. It is the same yesterday, today, and forever. His is not the likeness of men but the primal humanity itself which he retained even during his three days in the tomb, and which makes Christ to be of the same species as other men. Nothing human is alien to him, for the manhood of Christ is the basis of the manhood of every individual."

Not for a moment did he deny the Godhood of Christ. What he meant to show, and what he did so clearly show, was that from the Incarnation onward Christ in his humanity revealed the Divine Idea, the perfect example of what God intended from the beginning that man should be.

His disciples were overawed; they declared it the finest treatise ever delivered at the university. The officials who sat to judge his performance had only the highest praise. His critics, not immediately able to put their finger on what might be considered a flaw, remained silent.

One last hurdle remained. All doctors were required to testify as to his fitness for the degree. A single adverse vote would be fatal. This passed without incident.

On the eve of inception came the final ceremonious disputation held at St. Mary's. Eight days earlier he had been required to notify all regents and bachelors of the two questions to be discussed. A candidate was expected to solicit attendance by personal canvass, but this was unnecessary in Wycliffe's case.

Wycliffe and the presiding officer spoke first, followed by the argument of each bachelor in turn. This event concluded with a speech by the president in praise of the inceptor. Wycliffe now, according to custom, feted a host of friends, including Brut, Aston, Hereford, with cake and wine. This over, his friends made the circuit of the great and learned of the university, inviting them to attend the final ceremony on the next day.

He made his way to St. Mary's well before the hour for the final ceremony. Outfitted in his best robe, he felt that he looked the part he now played in what was one of the greatest, if not the greatest, events of his life. On this occasion he was expected to wear boots which came up to the middle of his leg. The other masters were only allowed to wear "pynsons," a kind of sandal or slipper. All these specific regulations made little sense, but they must be followed.

He took the seat designated for him on the left of Chancellor Thorpe. At the proper moment the chancellor arose and with the words *Incipiatis in nomine Patris,*

Filii et Spiritus Sancti, Amen, he placed the doctor's biretta on Wycliffe's head.

The words seemed to echo within his heart: "In the name of the Father, of the Son, and of the Holy Spirit." With a feeling of elation unknown to him before, Wycliffe now mounted the cathedra and gave a short address in praise of the Scriptures. The instructions had been emphatic that it must be brief.

Disputation over, a procession formed and moved to the high altar, from which they escorted the new doctor to his domicile. After a round of thanks to the masters, the day ended with a most elaborate feast. He determined that nothing, no anxiety, no begrudging of the expense should mar the joyousness of the celebration of the attainment of a goal toward which he had struggled for nearly twenty-six years. He threw himself wholeheartedly into the festivities.

25. May-October 1372
Conflict With Kenningham

The glow lingered for some days. "Now!" he exclaimed, "I'm free to take my place in my own lecture hall and, as a doctor of theology, to lecture upon the Scriptures."

For months he had worked on his *Postilla Super Totam Bibliam*. "I'll be the first man at Oxford," he cried, "to lecture upon the whole Bible. The most important book in existence, the source of truth, God's Law, Christ's Law. Upon what greater theme could one hope to expound?"

The Michaelmas term, when he would begin his lectures, was several months away. The time would not be spent with folded hands. The duke of Lancaster expected him to produce a tract now and then, and, when sent for, to come to London to discuss matters upon which he would write.

"I've neglected Ludgershall," he said. "I must spend time there. That responsibility must not be crowded out."

When in late summer he returned from several satisfying weeks in his parish, he concentrated for some days in putting the finishing touches on his first series of lectures. When he felt he could give his attention to other items, he picked up a small book recently sent to him which he had not yet examined.

A short time later Hereford came in to find Wycliffe pacing the floor of his study, muttering under his breath, quite upset.

"What can be troubling Oxford's most illustrious doctor of theology?" he cried.

"Certainly no joking matter," snapped Wycliffe. "Kenningham refuses to be silenced. I answered him adequately the first time, then with a brief tract the second time. Yet he persists."

"You could just let him have the last word, and ignore this attack," said Hereford.

"Some of the things he says require an answer. He makes preposterous statements I am not willing to let pass."

"He's highly respected, but so are you. He can't do you any real harm. Differences on philosophical views will never be settled. You won't change his mind, nor he yours. Ignore him."

"I can't do that. He continues to attack my views of Scripture. In some points here," he said, jabbing a finger at the page, "he twists my words so as to misinterpret my meaning. That is serious, and I must not let it pass."

"Of course you can't let that pass without challenging it."

"He's still courteous enough, addressing me this time as *reverendus magister meus et dominus*, taking notice of my newly-advanced standing. Yet in some of what he says he seems to poke fun at me. He is subtle. He would not be obvious."

"Perhaps you mistake what he says. I can hardly imagine such a distinguished man stooping to ridicule an opponent."

"You shall judge for yourself later, but let me now point out the areas in which he finds fault: You are familiar with views I have long held as to eternity of intelligible being. You know, too, that I have applied this to the text of Scripture."

"Yes, indeed. You taught me that the Word of God is divinely inspired and is the material form of the eternal Word."

"Because of that, I insist that each syllable of Scripture is literally true. He questions what I say and insists upon mixing his own ideas with the literal truth of Scripture."

The treatise was long and tediously involved with philosophical intricacies. Hereford confessed that he was not able at places to follow the arguments.

"*I admit,*" Kenningham had written, "*that many philosophers support Dr. Wycliffe's arguments. Augustine, it is true, adhered to the Platonists on the matter of ideas, but even his opinion was not conclusive. Out of respect for that learned doctor I refrain from criticizing his views.*"

"He is certainly bold," said Hereford, "to come so close to finding fault with Augustine."

"Agreed. Now for this paragraph, and you may see whether he stoops to ridicule. Read it for yourself."

Hereford read: "*How hard it is to find support against the opinion of so great a doctor! Against him my arguments are as much use as the stones which boys hurl at the Pleiades. As the starry Heavens differ from a spider's web, so do my arguments compare with the opinion of my master. Truly the imposing words of a doctor so famed for learning and eloquence almost defeat me. Neither Aristotle nor the great Augustine spoke thus, though both suffered much from those who contradicted them.*"

Hereford appeared shaken as he returned the book. "He must feel sure of his ground to be able to speak thus to you."

"Sure of his ground, yes—but I am just as sure of mine. One of us is wrong." Wycliffe laid the book on the desk in front of him.

"Then you will answer him? I begin to see the necessity."

Wycliffe struck the desk a firm blow with his fist. "Be assured, I shall answer him!"

26. October-December 1372
"Doctor Evangelicus"

Even such a task, however, could not dim his joy at beginning the lectures on the Bible. He rented a lecture hall, assuming that he would attract enough students to fill it, and posted notices as to the day and hour. As he approached the hall, he experienced a fleeting doubt. What if no one came!

He made his way to the raised area at the front upon which rested his chair, and placed his books and notes upon the podium. Only then did he raise his eyes to view his students. The room was filled to capacity with mostly younger men.

As his eyes swept the room, their excited chatter subsided and a deep silence fell. His heart swelled at the thought of the privilege that was his. He would open up the Word of God to these men as they had never known it before. What a responsibility! What a joy!

"I remind you," he began, "of the importance of the subject upon which we enter and of the spirit of humility with which you should address yourselves to it. Our first topic must necessarily be the argument for the being of God..."

He moved steadily through the first course, insisting almost daily to his students, "Much authority lies in tradition, but there is a higher authority. If there be any truth, it is in the Scripture; there is no truth to be found in the schools that may not be found in more excellence in the Bible." His beloved St. Augustine remained his authority in this.

Inevitably his philosophical ideas wove themselves into his teaching. His insistence on thinking for himself came through here as in his theology. Some students found his lectures difficult to follow. Yet attendance did not diminish.

As the weeks passed, his students gave him a new title. He smiled to himself. So I am now the "Evangelical Doctor."

Sometimes consciously, sometimes unconsciously, he moved in his lectures toward the necessity for reformation. Speaking of the importance of following God's Law, he said, "As you look about you, you see men showing greater concern to protect their private interests than to uphold the law of Christ. Otherwise they would destroy, as far as they have power, whatever is opposed to that law. But we see both prelates and civil dignitaries exalting and defending the laws and interests of men, placing them before the law of God."

His popularity grew. No doubt existed that he was the most highly esteemed doctor at Oxford. Yet not all were in agreement with him. Kenningham was not his only opponent.

Though differences arose between him and Woodford, they were able to keep their arguments on a friendly basis, due to the association they had enjoyed in their study of the Sentences. Each had much respect for the other. Woodford supported Kenningham in his opposition to Wycliffe, as did Uhtred Boldon and William Binham.

Only by furious writing in every spare moment could Wycliffe keep these opponents at bay.

"It will grow worse," remarked Wycliffe to Brut. "The direction my teaching is taking will make it inevitable."

"Just remember your sententiary oaths that you would teach nothing that is not orthodox. Be careful, and don't move too hastily," advised his friend.

"It hinges on what constitutes orthodoxy," replied Wycliffe. "I have less and less confidence in tradition and more and more in the Scriptures. By Scripture must orthodoxy be tested."

"You'll surely get into hot water if you press too hard on that point. Again I say, go slowly."

Wycliffe smiled. On an impulse he said, "Attend my lecture tomorrow, and tell me whether I am treading on dangerous ground."

"I just might do that," said Brut. "As for telling you what I think, I have no notion that it would do the slightest good."

He did come, and Wycliffe seated him where he could not miss a word. The lecture was on the nature of sin and particularly on the distinction commonly made between venial and mortal sins.

At first Brut could detect no hint of unorthodox treatment. Then he winced as he heard, "The terms 'venial' and 'mortal' are commonly in the mouth, not only of the people but of the prelates, men who know better how to extort money for sins than how to cleanse any man from them, or how to distinguish between mortal and venial, about which they babble so much.

"The Scriptures know nothing of such distinction. A sin may be called mortal when according to the judgment of God it is worthy of death. Thus it is the sin of final impenitence only, that is, the sin against the Holy Ghost, that is properly mortal. Any other sin, inasmuch as it is a sin that may be pardoned, may be called venial."

At length Wycliffe drew to a close, announcing that the next lecture would be upon grace. As he dismissed the group, some lingered, doubtless having questions. He called their attention to the presence of a guest and urged that they hold their questions for a later time.

Brut said nothing until they were again in Wycliffe's study. "I tried," he said, "to put myself in the place of your students. Much of what you said would be new and startling. I doubt they have ever had such an explanation of mortal and venial sins."

"True, but it is an explanation they need. The distinction between the two is of high moment in the discipline of the church. Anyone who is regular at the confessional cannot be ignorant of that. The tax on absolution is great or small as the sin to be absolved is accounted great or small."

"You held their attention. Significant glances were exchanged, and a few puzzled looks appeared as you flung aside the 'babble' of the prelates and applied the lash, as it were, to men who knew how to extort money for sins while doing little to reform the sinner."

"Do you then find fault with anything I said? Was not truth evident in each point?"

Brut scratched his chin thoughtfully. "Truth, yes, it was there. But you are asking for trouble from those in high places. It's the type of thing I feared when I urged you to be careful."

"You realize that I cannot tread gently when I'm sure of my position. It's the familiar battle between tradition and the Scriptures. The Scriptures do not support a distinction such as tradition makes between mortal and venial sins, nor does it support many other points on which tradition insists."

Brut was distressed. "It's not the truth of what you say that disturbs me, but the fact that you are determined to say it, whatever the consequences. The consequences may be rather grim."

"Face it, my friend," cried Wycliffe in an impassioned tone, "reform is needed. Perhaps, as Mordecai suggested to Queen Esther, I have come to the kingdom for such a time as this. If I proclaim the truth from the lectern, I may build up an army to do battle for reform. Nothing I said can be construed as heresy."

Brut's tone was warm and his eyes seemed bright with unshed tears as he laid his hand on his friend's arm. "I know, Wycliffe, I know. It's your God-given nature. Others recognize the need for reform, but few dare throw themselves into the struggle against such overwhelming odds. You fight a furious battle—a war with words rather than with sword. You have powers none of us possess. We can but back you up and follow where you lead. That you can count on."

27. 1373—Dangerous Topics

In early 1373 Pope Gregory XI engaged in his own private war with certain Italian groups which manifested nationalist leanings. Needing funds for this effort, the pope demanded from the clergy of England the sum of 100,000 florins. One-tenth should be paid immediately to his Florentine agents at Bruges. At Easter they must pay one-half of the amount, the balance at Michaelmas.

This news greeted Wycliffe as he left his lecture hall one snowy morning. "Interesting!" he cried. "His Holiness is always thinking up schemes by which to draw away money from England. In this case he will be disappointed. How can the clergy pay that amount when some have yet to pay their part of the 50,000 pounds set by Parliament? On top of that, the king is about to demand another tenth needed for the French war."

He was right. The demand was impossible. The king's taxes took first place. To Wycliffe's delight, king and prelates turned a deaf ear to the pope's demands. No immediate payment was made, nor was any made at Easter.

In early summer the king issued a writ for the removal of all alien friars. A token effort was made, but matters moved slowly and with a great deal of complaint.

In July Wycliffe published a paper to which his opponents reacted immediately. The material was largely what he used in his lectures. Had it been merely a question of his philosophy, no problem would have arisen. Many shades of philosophy were debated at Oxford. But because he dared to bring his philosophical convictions into lectures on the Scriptures, some began to question his orthodoxy.

"Ridiculous!" cried Wycliffe. Ridiculous or not, he soon became aware that his teaching was being monitored, his words weighed and questioned. "This is what Brut warned me of," he said grimly. "I'm sure it will continue."

In the summer patrons of parish churches complained loudly that their duties were taken out of their hands as the pope filled benefices with mostly foreign and absentee appointees. The king appointed a commission to Avignon to discuss these matters with the Roman curia. At the same time he extended to Oxford the order to remove all alien friars.

"I understand the wisdom of the order in general," cried Wycliffe, "but I regret that it catches some of my close friends."

He entered his second year of lecturing with the same zest as before. Increasing numbers of students attended his lectures, seeming to drink in every word. He was told that in their small groups at night they discussed, often until dawn, what they had heard. Though some were disturbed, all were challenged to examine the teaching, compare it with what they saw practiced, and decide on which side the truth of the Scriptures lay.

He taught upon grace: "Only God can forgive sin. It is plain to me that prelates who grant indulgences commonly blaspheme the wisdom of God, pretending in their avarice and folly that they understand what they really know not."

He declared in impassioned tone, "These sensual simonists, selling sacred things and offices, chatter on the subject of grace as though it were something to be bought and sold like an ox or an ass. By so doing they make merchandise of selling pardons. Thus the devil avails himself of this error to introduce into the schools heresies in morals.

"All lordship depends upon God, thus any lordship depends on grace. Only those justified by God can be said to have a valid right to lordship. Those in sin forfeit their right, and should have their possessions removed."

At table his students talked only about what they had heard in the day's lecture of the Doctor Evengelicus. Others besides Brut, however, urged him to tread carefully. He was stepping on important toes, making enemies he could ill afford.

With reckless insistence he continued in the same direction. "Morality cannot possibly admit such errors as we have spoken of earlier. Morality rests on a foundation in the very nature of things. Its principles are immutable and eternal. It is right, not because God wills it, but God wills it because it is right. It is not possible that there should be a divine mandate calling upon us to violate the divine laws. But if there were, a man would not be bound in such cases even to obey God."

Brut's concern continued. "I shudder," he said, "when I hear you suggest a case in which man would not be bound to obey God."

"You must know," cried Wycliffe, "that putting it like that mutilates the statement and gives a meaning I never intended!"

"I know that, and you know that, but the statement will be taken out of context and twisted to your hurt. Count on it!"

To realize that his teaching could be so misrepresented hurt and distressed Wycliffe. Then hurt gave way to anger. "Let them do their worst," he cried. "For me there is no turning back. I can only go forward, declaring the truth as God reveals it."

"I'm with you," said Brut, with a sigh. "But you must realize it's a dangerous path. Where will it eventually lead?"

In November members of Parliament made their usual complaint about papal provisions and the presence of alien clerks, who continued to remove treasure from the realm, in spite of efforts to prevent it. Their betrayal of national secrets was a danger to the realm. The king replied that the commission at Avignon would deal with these matters. Action as to the pope's demands must await the return of the commission.

On December 26 Gregory XI renewed the grant to Wycliffe "of a provision lately made to him of a canonry of Lincoln with reservation of a prebend, possession of which he has not yet obtained." He also received permission to retain the canonry and prebend in the collegiate church of Westbury.

No one thought for a moment, least of all Wycliffe himself, that this was due to any special interest of the pope in Wycliffe. "His Holiness is dealing with the usual list of requests of the university on behalf of successful doctors," said Wycliffe. "What matters the how or why? At least the grant is renewed. I get to keep Westbury and Ludgershall."

Perhaps it was a good omen that the year closed with such tidings.

PART 3

Mounting Conflict with Ecclesiastical Powers
(1374–1378)
"The battle has just begun!"

1. January-April 1374—Surprise Appointment

"You always seem to be up on the news," said Wycliffe as Aston came into the study one bright winter morning. "I hear the Avignon deputation has returned. Have you heard any report as to what, if anything, they accomplished?"

"Nothing official," said Aston. "It seems the pope made vague statements with regard to the complaints, indicating that some change would be made as to provisions, that is, making appointments on his own to English benefices. He still requires the tax from the clergy and renews the demand for the tribute due on King John's account."

"That means," said Wycliffe, "that they accomplished nothing. His Holiness has made promises before. They are worth little. His demands are still outrageous."

"It seems," said Aston, "that the king is taking action that may shake the pope up. He has ordered an accurate count made of benefices held by aliens appointed by the pope. He wants to know, too, the value of each and whether the aliens are resident."

"I think it will cause the pope some anxiety to hear of the king's search for such information," said Wycliffe. "The report will reveal a large number of benefices held by cardinals."

The king requested of the pope that a commission convene at Bruges to deal with remaining matters of dispute. Pope Gregory was quick to respond that he would have three nuncios at Bruges on June 24 to meet with the king's appointees.

"The question is," said Brut, "whether another commission will accomplish anything more than the one at Avignon."

"Time will tell," replied Wycliffe.

Almost at once Wycliffe received a summons from the duke of Lancaster. Wycliffe assumed the call had to do with the matters in which he was occasionally engaged on behalf of the duke.

Although Lancaster maintained an air of arrogance toward all but a few close associates, he manifested a friendly cordiality and respect toward Wycliffe. After a pleasant exchange of greetings, he announced, "The king is pleased to appoint you on the commission to Bruges."

After a momentary feeling of shock, Wycliffe managed to reply, "It's an honor indeed that his majesty bestows upon me."

"You should know that your name appears second in position, which indicates the confidence the king places in you," said the duke.

"I shall do my utmost to merit that trust."

"Let's hope accord may be reached. The pope will grant no more than he is forced to. My father does not wish to anger him unduly, as there are other considerations."

Wycliffe thought grimly to himself, *Other considerations, indeed!* He well knew that king and pope split the income from unassigned posts. Benefices were often left vacant for long periods for the purpose of fattening the royal and papal coffers.

"When will the meeting convene?" he asked.

"Sometime after the end of June, perhaps as late as August. The pope mentioned June 24, but the date is not firmly fixed."

Abruptly the duke proceeded to another subject. "A benefice has become available which I think may interest you."

Wycliffe said nothing, but his expression registered surprise.

"Its patronage lies in the hands of the crown, as Henry de Ferrers of Groby, a ward of the king, is but four years old."

Wycliffe remained silent, though his mind was active. *De Ferrers of Groby? Who is de Ferrers? Where is Groby?*

"I speak of the parish of Lutterworth, no great distance from Leicester. It would be convenient to have you near when I am in residence at Leicester."

Wycliffe started to speak, hesitated, then said, "I shall express my feelings honestly. My first thought is that it would put me at a greater distance from Oxford than does Ludgershall."

"You would be under no obligation to reside there on a permanent basis." The duke gave a little laugh. "No more will I often reside at Leicester castle, but at times we may meet there more conveniently than in London. The value of Lutterworth is considerably more than that of Ludgershall. I would be pleased to see you accept this favor from the king's hand, perhaps as a small reward for your willingness to represent him at Bruges."

"Inasmuch as it's still in the diocese of Lincoln, I can anticipate no objection on the part of Bishop Buckingham."

"You agree to accept the benefice, then?"

"I appreciate the honor and am happy to accept."

"You will not regret it. The parish consists of some 400 souls, I believe, among them several prominent families. Some have holdings there, but live part of the time elsewhere."

"Are there serfs?"

"My understanding is that a large part of the parish land is held by one lord and is tenanted partly by serfs and partly by free men who rent from him. A number of burgesses own land and govern themselves. The ancient church has a comfortable rectory."

2. April 1374—Lutterworth

Wycliffe returned to Oxford in somewhat of a daze. "Just when I think my life is pretty well settled on one course," he said, shaking his head ruefully, "something comes along to upset it. I seem always pulled in some new direction."

He had little time for such meditations, for events moved rapidly. In the first week of April Wycliffe received instructions from Bishop Buckingham to proceed to Lutterworth for his institution.

"I don't want to make that journey alone," he said. "I think it would be well for Purvey to go with me." John Purvey was a young student who regularly attended his lectures and who had helped him with secretarial work.

"Purvey," he said when the young man appeared, "you've made yourself useful to me, and I've come to depend on you. I'd like you to accompany me on a journey."

"I'm quite willing, Sir, if I can arrange to be away from my studies. Where is it we're to go?"

"To Lutterworth for my installation as parish priest. I need company on the way, and you might as well look this new situation over along with me. You may see more of it in the future, if you continue to assist me."

As they rode northward, Wycliffe reflected upon the fact that he would not complete his current series of lectures before the end of the term. Yet he could not disguise the elation he felt at the thought of what lay before him. Fillingham...then Ludgershall. How different would he find Lutterworth? Then the commission to Bruges!

In the early afternoon of the second day Wycliffe called out, "We must be almost there. Surely this stream is the river Swift."

A narrow wooden bridge with high sides led across the river. Here Wycliffe paused. The road sloped upward toward the low hill upon which the town stood. "There!" he cried, "See above the housetops? That spire undoubtedly belongs to St. Mary's church."

As they moved on, Wycliffe gave a sigh, which he hoped Purvey did not notice. He was tired, in spite of the excitement he felt. Could he be getting old at 44 years?

Purvey's anxious eye did not miss the droop of Wycliffe's shoulders, nor the sigh. As he dared to voice his concern, Wycliffe cried testily, "Stop fussing about, Purvey! You act as if I'm an old man." Regardless of his feelings, he would not admit to weariness unless his situation became desperate.

The road from the river led up the hill into High Street. A fine looking house stood to the left amid well-kept grounds. Farther along, market stalls stood on either side of the cobbled street. They would learn that Thursday was market day, and that Lutterworth took pride in the fact that it had had a market by grant of the king since 1214.

They turned west into Church Street, where a number of small cottages appeared on the right and left. As they reached the iron gates leading into the churchyard, Wycliffe dismounted and gave his reins to Purvey.

"Do what you like for the next little while," he said. "I wish to visit the church alone."

He took the path around the north side. At the west end, he stopped and caught his breath. "Bluebells!" he exclaimed. "Just coming into bloom." His heartbeat quickened at the sight of such beauty spreading across the churchyard into the meadow beyond.

He circled the church and approached the main entrance at the south side. The heavy oaken door yielded reluctantly, requiring a strong tug before he could enter. He stood in the south aisle until his eyes became accustomed to the dimness.

He walked slowly to the rough stone baptismal font just in front of him, reaching out to touch it. Its similarity to the one in the Wycliffe church brought a wave of nostalgia. Shaking off the feeling, he continued down the nave toward the chancel.

There was little stained glass. Above the high altar three narrow lancet windows stabbed slits for light to enter. He stepped into the chancel with its rows of choir stalls. Continuing toward the altar, he climbed the steps and knelt for some moments in prayer. The service of institution would take place on the morrow. Today, here alone with God, he consecrated himself to his new work.

The two-tiered pulpit, with its impressive carving, would put him above the congregation as he preached. "Good!" he murmured. "Preaching is the most important part of the service. Standing there will permit me to command the attention of the parishoners." With some displeasure, however, he observed the raised pews set aside for the lord and other notables. "Why should any group be seated in a higher position than others? They might read what James says in the New Testament about that."

The heavy door closed behind him, and he stepped into the sunlight. Purvey came up from where he had waited a few steps away, having tethered the horses at the gate. Together they went to the rectory, a sturdy, well-built structure, located back from Church Street in front of the churchyard to the north.

A number of people had assembled to greet the new priest. He found Bishop Buckingham engaged in conversation with a stately lady, whom he introduced to Wycliffe as Lady Isabel, mother of young Henry de

St. Mary's Church at Lutterworth, near Leicester

Ferrers, lord of the manor. A hasty search produced that young man, who had wandered into the garden. His mother patted his hair into place and presented him to Wycliffe. With some prodding from his mother, he made a polite little speech of welcome which had been carefully taught him.

The bishop officiated at the service of institution next day. To Wycliffe there was a deep sacredness about being inducted into a parish as its priest. Feeling the weight of the responsibility laid upon him, he added a silent prayer to that spoken by the bishop, asking God to make him a true pastor to these people.

He remained a few days making preliminary acquaintance with the people of the parish. It was an all too brief introduction, but he hoped to be back for part of the long vacation. As soon as possible he would appoint a curate.

3. April-May 1374—Council at Westminster

Soon after his return from Lutterworth the report on the alien clergy appeared. The list filled several pages, and few if any were resident. Only a small number had ever visited England. They drew 50 pounds and more a year, some as much as 100 pounds.

"The knowledge that the king has this information surely must trouble the pope," said Wycliffe. "It gives the king a shiny new weapon to use against his Holiness when he needs it."

After a few weeks of lectures came another interruption. He was called to Westminster to take part in a council to consider anew the question of papal tribute. The results of this meeting would be reported by the embassy the king was sending to Bruges.

Wycliffe had to admit, though only to himself, that he was beginning to relish these calls to Westminster.

I can catch up on the lectures. Even at Westminster I will surely find spare hours to continue writing. I mean to keep Purvey at hand as much as possible.

Prelates and barons made up the council, along with representatives of the various religious orders. It was not a Parliament, since the Commons were not present. It was assumed that this matter was not within the range of their concern.

The Black Prince and Archbishop Wittlesey presided. Knyvet, the chancellor, opened the proceedings. He stated the pope's claim that, as vicar of Christ and lord spiritual, he was general lord of all temporals, and especially in the realm of England, because of the gift of King John.

The prelates must now decide the spiritual claim. The barons would render a decision on the temporal claims on the morrow. Having stated this, Knyvet turned to Wittlesey and said, "My lord archbishop, what do you say?"

He gave what was the expected answer for one in his position. "We cannot deny that the pope is lord of all." The other prelates assented to this judgment.

The provincial of the Dominicans refused to be trapped into a hasty answer. He complained that the meeting had not been opened according to the custom of his order. Neither mass nor the hymn *Veni Creator Spiritus* had been sung. Until this was done, no answer could be given on so difficult a question.

Uhtred Boldon of Durham had no hesitancy about answering. He asserted with boldness the papal supremacy in spiritual and temporal spheres, quoting the favorite text of Hildebrand, "Lo, here are two swords."

The Franciscan spoke, quoting the counter-text, "Put up thy sword again." He argued that Christ had neither possessed temporal dominion nor bequeathed it to the apostles. He justified his arguments by citing passages from the Scriptures, from the doctors, from the example of the religious orders, and from the confessions of popes themselves. In aspiring to earthly dominion, the pope was the successor not of Peter but of Constantine.

The Austin friar followed along the same lines. The pope, he said, carried the keys; the Black Prince, like St. Paul, the sword. "Wield your sword, and Peter shall recognize Paul."

Wycliffe could scarce restrain a chuckle, so pleased was he with these last replies. The archbishop showed an opposite reaction, as his muttered words and stormy looks indicated.

The next day the archbishop expressed himself by sneeringly remarking, "The assembly would have been better off without friars, as also the country itself."

In anger the Black Prince replied, "If we had listened to your counsel, the kingdom would have been lost."

The archbishop, who appeared quite ill, now refused to give any answer at all.

The prince, also ill and worn with disease, cried, "Answer, you ass. It is your business to inform us."

In a feeble voice the archbishop replied, "I am quite willing that the pope should not be lord in England." The other prelates gave assent to this.

Uhtred also had second thoughts and decided to agree.

"What then becomes of the two swords?" mocked the prince.

"My lord," came his reply, "I am now better instructed."

The barons gave their verdict on the "gift of John" in several lengthy speeches, all to the same point: King John had had no right to give the kingdom to the pope. Therefore, the gift was invalid, and no payment should be made.

This reply the envoys would report to the pope. They would receive other instructions later, for this was only one of the matters to be dealt with by the commission at Bruges.

4. May-June 1374—Facing Opposition

A number of things called for Wycliffe's attention once he again reached Oxford. He must notify the bishop that he was relinquishing the benefice of Ludgershall. Buckingham knew this, but would do nothing about it unless Wycliffe pushed him.

"I must not neglect the search for a curate for Lutterworth," he said. "I can't be certain when I'll be able to return there in person for any length of time. Purvey ought to be able to locate a man for me."

He discovered that Uhtred had attacked his teaching in some recent lectures, maintaining that the rule of the priest is preferable to that of layman. He held that in no circumstance could any lay power have the right to judge the priesthood. Furthermore, anyone who dared to teach or by any means induce the lay power to despoil the church of its endowments was acting for the ruin of king and kingdom.

"I need not spend much time on my reverend doctor *et magister specialis*," said Wycliffe to Brut.

"I remember," said Brut, "that you encountered him when you were master of Balliol."

"I made reply to these same objections on the part of Woodford not long ago. A simple tract should take care of it."

Enlisting the aid of Purvey as scribe, he wrote, *In my opinion the patron should act against a scandalous priest by depriving him of his endowments only if the bishop fails to do his duty. As for the management of church property, it would be better left in the hands of selected laymen, that the clergy may give full attention to their spiritual duties.*

Brut dropped by again later. "I hear that a Benedictine monk, a doctor, has published against you. What's this about?"

"It's William Binham," said Wycliffe in disgust. "He entered Oxford about the time I did and took as long to get his doctorate. He has made a violent attack on me in a book called *Against Positions of Wycliffe*. He says I tear to pieces the theology of the old theologians."

"I remember him. Strange that he reacts so strongly. He must expect a reply, and I am sure you will not disappoint him."

"Oh, I'll answer him. Not only has he attacked me, but, in spite of the clear action taken on the matter of the tribute, Binham has had the effrontery to continue to defend the pope's claim. He maintains that by the non-payment of this tribute the king of England has forfeited his right to dominion in England. He challenges me to argue the point. How can I refuse?"

"You realize that harm could come from it. The action of the council is official. Why not just reply to his attack on you, and let the matter of the tribute alone?"

"And have this monk believe I could not refute every point he makes? Have him think the pope really has a right to make such demands of our sovereign?"

"By drawing you into the fray, he singles you out as one who dares defy the pope. An answer delivered by the council headed by the prince and the archbishop is quite different."

"That may be his intention. You know the feeling of his order toward me because of the Canterbury Hall affair. The learned doctor no doubt intends at the same time to obtain favor in the pope's eyes for himself and his order."

"So refuse to take up the challenge. You could lose your benefices, you know. Is it worth it?"

Wycliffe rose from his chair and paced the room. He could *not* afford to lose his benefices, but was there really any likelihood of that happening? Love of a fight won out. "How would it be if I managed to dispute, yet avoided danger?"

Brut laughed. "I might have known you would think of something. How do you propose to manage this?"

"I'll state that I am an humble and obedient son of the Roman church, which, of course, I am. I'll declare it my intention to assert nothing that may sound injurious to the church or reasonably offend devout ears."

"A mild enough beginning. Almost *too* mild to be in character. But in refuting the monk's declarations you will of necessity offend certain devout ears."

Wycliffe smiled enigmatically. "Trust me. I intend to refer the learned doctor to opinions which I will maintain I heard expressed by lay lords in a certain council. If he wants to identify the council, that is his privilege. The arguments of these seven lords are entirely convincing, and the doctor will not be able to refute them. I shall be under no necessity of mentioning that my own thinking is in absolute agreement."

Again Brut laughed. "My admiration for you grows daily. I have no doubt that the opinions you will attribute to these lords will not match exactly the words they spoke, but with your skill in the use of language, you will be excused for a bit of judicious editing. Who else would dare attempt it? You might pull it off. When you do, the result must be published. This will add to your fame."

"Publication is easy if one has financial means. Scriveners, parchment-makers, and illuminators in Catte Street charge dearly and demand immediate payment for work done."

"You'll manage. Money is not the problem to you it was several years ago. Not that there is ever enough. Besides, think of the income from the sale of the treatise."

When Brut had gone, Wycliffe moved a bit reluctantly toward his desk. He would not wait for Purvey, but would write the reply to Binham with his own hand. *In times past*, he said to himself, *he and I were more or less friendly rivals. When we disagreed, no ill-feelings arose. He has brought an end to that by his vicious attack. This matter is too serious for kindly feelings.*

Anger built up as he thought of Brut's suggestion that replying to Binham could cause him to lose his benefices. "That may be what Binham hopes for," he muttered. "I addressed Uhtred with courtesy, but I feel no such obligation to Binham."

Picking up his pen, he began a preliminary draft, letting his feelings spill onto the paper without restraint. He concluded his refutation of the attack on his own teaching with the caustic statement, *If any monk does not keep the poverty of his first profession, I dare to say that he is not a follower of St. Benedict but a dangerous apostate, a disciple of antichrist.*

His pen moved slowly at first, then more rapidly. As daylight failed, he paused to light a candle and to close and bar the door against a chilly blast. His mind raced, and his pen had difficulty keeping pace. The hour grew late. He had now completed the speeches of the first five lords. He paused to flex his stiffened fingers, but dared not stop and risk losing momentum.

He smiled grimly as he realized that he attributed much of his own thinking upon dominion and grace to the sixth lord. What matter? The lords were anonymous. Neither he nor anyone else could recall every word spoken. Moving on, he was only half-aware that the ringing challenge of the seventh lord expressed his own views of constitutional history and practice.

With a triumphant gesture, he cast down his pen. He gathered the scattered sheets, crying, "Done! Not yet in finished form, but the arguments are there. Binham will go down in ignominious defeat in the face of this evidence."

5. July-September 1374—Bruges

In July Wycliffe hurried to Lutterworth to spend a few days before leaving for Bruges. He had found a man, a very young man, by the name of John Horne, to serve as curate. He wanted to help him get settled and started in the right direction.

Hardly had he returned to Oxford when the summons to London came. The commission consisted of seven members, Wycliffe being the only theologian. John Gilbert, bishop of Bangor, headed the commission. He and Sir William Burton had been members of the deputation to Avignon. Wycliffe's name was second on the list, as Gaunt had told him.

The day before their departure, the formal commission was issued, investing them with plenary powers to conclude a treaty with the pope's representatives on the pending points such as would both ensure the honor of the church and uphold the rights of the English crown and realm.

Wycliffe lay awake pondering the purpose of this mission and his part in it. He had told the duke he appreciated the honor, but had then hardly realized its scope.

"A royal commissioner!" he exclaimed. "How incredible that John Wycliffe be involved in diplomatic transactions with the papal court, charged with the duty of protecting the rights of the crown and the interests of the kingdom. I shall deal face-to-face with the plenipotentiaries of the pope. A high honor, but more, a grave responsibility. May God give me wisdom."

On July 27 they sailed. At the hour of departure the excitement of the journey displaced all deeper thoughts for Wycliffe, who had never left the shores of his native land. He watched the coastline recede until it disappeared.

Hours later the low, flat shores of Flanders came into view. The ship entered the mouth of the Zwijn and moved slowly up the river to Bruges.

"I can't believe those mountainous piles of merchandise," cried Wycliffe, as the ship drew near the dock. "They must come from the ends of the earth!" He was fascinated by the bustling activity, the number of ships loading and unloading, the general din, punctuated by shouts in languages unknown to him.

His wonder grew as his party entered the city. "You must know," said Gilbert, "that Bruges is one of the leading cities in Europe, its center of commerce and banking."

"Yet I am unprepared for this vast geographic extent and milling multitudes in all places, even at midnight," said Wycliffe. London he had seen, but Bruges was twice as large.

He discovered not only a large colony of Englishmen, but permanent settlements of foreigners from every nation, giving their names to streets and whole districts.

Bruges boasted a magnificent cathedral and an almost equally outstanding castle. But surpassing both these in importance if not in splendor were the Cloth Hall and the Belfry. The Belfry's carillon called the artisans to work each day, or to arms if any attempt was made to invade their rights. A strong civic spirit prevailed. The burghers assumed control of all public affairs.

The first few days were taken up with formalities. Entertainment at elaborate meals seemed essential. Notables of the city attended, and they reciprocated in even more ostentatious style. Visiting dignitaries, church officials from all over Europe, invariably appeared.

Wycliffe made the acquaintance of people of diverse backgrounds and opinions. He soon became aware of shallowness, preoccupation with position and wealth, and bowing to political expediency.

However, in these dinner table conversations he found a few who showed interest in the things he talked about—the need for reform in the church, the problem of excessive wealth in the hands of the higher clergy, both secular and religious. The attention given him by his listeners led him to express his views with eagerness. Eventually he realized the listening was mostly a matter of politeness and curiosity.

He found the official sessions disappointing. Discussion wandered from the points under consideration. The old arguments were reviewed, with no conclusions reached and no progress made.

After gaining the floor and voicing his opinions a few times, Wycliffe gave up, admitting with a sigh, "My recommendations are being brushed aside, not only by the pope's men, but by my fellow countrymen. And I begin to understand why: If my ideas were accepted, the outcome would be to the liking of neither king nor pope."

After several weeks it became obvious that they dealt with irreconcilable elements. Neither side wished to push matters to an extreme. Giles Sancho, pope's nuncio, announced that he must return to Avignon for further instructions. So, with nothing actually accomplished, the meetings adjourned to a future unspecified date. On September 14 Wycliffe was back in England.

6. September 1374—Disillusionment

Gilbert would make the report to the king. Wycliffe had no wish to tarry in London. Once more at Oxford, he hired his old rooms at Queen's and remained in seclusion for some days. He preferred to deal with his disillusionment alone.

I may as well face it, he thought. *My services at Bruges were of no value. The whole conference was an exercise in hollowness and futility. I went as the king's man, and so I continue to be, but it seems as if the king is not in earnest over this business.*

He considered the attitude of the pope, as mirrored by his nuncios at Bruges. *Obviously he will agree to no great changes. Any concessions made will mean little. There must be a means of stirring crown and Parliament from their lethargy with regard to the pope's greed, and I mean to find it.*

Finally the time came for him to end his solitude, to take action. He sent for John Purvey to aid him in reworking and polishing the replies written earlier to Uhtred and Binham. This might be the opening wedge for what he hoped to accomplish in stirring public opinion.

"Brut urged me to publish this," he said. "It will provide the beginnings of a larger work to come later, but this much must get into the hands of readers without delay."

After viewing the work with satisfaction, he handed the sheaf to Purvey and pushed him toward the door. "Hasten to Catte Street and put it in the hands of the scriveners. Tell them to work quickly but accurately and to make copies sufficient for a considerable number more than what will be needed here. Copies must go to the London market. Haggle with the binders over their price, but agree to what seems reasonable."

Hearing that Aston and Brut had arrived at Oxford, Wycliffe contacted them. They would be eager for news from Bruges, and to them he could express his disappointment and frustration.

"I understand more clearly now," he said, "what the duke meant when he said the king could not press too hard on the pope, because of other considerations. I knew something of those 'other considerations,' but the full extent is now clear. The conference at Bruges was little more than a farce."

His friends listened quietly as he poured out the details of the conference and the bitterness and disillusionment he felt. When he had finished, they seemed reluctant to speak.

"In all those weeks, then, was nothing of a positive nature accomplished?" asked Aston.

"Apparently it was not intended that anything be accomplished."

"Wycliffe," said Brut, shaking his head, "you're out of your element in politics. You're too honest. As a negotiator you'll never make it. Stick to your proven realm of excellence."

"I'm not ready to give up yet. The king's mistaken judgment must not be allowed to sway those he commissions to act for the good of the realm. I saw no other course than to expend all my efforts to the carrying out of the commission."

"And your fellow-commissioners, either out of fear or hypocrisy, stalemated any satisfactory conclusion," said Aston.

"I suppose I learned, too," said Wycliffe, speaking slowly, "something more of the power the pope wields, of his pride, his covetousness, his ambition, his tyranny, and his willingness to connive at any scheme which furthers his ends."

7. October 1374—Poor Priests

In spite of protesting that he was not giving up, he made no effort to renew his contact with the commission. The urgent necessity for more preaching of the Gospel weighed upon him. He determined that the time was ripe for putting into effect a long-cherished plan. Brut had gone, but he called Aston and Hereford.

"Think of men with a fiery zeal for preaching who would go out through the countryside bringing Christ to the people."

"Sounds like a description of the friars," said Aston.

"No, no, not the friars. Not that kind of preaching with its fables and myths and distortion of Scripture. You two will do for a start, but I'll need more. Who else is available?"

"Couldn't you tell us a little about what you have in mind?" asked Hereford.

Wycliffe had intended to wait until he could gather a larger group to unfold his plan, but his excitement could not be restrained.

"Do you recall," he asked, "in Luke's Gospel how Jesus sent out the seventy?"

After a thoughtful moment Aston's face lit up. "He sent them out two by two to preach. They were not to take purse or scrip or sandals."

"Right," said Wycliffe. "You will not go out begging as the friars go, but as poor men, without money or other possessions. Your badge will be the Gospel you preach. As a token by which you may be recognized and distinguished from the friars, you will wear a simple russet robe. In your hand you will carry a staff. You will accept no gift other than food and lodging."

Aston's face continued to glow, but Hereford seemed puzzled. "Where will we go? How shall we find preaching points? What of our other commitments?"

"Don't expect answers to all questions at once, Hereford. You will preach in parish churches or church-yards. At times you may find it convenient to preach in the marketplace, as the friars often do. Or in the street corners, or the fields—wherever you find willing listeners."

"As to other commitments," put in Aston, "I assume this will not be a full-time occupation, at least not at first. All of us have time we can give to this venture—a day, a weekend, perhaps a week or a month at times. Opportunities will not be lacking. Will you give us instruction as to what we are to preach, how we are to operate, that there may be some uniformity?"

Wycliffe smiled. "You are getting the idea rather clearly, Aston. I have some materials prepared, and you will help me to prepare more. You will make liberal use of Archbishop Thoresby's *Lay Folks Catechism*, with which you are familiar. The Scriptures will be basic, using certain chosen portions at first. I have sermon outlines of which you may make use."

"I perceive," said Aston, "that you've had this project in mind for some time and have laid careful plans."

"The general outline, but not all the details. We'll start small. Suggest two, or perhaps four, who might join you two."

Hereford responded eagerly. "On my way in I saw Thomas Brightwell and Robert Alington, who have rooms here near you."

"There's Purvey," said Aston.

"Purvey has yet to be ordained to the priesthood. I will, of course, make an exception of Brut when he appears."

"Lawrence Bedeman, then," said Aston.

"I'm not sure William James is here at present," said Hereford, "but John Aswarby should be available."

"All those are good men, true lovers of Christ, knowledgeable in the Scriptures."

An enthusiastic group of six gathered that evening. Wycliffe cautioned them to remain silent about this venture. "It may be frowned upon by the bishops. A quiet beginning is best."

He stressed the care they should give to their personal lives. "As priests you are to live holy lives. Make it your aim to excel other men in holy prayer, in holy desire, and in holy speaking. In conversation as well as in preaching, keep Christ's word and his praise always in your mouth. Despise sin in any form, setting an example to others. Avoid all questionable deeds, that no man may find reason to blame you."

The men sat with thoughtful expressions. Hereford murmured, "What a responsibility! We'll be in the public eye in a new way."

"See that your life is a true and open book," Wycliffe continued, "in which the soldier and the layman may learn how to serve God and keep his commandments. For the example of a good life, if it be consistent, strikes ignorant men more than open preaching with the word alone."

"You're saying that a good life is more effective than preaching?" asked Alington.

"The two must match. No matter how good the preaching, failure to live a Christlike life can destroy its effect."

He supplied them with a Latin commentary on the Sermon on the Mount, which they were to put into English for use with the people. In addition they received passages of Scripture which he had translated into English, each with a short explanation. He saw to it that each had a copy of the *Lay Folks Catechism* in English.

"Teach the *Te Deum* and the Athanasian Creed in English," he said. "You have much more material than you will need this first time. Use the Scripture passages for your sermons. We'll know how to plan further on the basis of this experience. Mingle freely with the people, talking with them of Christ and the Gospel when the preaching is over."

"What about food and a place to stay?" asked Aswarby.

"You will almost always find hospitality in some home. Accept it, no matter how humble. Share the simple meals of your host. Should you chance to be offered nothing, seek what shelter you may find. If you go hungry one day, remember that you are not the first to do so. On the whole, however, you may count on God's leading and blessing."

The teams were eager to be off, but Wycliffe held them back. "Think over what has been said tonight," he said. "Study the materials and, with your partner, plan your first sermon as best you can. It will be different from preaching in the University Church. Spend time in prayer. Be sure you understand the commitment and that you feel ready to undertake it."

They decided to meet again on the two following evenings. Villages in the area were considered and a tentative itinerary marked out for each team.

"How long shall we expect to be gone?" asked Hereford.

"Judge by how things work out," said Wycliffe. "Perhaps two or three days for this first venture. The Michaelmas term is almost upon us, and most of you must return to your studies."

On a bright October morning Wycliffe committed them to God in prayer and sent them out, two by two, in their different directions. A great joy filled his heart.

He now applied himself furiously to writing, often working far into the night. He expanded the topics he had touched on in lectures for the past two years— dominion and grace and the related subject of disendowment of the clergy. When he took up anew his lectures on the Scriptures, he would find further opportunities to introduce these topics about which he had a growing concern.

His "poor preachers" returned, weary in body but still eager in spirit. He listened to tales of success, of disappointment, of frustration, and of apparent failure. They had preached and they had taught...and each admitted that he had learned much. Not one wanted to quit. He would give additional instruction before they went again and perhaps enlarge the group.

"This may be the beginning of a movement which, under God's hand, can change the face of England," he cried.

8. November-December 1374
Lutterworth Visit

He pried himself loose from his labors long enough to spend a few days at Lutterworth in November and found his timing propitious. His young curate, John Horne, needed encouragement.

"The parishioners want to know," said Horne, "what they can and cannot, should and should not, do on the Sabbath. I am afraid many of them want to be told they may do as they please."

Wycliffe preached a sermon they would not soon forget. "I give you three manners of occupation for the Sabbath," he told them. "First, keep it in *thinking*. Meditate on the greatness of God, that he is *Almighty*, for he made the world out of nothing; that he is *All-knowing*, and governs all wisely; that he is *All-good*, for he makes all work for good for men who faithfully love him; that he is *All-just*, rewarding good deeds and punishing trespasses; and that he is *All-merciful*, readier to receive sinful men to grace, that would truly leave sins, than they are to ask mercy."

He urged them to think upon the greatness of creation, of God's kindness in sending his Son to suffer for us, of the glorious resurrection, and of the coming of the Holy Spirit.

As the second occupation proper to the Sabbath, he gave them *speaking*. "Confess your sins to God, cry heartily to him for the grace and power to leave sin, and to live in virtue. Then speak to your neighbors, to bring them to better living."

Having told them to *think*, then to *speak*, he now gave them something to *do*. "Be careful to attend public worship. Endeavor to bring pure motives to the service of God, so that the mind may be in its best state for attending to the duties of that day."

When he urged that there be little indulgence in the pleasures of the table on the Sabbath, he noticed some raised eyebrows and doubtful looks. "This is important," he insisted. "When the stomach is over-full, drowsiness is likely to take over, and discourage further spiritual activities."

He added, "Visit the sick, especially those whom God has made needy by age. As you are able, relieve with your goods the feeble, the crooked, the lame. The Gospel bids us do so. Men should not be idle but busy on the Sabbath about the soul as on the week day about the body."

Later he said to Horne, "I preached the sermon to you as well. It answers the questions they ask about the Sabbath, and it gives you a model to follow. You must set an example."

9. 1375—On Dominion

At the beginning of Advent he delivered a carefully-prepared sermon in St. Mary's, the university church. As he spoke and felt the attention and approval of a large audience, he found it an exhilarating experience. Quite different, in some ways, from preaching at Lutterworth.

Perhaps Brut was right. Oxford may be where I belong, with opportunities for lecturing, preaching, writing. With Lutterworth added, that should be enough. And yet... He shook his head uncertainly. *I suppose I may be reaching for the moon, but there are wrongs to be righted, errors to be corrected, battles to be fought and won...for God, with his help.*

In the first weeks of the new year Wycliffe struggled to put in publishable form two related works he would call *De Dominio Divino* and *De Civili Dominio*. He had for some time expressed the major ideas in lectures and in public debate. Conversations with students and friends helped him dig deeper and expand his views. "*Dominium*—lordship. How can anyone fail to see that lordship is the prerogative of God? All belongs to him and is under his control," he insisted.

All men, through the fall, he wrote, *have forfeited divine approval, and with it, all right to the possessions of this world, in common with any hope as to the possessions of a better world to come. As for those who avail themselves of the mediation of Christ—this lost right as to present and future blessing is, for his sake, restored. But all other men hold possession even of present things only by the divine sufferance. Men should know that all goods they have belong to God, and they are but his naked servants.*

He denied the theory that God had committed all dominion, temporal and spiritual, to the church or to any supposed successor of St. Peter. He drew heavily upon Fitzralph for support, and he quoted often from Augustine.

Lordship is committed directly by God to men, but only in grace. One in grace is, theoretically, lord of all, along with others likewise in grace. Wycliffe never pressed this point to the extent of advocating communism of worldly wealth.

It was a theory, and he recognized its utter impracticability at present.

On the other hand, he maintained, *no one, cleric or secular, king or peasant, has true dominion over anything, whether inanimate objects or animate nature, while in a state of mortal sin.*

Upon these views and others which he expressed in his writing at this time, Wycliffe based his arguments for the disendowment of the church.

Monasteries and dioceses hold enormous wealth in gold, silver, land and landed estates. They hold control over the serfs who dwell upon the land, of whom they make full use in cultivating the fields for the production of food, in herding and shepherding cattle and sheep, and as domestic servants within the establishment.

He held that it is not only wrong for them to possess this property, in view of the teaching of Scripture as to apostolic poverty and of the vows of poverty most of the monks had taken, but also the use they make of it is wrong. They hoard it and use it for their own purposes instead of helping the poor. In caring for these vast possessions and in spending time in secular positions, they woefully neglect their spiritual duties.

As Wycliffe wrote on and on, the parchment pages piled high. These works on Dominion would be no brief tracts, but a small part of a larger work beginning to take shape in his mind. Other duties pressed, but he returned to the writing whenever time permitted, for ever more strongly did the rightness of his ideas grow in his mind.

The duty of imposing order on the chaos which reigns in the church rests with the lay authorities. We cannot look for a piecemeal reform within the church, for all the clergy are contaminated in some way by failure to observe Scriptural precepts. As the lay authorities caused the trouble by their endowments, they must cure it. The king is chiefly responsible for putting his house in order. Should he fail, Parliament must undertake the responsibility.

He knew he was treading on dangerous ground. He hesitated before making the next statement, then plunged on. *If Parliament fails to do its duty, the common people should be prepared for direct action.*

Aston came in one May morning from a trip to London. "I suppose, as usual, you have news," said Wycliffe. "What now?"

"As more or less expected, Sudbury has been appointed archbishop of Canterbury. Would you hazard a guess as to who is to be translated to the see of London?"

"Not Courtenay, oh, please, not Courtenay!" cried Wycliffe.

"I'm sorry to tell you that Courtenay it is. This leaves several bishoprics vacant. What about Worcester for you?"

"No bishopric for me," replied Wycliffe. "Remember, I was dropped from the negotiations at Bruges. I received my 'reward' earlier—Lutterworth. Others more active in the king's service will receive these appointments. I still wait for my Lincoln canonry to materialize. It's all I can expect."

Wycliffe learned that the prebend of Caistor had become vacant, a lucrative benefice worth sixty-eight marks. "Surely," he cried, "this is for me. The pope will not by-pass me again."

With the inner asssurance that he would receive this benefice, he inquired into the amount of the first-fruits. It proved to be 45 pounds. Even though in line for the appointment, he would need to pay this to the pope before a final word was given.

Almost in despair, he considered avenues he might follow in seeking to borrow the money. How could he bear to lose this appointment for the lack of 45 pounds!

Possibly by the end of the year the money would become available.

10. January-April 1376—Of Disendowment

Wycliffe exulted in the confidence that the prebend of Caistor would be his. When witnessing an official letter, he even signed himself "canon of Lincoln." Then the blow fell. The pope granted the prebend to Philip de Thornbury, illegitimate son of Sir John Thornbury, an English leader of mercenaries in the pope's service in Italy. In payment of his debt to the father, the pope had granted a general reservation to the son, which took precedence over Wycliffe's special reservation.

Wycliffe was too shocked for speech at first. When he found words, his wrath caused him to go to extremes. "Why should I, a prominent and deserving scholar at Oxford, be passed over in favor of an idiot from overseas who has no intention of setting foot in England and has already received a license for non-residence? I consider this an insufferable insult."

In vain his friends pointed out that the young man was not an "idiot," but a man of some ability and standing, whose name happened to be higher on the pope's waiting list. The incident rankled, and added to his growing animosity toward the hierarchy.

This evidenced itself in his writing, which he continued to pursue furiously. He never hesitated to use his old friends as sounding boards, Hereford, Aston, Purvey, as a rule. Another strong supporter had recently appeared, Philip Repyngton, an Augustinian, an attractive young man, already highly esteemed at Oxford for his moderate and kindly bearing.

Repyngton listened one day as Wycliffe expounded upon the need for disendowment: "Appropriation of parish churches is so often made to worldly bishops and abbots. Does one of them do the office of curate in these parishes? Does he preach or teach or give the sacraments? Does he offer help to poor men?"

"I see your point," said Repyngton, "but surely a bishop or an abbot could not turn from his responsibilities to fill the post of curate in every church given as endowment."

"Must he set an idiot for vicar or parish priest? Many such a one you will find who cannot or will not do the office of a good curate, yet the poor parish is saddled with him."

Repyngton agreed with Wycliffe's doctrine of evangelical poverty and its application to the "possessionate clergy." "But how," he asked, "can it be brought about, even in a modified way? It's unthinkable to expect the church to be utterly deprived and reduced to total reliance upon alms and voluntary gifts."

"Perhaps for the foreseeable future. Yet one must aim high and ask for more than one expects to receive immediately. As to how to accomplish it, that is the responsibility of the king, as I've said before. All property should be under the control of king and nobles. Nowhere in Scripture is there even a hint of temporal lordship in the hands of spiritual leaders."

Wycliffe moved on in his writing to the matter of clergy in lay office: *These lordships that clergy hold so falsely against God's law and spend so wickedly should be given by the king and wise lords to poor but able gentlemen who would justly govern the people and maintain the land against enemies.*

In writing upon the right of lay leaders to deprive sinful priests of their endowments, he admitted that such action would result in excommunication of the lay leaders. *However, such excommunication,* he added, *except for strictly spiritual* offenses, was meaningless.

Coming to the close of the second book of *Civil Dominion*, Wycliffe waxed almost poetic: *Oh, how happy and fertile would England be if every parish church had as of yore a saintly rector residing with his family, if every manor had a just lord with wife and children! So much arable land would not lie fallow nor there be so great a dearth of cattle. The realm would have every sort of wealth in abundance, as well as serfs and artisans.*

He gave a rueful sigh. "How sadly the ideal contrasts with the actual! That, too, I must report. That done, this must be published."

Before beginning the third book Wycliffe made a hurried trip to Lutterworth, where he found Horne handling things well. *But so young!* said Wycliffe to himself. *A Timothy. I must bring him up right, only I get little opportunity to work at it. A good man, but he needs guidance.*

Wycliffe exhorted his people warmly as he preached on the importance of putting God first, of worshiping, loving, obeying him. "Never forget," he said, "that when you were a child of wrath and of hell for the sin of Adam, Jesus Christ, who is both God and man, laid down his life to bring you out of that prison.

"He gave not as ransom for you either gold or silver or any jewel, but died a painful death on the cross, giving his own precious blood which ran out of his heart to buy your soul out of hell to the bliss of heaven. That must move you to have a mind for God, and to worship him in thought, word, and deed."

He found an impatient Brut awaiting him at Oxford. "I thought you'd never come," he growled. "So long without a visit, then it seemed I might have to leave without seeing you at all."

In his deep joy at this reunion with his old friend Wycliffe wiped away a sudden rush of tears. "What news do you bring from the great world outside Oxford?" asked Wycliffe,

"All London and Westminster is abustle with preparations for Parliament. The noise in the streets was deafening as the trains of gentlemen and their retainers crowded in."

"I'd like to be there, noise and all," cried Wycliffe.

"It was expected that the king himself would be present at the opening of Parliament," said Brut. "I doubt he will make more than the one appearance. Gaunt will preside after that."

11. July-September 1376
Unexpected Summons

After sitting for nearly three months, Parliament finally adjourned. The death of the Black Prince on Trinity Sunday had caused a brief interruption.

Wycliffe had reason to rejoice over the actions of Parliament. "They're calling it the 'Good Parliament,'" he said. "And such it was. It's almost unbelievable that some of the men in high office were accused and condemned of fraud and worse. Several were fined and removed from office, some were imprisoned."

"It does seem strange," remarked Purvey, "that Lancaster was not included on the new council named for the king."

"That was a mistake," said Wycliffe. "Possibly some still fear he has designs on the throne when the old king is gone. They need not fear. He's loyal to his brother's son."

"It was that fear that caused the Commons to insist, after the Black Prince's death, that the king produce the boy in Parliament and acknowledge him as his heir," said Purvey.

"An unnecessary move," said Wycliffe. "But let's get this tract I've called *De Daemonio Meridiano, The Devil's Noonday*, ready for publication."

"You're again attacking wealthy prelates and priests in this one," said Purvey, picking up his pen.

"What I'm saying applies to the religious orders as well, notably the monks. Perhaps I'm being repetitious, but that's sometimes necessary to make a point. By their worldliness and neglect of spiritual duties they are sinning against the Holy Trinity, ruining the land, and robbing the poor of their rights."

On a day in late September he sat at his desk laboring to establish from the Scriptures the fact of the complete poverty of Jesus and the apostles. "From this," he maintained, "it follows that the clergy should neither bear civil rule nor hold property except for the poor."

At this point he looked up from his work. "Purvey, by the time I finish this third section of *Civil Dominion*, the whole will come to something like 1,000 pages. It is well that I am publishing it in parts. If it appeared in one volume, not only the size but the price would frighten the prospective reader."

"Is this section about ready for publication?" asked Purvey.

"Another week or two may see it finished, barring unforeseen interruptions. The end of September at the latest."

The unforeseen interruption came in the appearance at Wycliffe's door of a messenger. "Ah, Sir," he cried, "I was told to deliver with all haste this letter entrusted to me. For my pains I am to receive five shillings, and that alone speaks of its importance. See, it bears the king's own Privy Seal."

Dated September 22, the communication instructed "Master John Wycliffe, clerk," to appear before the king's council. Puzzled at this summons, Wycliffe sent the messenger on his way and made hasty preparations for his own departure.

Since Brut was concluding a visit to Oxford and was ready to return to London, the two could travel together. A strong hint of autumn hung in the air as they rode out the next morning. The trees showed tinges of brilliant colors, the full splendor of which would appear in a few weeks. Along much of the way they could ride side by side, with Wycliffe's man following.

"Remember our old walks on a day like this?" asked Brut.

"Sometimes you had to drag me out, but what a miracle it worked in body and mind. I'll never forget."

"It meant as much to me. Even in my absence you should get out like that occasionally. It would keep you from getting too intense about your lecturing and writing."

"What do you suppose this summons before the council means?" asked Wycliffe. "It was Lancaster's man who brought it, yet Lancaster is not on the new council appointed by Parliament."

"Don't fool yourself that the new council will stand. Lancaster is back at the king's side. Doubtless he has the king's ear as well since the death of the Black Prince. As to your summons, you will find out soon enough."

"Will the actions of the recent Parliament not be upheld? Many of them pointed to changes for the better. The Parliament is known as the 'Good Parliament,' which is just what it was."

"When you get to London and Westminster, you'll find different talk. Lancaster means to undo all that was done. I fear you face disappointments."

"I'm shocked," said Wycliffe. "I can't believe Lancaster means to set aside what was accomplished. He upheld all the actions taken."

"Wycliffe, you are the most outstanding philosopher and theologian at Oxford. Your wisdom in your own fields is incontrovertible. But you live your life in the tight little world of the university with your head in your books. There is much in the outside world of which you are ignorant. You are in for some surprises, even some shocks, when you begin to breathe other air than the rarified atmosphere of Oxford."

Wycliffe bristled. "I'm not a child, Brut. I do get out and away from Oxford. I spent two years and more at Fillingham. I was at Ludgershall any time I could spare. The same is true of Lutterworth. I observe what goes on; I am aware of the ills of the world. Those weeks at Bruges opened my eyes to much."

"You know what goes on in the church and in ecclesiastical circles, but there is much of which you are unaware. People are not always what they seem. Of course the duke upheld the actions taken by Parliament. What else could he do? That doesn't mean the actions pleased him."

"Some things about the duke I cannot countenance, but he does have admirable qualities, and he is in a position of power."

"He has an admiration of you," said Brut. "He must read all that comes from your pen, so he is aware of your thinking. I just don't want him to take advantage of you, using you for *his* purposes, which may not turn out to be *your* true purposes."

Wycliffe shook off his irritation and gave Brut a smile. "I do need taking down a peg now and then, and you are the one to do it. I don't think you need worry. We don't even know why I'm called. I don't intend to enter into any nefarious business."

When they neared the city, Brut headed into London, while Wycliffe continued on to Westminster.

Before parting they arranged to meet the next day so that Wycliffe might enlighten Brut as to the outcome of his appearance before the council.

"I don't know why I find myself in such a state of high excitement," said Wycliffe as he approached the meeting place. "Is it a premonition that some startling new venture lies ahead?" When the moment came for him to enter the council chamber, he managed a degree of calmness.

The king was not present, but Lancaster represented him and was in full charge. Wycliffe looked about him and was surprised to see not one of those who had been named to the council by Parliament. His thoughts, however, were soon drawn elsewhere.

They had not called him to ask his opinion on any matter. Indeed, it appeared he was expected to say little. Lancaster referred in complimentary phrases to his most recently published works, his words echoed by others present. References were made in guarded terms to the recent Parliament and its actions.

When they came to their business with Wycliffe, he could hardly believe what he heard. He tried to subdue his excitement, feeling sure his pleasure must radiate from his countenance. With no hesitation he accepted the proposition Lancaster presented.

He could hardly recall how the meeting ended, but he must have given proper responses. As he was dismissed he stumbled out in a euphoric daze and rode off in search of Brut.

12. September-November 1376 London Preaching

Brut listened in silence as Wycliffe poured out his story. He remained silent when Wycliffe came to a halt. When Wycliffe focused his eyes on his friend's face, the lack of response he saw there startled him. "Brut! Do you hear what I am saying? Don't you share my joy at the opportunity that has come to me?"

"I hear you, my friend. I'm trying to think through what you have said. I'm not yet sure that it is cause for joy."

"An opportunity to preach in all the churches in and around London, and with specific instructions to preach on the subject of disendowment of the clergy—this is not cause for joy?"

"I hate to throw cold water on your delightful prospect, but I'm not sure it's a good or a wise thing you are asked to do."

"Not a good thing to preach to the population of London on the theme that has been uppermost in my mind for so long? The subject I have talked of, preached about, lectured on, written countless pages on at Oxford—and now this chance to reach a wider audience, with the blessing of the king's council? Brut! What objection can you possibly offer?"

Brut let out his breath in a long sigh. "More than one objection comes to mind. You say they spoke of Bishop Wykeham, an exceedingly wealthy prelate, a proper subject for disendowment. What they did not say is that Lancaster believes Wykeham was behind the impeachment actions brought against his friends in the recent Parliament. He is out to destroy Wykeham."

"I find that hard to believe. Wykeham is only one against whom I will preach for disendowment. I need not name names. The truth applies to most prelates, as to other ecclesiastics."

"I feel that you will put yourself in a dangerous position. Much can be said in the climate of the university which will not be tolerated elsewhere. You will be preaching in Courtenay's diocese. Since you are commissioned by the council, he will not dare to stop you, but he can make trouble for you."

"What I will preach is what I have already written and published. Courtenay has surely read every word with a critical eye. If he's going to object, he has his ammunition already in hand. Dangerous? Proclaiming the truth is often dangerous. I am not a heretic. Courtenay can never pin that charge on me."

"Seeing your determination, I withold further objections," replied Brut. "Perhaps I'm wrong. I pray this opportunity may be all you expect it to be. You do preach the truth, and your plea for disendowment is valid. Whether it can come about in our time is debatable. Preach, Wycliffe! Preach with all the power God gives you, and may his blessing be upon you."

Putting aside Brut's warnings, Wycliffe entered upon what promised to be several glorious weeks. He preached in one church after another, and found his message received with enthusiasm.

To the people themselves he preached against greed and seeking after wealth. "*Godliness with contentment is great gain,*" he would quote from Paul's first letter to Timothy. "*Having food and raiment, let us therewith be content.*"

He would continue in that vein for a bit, saying, "Paul also tells us, '*They that will be rich fall into temptation, and a snare, and into many foolish and hurtful lusts, which drown men in destruction and perdition.*'"

Having warned his hearers as to their own lives, it was a natural step to turn to examples of those who did not live according to Scriptural precept—the bishops and rich clergy and monks, who neglected spiritual duties to accumulate and increase worldly wealth.

"Christ and his apostles were not rich men; indeed, they lived from the gifts of their followers.

The apostle Paul worked for a living while he preached the Gospel.

"Endowments which come to the church are for God's work, for the relief of the poor and needy, not for the luxurious living of the prelates. While they thus hold what does not belong to them, they are thieves and have no right to the offices they hold."

He was conscious of the breathless attention his hearers gave. "Such wealth should be under the control of the civil government. Then it would be rightly administered, and the clergy could concentrate on preaching the Word of God and extending Christ's kingdom, while setting an example of holy living."

People thronged to the churches. Crowds followed him in the streets. He was told that quotes from his sermons formed the basis of conversation in marketplace and alehouses. His name met with applause whenever mentioned.

He disregarded a mild but growing rumbling of opposition. *I have these people in the palm of my hand*. It was a dizzying sensation.

Then came a break in the routine. The body of the Black Prince had lain in state at Westminster for four months. His desire had been to be buried at Canterbury, the shrine to which he had been especially devoted.

The coffin, drawn by twelve black horses, moved through the streets of London and across London bridge, followed by a throng of dignitaries, including Wycliffe. His body was laid to rest behind the high altar near the shrine of St. Thomas. His shield, helm, jupon, scabbard, and gauntlets were hung above the completed tomb.

Wycliffe, looking upon these relics of the battlefield, thought back thirty years to the victory at Crecy when the valiant Black Prince, a lad of fifteen years, had first become the idol of the nation. So much had happened, so many changes!

Back in London, Wycliffe descended with a jolt from his previous exuberant state. At Westminster actions of the recent Parliament were being ridiculed. The "Good Parliament" was declared null and void, and its actions erased from the books. The condemned men were back at their posts.

Puzzled and distressed, Wycliffe preached on, but he began to listen more closely to what he overheard at meals or in chance conversations. Brut's prediction as to Bishop Wykeham's fate began to come true. Wycliffe squirmed over what he heard. In this case had come a result for which he had preached, but the circumstances and the reason behind the action stirred doubts in his mind which he had difficulty in quieting.

Lancaster and the Great Council were determined to destroy Wykeham, bishop of Winchester. Charges of misconduct were brought up against him, dating back to his chancellorship ten years before. He was deprived of his temporalities, forbidden to come within 20 miles of court, and was told he must appear for trial in January.

The man suffered. He moved about through his diocese, with no house or goods left, largely deserted by those who had served him. Students at his recently established New College at Oxford were forced to go home, for there was no money for their maintenance. This last disturbed Wycliffe greatly. Surely suppport of a college was money well-spent! Disendowment—but he had not considered such a situation as this.

Wycliffe had no opportunity to see Lancaster before he returned to Oxford. "In any case, what would I say?" he asked himself. "Allied as I am with him, I could hardly afford to speak out as I would like on the things that have come to pass. But how I wish for some explanation, some reassurance."

Again at Oxford, he looked back with satisfaction upon his preaching and its effect upon the populace of London. He tried to stifle the qualms he felt about the Wykeham affair. He preached at the University Church on November 23, then threw himself into preparation of lectures and writing, hoping that filling his mind with necessary occupation would help.

In December he learned that Lancaster had summoned Parliament to meet in January. What would this mean?

13. February 1377—Ominous Summons

On a brisk afternoon in February Wycliffe entered his rooms at Queen's feeling rather pleased. "Good attendance today," he remarked, "and the lecture went well."

Some inner voice—his conscience, he assumed—said, *Not all students agreed with you, and they stated their objections.*

"Ah, but this is good," he replied. "It gives me an opportunity to employ my dialectical skill in seeking to convince them. In many cases you noticed that I was successful."

His conscience continued to needle him. *Don't I detect something of personal pride here?*

"You may be right," he said reluctantly. "Yet most of all I want to bring these men to a knowledge of the truth." He sometimes had a great deal of trouble with this inner voice.

He settled down to work on his next lectures. Before he had progressed far, a knock came at his door, and a visitor entered.

"Aston!" he cried. "How good to see you! It seems a very long time since I've had the pleasure of your company."

"Through no fault of mine. When you spend weeks on end in London, how can you expect the undoubted pleasure of my company?"

"I've been back for two months now," replied Wycliffe. "It's you who have been away."

"It's those weeks in London I'm eager to hear about. You went at the call of the duke of Lancaster. Did he give you the assistance you needed? Was he satisfied with the results?"

"You come right to the point. I must try to do as well. The duke neglected no detail. He wanted me to preach in as many churches as possible. Arrangements were made in advance, and the fact that I would preach well-publicized. I did not see him before leaving, but I believe what I accomplished would satisfy him. I was a guest at his magnificent London palace, the Savoy, but I rarely saw him. I went and came on my own."

"Didn't the bishop of London object to your preaching in his diocese? If you preached on the disendowment of the clergy as the duke requested, Courtenay could hardly have taken it calmly."

"What could he do? The king's council called me. And think of John of Gaunt's position. Consider his power in this realm."

"Power he has but not popularity. You must have softened your message. Presenting disendowment and dominion as you do in your lectures would be dangerous."

"You should know, Aston, that when I reach a conclusion, guided as I seek to be by God's Word, I speak. My convictions will not allow me to be swayed by consideration of possible consequences. Wrongs in the church must be reformed. How are people to know the teaching of Scripture unless it's proclaimed? They are blinded and misled by the fiends of Satan who refuse to preach or who preach error."

"I should have known," said Aston. "Yet in spite of the protection of Lancaster, I fear for your safety. London is not Oxford. Courtenay, too, is a powerful—and dangerous—man."

"Safety! You and Brut keep harping on safety. Since when has it been *safe* to defend the truth? Do you forget what happened to our Lord, who *is* the Truth? Or to Stephen or James or Paul? I had already made Courtenay an enemy by last year's activity, if not before. He hates Lancaster, and the feeling seems to be mutual."

Aston started to comment, but Wycliffe rushed on. "Anyway, Courtenay has had a problem of his own to settle. You remember that the pope, when at war with the state of Florence last year, excommunicated all Florentines."

"He invited all princes and cities to seize their goods. Our king's friendship with Florentine merchants in England moved the council to ignore the pope's wishes and suppress his bulls."

"That's where Courtenay ran into trouble. The pope began to mutter about interdicts. Since many Florentines live in the London diocese, the pope ordered Courtenay to publish the bulls."

"I suppose that rather put Courtenay on the spot. You mean he finally decided to give in to the pope?"

"In early January, he had the effrontery to publish the bulls at Paul's Cross. As a result some of the London business rivals of the Florentines began to plunder their warehouses."

"That must have caused an uproar. How did the council react to that?" asked Aston.

"The chancellor summoned the bishop and asked why he had published the bulls without knowledge of king or council. Courtenay's reply was, 'Because the pope ordered it.' The chancellor gave him the choice between suffering confiscation of his temporalities or recalling his words with his own mouth."

Aston let out a whistle. "That *is* a comedown for our friend Courtenay. Did he actually recall the bulls?"

"They spared him the indignity of doing it in person. When members of Parliament gathered on January 27, they were treated to the spectacle of Courtenay's proxy at Paul's Cross explaining away his master's action, after which an official spoke, denouncing papal usurpations."

"The bishop's action may have shocked the city fathers, but it no doubt raised him in the estimation of the London merchants. They harbor an understandable hatred of the foreign traders."

Wycliffe shifted in his chair and stretched his legs. "This cold gets into my bones a bit."

"If Parliament has been in session since January 27," said Aston, "we should soon have news of the action there."

A clatter of hoofs on the cobblestones outside, followed by a rapping at the door interrupted their conversation. Wycliffe's servant answered, returning with a document for his master.

Wycliffe turned it over in his hand. "Interesting! It bears the seal of the archbishop of Canterbury. What business can he have with me?" As he broke the seal and read, he frowned.

"What is it?" cried Aston.

"Looks pretty serious. I'm summoned to London to appear at St. Paul's before the Convocation of the clergy on the 19th of this month of February."

"As I feared!" exclaimed Aston. "What is the charge?"

"I am charged with 'maintaining and publishing a variety of erroneous doctrines.' Courtenay's work!" he cried, springing up from his chair. "The archbishop is a mild man. He would never have taken such action. Courtenay goaded him into it."

He paced up and down the room. "It was too good an opportunity for Courtenay to resist. He dared not take action against the duke of Lancaster. This way he not only strikes at me but at the same time delivers an indirect blow at the duke."

"They say Courtenay is driven by two strong motives, one in politics, one in religion," said Aston. "The first leads him to fierce opposition to John of Gaunt, the second to hatred of all heretics. He can't bring a charge of heresy against *you!*"

"You underestimate the bishop of London. He will almost certainly make the attempt. I see no way he could succeed." Seating himself heavily in his chair, he struck the top of his desk with his fist. "Still, to go lightly before this body would be foolish. I must arm myself against any line they may conceivably follow."

"Time is short, Wycliffe. The 19th of February is only a fortnight away. You must develop the strongest defense possible. What help may I offer?"

Wycliffe stirred uneasily. "I must work at it alone at first. Plan to remain in Oxford. Is Hereford here? And Repyngton? I hope Brut is available. Get the word around, and report to me when I call."

After Aston left, Wycliffe found his rage mounting. *It had to come to this! Courtenay's eye has been on me for some time. My preaching in London, which he was helpless to prevent, brought him to the end of his tether. I had hoped the storm would not break so soon.*

He seized his coat and cap and hastened to the banks of the Cherwell. An hour of strenuous walking might calm his spirit somewhat. Returning to Oxford, he sought the chapel at Merton college, one of his favorite spots for prayer.

14. February 1377—Preparation

Two days later a missive from John of Gaunt arrived by special messenger. The duke wished to reassure his friend as to the ordeal before him. It was a perilous situation, but he was taking steps to insure Wycliffe's safety. *I will accompany you personally*, he had written. *You are not to be anxious.*

Hereford, Aston, Repyington, and Brut came to him on Monday before he was to face the bishops on Thursday. They expressed relief upon hearing that he would have the duke's support.

"They say," said Hereford, "that those who serve John of Gaunt may expect his protection. That is well in this case, though such a connection is not always a desirable position."

"It's his policy," said Wycliffe, "to treat as his own the quarrels of those who work with him. He counts it a point of honor. I don't go along with all his schemes, but in matters on which we agree, it's an advantage to have him as a friend."

Brut cleared his throat. "I want to say something, Wycliffe, which I hope you will take to heart. You tend to brush off such advice as I will give, but I implore you to listen. You should strive to keep your temper. The bishops will say things that anger you, and anger sometimes leads you to unwise words and actions." He paused as if trying to decide whether to continue.

"Go on," said Wycliffe, testily. He did not enjoy having attention drawn to a fault of which he was all too conscious.

"I implore you to control the vehemence of your language. You will not help your case by hurling vile epithets at your opponents, no matter how well deserved."

Knowing Wycliffe's touchiness on this subject, Hereford hastened to speak. "Brut is right. The situation is far more dangerous than you may imagine. You have voiced your suspicion that Courtenay takes this means of striking at John of Gaunt.

"Consider his reasons for striking not merely at John of Gaunt but at *you*. In the very heart of his diocese you denounced worldly prelates in bitter terms. You found a multitude of receptive ears for your message. He will not forgive you for that. The members of Convocation will back him strongly."

"Courtenay is not dependent only upon your sermons in London for knowledge of your teachings," said Repyngton. "He will have read your published works."

Wycliffe sighed deeply. "What you say can't be denied. Courtenay has declared war, and the lines are drawn for the first battle." He frowned and reflected for a moment. "In London I preached a relatively moderate disendowment."

"You know you have our full support," said Aston. "As radical as these views may seem, you have practically the whole university behind you."

"You can hardly say that, Aston. Courtenay is not my only enemy. There are those here who wish me silenced."

Wycliffe went over with them the material upon which he expected to be examined. In scholastic fashion, they tried him with questions, raising every objection an opponent might be expected to use. He was able to refute them on every point.

"I hardly see how Convocation can find heresy in your statements," said Hereford. "They will not approve of nor agree with them, but these matters attack no doctrine of the church."

"Still, I feel uneasy," said Brut. "Which of us should accompany you? Or should we all go?"

"I considered that," replied Wycliffe. "I think it best that none of you go. There is no cause for you to align yourselves with me outside of Oxford, not at this point. My man will attend me. The duke will have made any arrangements he deems necessary."

Early the next morning he rode out with his servant toward London. The day was cold, but clear. The roads were hard enough to give the horses firm footing. Wycliffe did not mind the crispness of the wind in his face. The coldness that clutched at his heart was another matter. His confidence in the rightness of his position did not waver, but he would face a formidable foe.

15. February 1377—Abortive Confrontation

Wycliffe arrived on Wednesday afternoon to find the duke occupied with business of Parliament. He had left a message setting time and place for Wycliffe to meet him the next day. Again he insisted, "You need not worry. All will be well."

Wycliffe found it hard to take seriously these words in light of what he encountered on the streets. It seemed as if the whole population of the city milled about with angry shouts. To his horror, the name he distinguished again and again in their furious outcry was that of the duke of Lancaster.

Parliament had been in session for three weeks. On this very day John of Gaunt had introduced into Parliament a bill which, if passed, would remove the government of the City of London from the hands of the mayor and put it in the hands of the king's marshal. The demonstration was in protest of this.

Wycliffe began to wonder about the value of the duke's support. *A few weeks ago I had these people solidly behind me. Popular support can sway a decision. What will happen when the citizenry find the hated enemy defending me?*

Next morning he set out through the narrow streets toward the house of the Blackfriars, where he was to meet the duke. He wore his best black robe, which was designed with fulness from shoulder to ankle, belted at the waist. It gave the appearance, he was told, of elegant simplicity. His beard, well-groomed as usual, added to his dignity. Behind him his servant bore his books and notes. Conspicuous among them was a Latin Bible.

Minutes after Wycliffe's arrival at Blackfriars the duke and his retinue appeared. They had come by river from Westminster to the Blackfriars landing. John of Gaunt approached in his usual self-assured manner.

He greeted Wycliffe with enthusiasm, but his smile, after the greeting, gave place to a serious expression. "As happy as I am to see you, Wycliffe, I regret the circumstances. I feel responsible. This is Courtenay's work. He will take any action which might be offensive to me, and he knows of our friendship."

"You must not blame yourself," said Wycliffe. "Courtenay has stored up wrath against me on several scores."

"In any case, we are here to protect you. You need not have an anxious thought. You have nothing to fear."

He presented Wycliffe to Lord Henry Percy, grand marshal of England. Consternation gripped Wycliffe. This was one of the names shouted with such murderous rage by the citizenry of London. It was he who proposed to supplant the lord mayor and take the rule of the city. Still, the power of his position was indisputable. He hoped the duke knew what he was doing.

Four doctors of divinity had come at Gaunt's call. They represented the four mendicant orders at Oxford. Their function was to assist Wycliffe in the defense of his doctrines. The rest of the party consisted of the duke's armed men.

The hour approached noon. Wycliffe was to present himself at the church in the early afternoon. As they turned to move on to St. Paul's, they found a noisy throng crowding the street. Lord Percy led the way. Behind him came Wycliffe with Gaunt at his side, followed by Wycliffe's man and the four doctors. The armed men brought up the rear.

Their difficulty in approaching the church was as nothing compared to what they faced upon arrival. The churchyard was filled with people, pushing, shouting, all trying to force their way into the cathedral. Only with great effort did Percy open a path for Wycliffe and the duke to reach the entrance.

The duke held Wycliffe's arm and guided him, murmuring, "Let not the sight of these bishops cause you to falter in upholding your faith. They know but little. As for this unruly throng, do not fear them. We are here for your defense."

Wycliffe pulled himself to his full height as he stepped across the threshold. He made no reply to Gaunt's utterances, but fear was the farthest thing from his mind. The "unruly throng" at the church had gathered because of their adherence to him. These were the people to whom he had preached a few weeks before.

Once inside, they faced a solid wall of humanity. Lord Percy found that his words had little effect. In the arrogant manner of a long line of Percys, he pushed aside the merchants and apprentices who stood in his way, causing resentment. His threat that he would use his silver-tipped staff as more than a symbol of his high office did nothing to improve the situation.

As those in his path recognized Percy and the duke, a change took place in the mood of the crowd. They seemed to forget that they had assembled to champion Wycliffe. The enemy was in their midst. Ugly mutterings spread, fists were raised, threats were shouted. The din reached disgraceful proportions in what should have been a holy place. Wycliffe was stunned at the swiftness with which the situation had assumed so ominous a character.

Percy redoubled his efforts to open a passage, raising his voice to be heard above the hubbub. Slowly Wycliffe and Lancaster moved forward. The aisle of St. Paul's was said to be the longest of any cathedral in existence. After this journey down it, Wycliffe had no inclination to dispute the statement.

They finally reached the Lady Chapel behind the high altar, where the august body awaited Wycliffe's arrival. Archbishop Sudbury was present, but Courtenay was to preside. Besides the bishops and other high clergy, a number of knights and barons had come to witness the proceedings. The crowd surged in behind Wycliffe's party.

Bishop Courtenay's expression revealed perhaps a touch of anxiety, but certainly displeasure at seeing Wycliffe accompanied by two such powerful men. He turned toward Percy and said, "If I had known, my lord, what mastery you would assume in this church, I would have taken measures to prevent your entrance."

The duke spoke up in a cold tone. "He shall keep such mastery here, though you say nay."

The duke and Percy seated themselves. Percy turned to Wycliffe, who remained standing, and said, "Sit down and rest yourself. You have much to answer and will need a soft seat."

Courtenay cried, "It is unreasonable that one cited to appear before his judges should be seated during his answer. He must and shall stand."

"I find it astonishing," cried the duke, "that a learned doctor of England should be refused a courtesy to which his age alone entitles him."

Courtenay made a heated reply. The crowd pushed closer, and excitement increased. The duke assailed the bishop with yet more angry words, for which the bishop returned taunts and insults.

The duke said, "You are very arrogant. Take care, lest I bring down not only your pride, but that of all the prelates in England."

"Do your worst, Sir," replied Courtenay.

"You are insolent, my lord," cried Lancaster. "You think you can trust in your family, of whom you speak so boastfully. But they will be in no condition to help you. They will have enough to do to protect themselves."

Courtenay replied, "My confidence is not in my parents nor in any man, but only in God, in whom I trust, and by whose help I will be bold to speak the truth."

The duke disdained to answer, but muttered in a low tone, "I would rather pluck the bishop by the hair of his head out of the church than take this at his hands."

Wycliffe stood aghast. Even through the general confusion, the duke's unwise remark was overheard and passed through the crowd. Confusion escalated to uproar, the citizens of London crying that they would not have their bishop treated so. They made an attack on the duke and Percy, making it necessary for the duke's men to step in to protect their master and his friends.

All hope of restoring order vanished. The sitting of the court was suspended before it had even begun. The duke and Lord Percy made their escape, taking Wycliffe with them. Once outside Lancaster said to him, "It is not safe for you to remain with us. Return to Oxford with all speed."

Wycliffe needed no second bidding. Within the hour his servant had brought the horses. Only when they had passed through the city gate did Wycliffe begin to reflect upon the incredible events. He thought ruefully, *Brut need not have worried about my language. I had no chance to utter a word!*

16. February-June 1377—Repercussions

Wycliffe heard nothing further as to his trial. Apparently the matter was dropped for the present. But he heard much as to what took place regarding Lancaster and Percy and the Londoners. An excited eyewitness had hastened to Oxford to report.

The day following the uproar, the citizens of London had met to consider what steps they should take to protect the city against the proposed change in government. Too, they must decide how to respond to the insults to the bishop.

Two lords burst in, crying that the lord marshal had taken a prisoner and had him under guard at his residence in the city.

"That Lord Percy would dare take such unauthorized action brought things swiftly to a head," reported the witness. "The meeting broke up as the infuriated citizens rushed out for their armor and weapons. An undisciplined mob joined them as they headed for the marshal's house.

"They broke down the gates, freed the prisoner, and burned the stocks in which he had been fastened. They searched every corner of the great house, slashing at the hangings, hoping to find the marshal."

"It was well that they did not," exclaimed Wycliffe. "He would certainly have lost his life."

Assuming he would be with the duke at the Savoy, they had rushed off in that direction. Failing to find their quarry at the Savoy, they were about to burn the palace when Courtenay himself appeared and persuaded them against such action. They satisfied themselves by reversing the duke's arms displayed at Cheapside.

"That of course signified their accusation that he was a traitor." said Wycliffe.

Someone had shouted that the duke and the marshal were at dinner in the house of Sir John Ypres. As they turned in that direction, one of the duke's men hastened off to warn his master of the approaching mob.

"With no delay," said the witness, "the duke and Percy rose from the table and hurried to the river. Crossing to Kennington, they found safety in the house of Prince Richard and his mother." No further news came for a while. The affair dragged on.

The citizens held firmly to a demand that Bishop Wykeham, whatever the charges against him, have a fair trial. They cried that they would have the traitor, Lancaster, wherever he was found. At last peace seemed about to be restored. The bill against the city's liberties was withdrawn.

As Convocation still sat, Lancaster made a plea that they excommunicate the anonymous parties who had posted lampoons against him about the city. With reluctance, they agreed.

This disturbed Wycliffe. "I have preached for some time that excommunication for other than spiritual offenses is not permissible. The bishops have excommunicated anonymous persons for a personal offense against Lancaster's pride!"

Now came the amazing news that Pope Gregory had returned to Rome. "Only a handful of cardinals accompanied him," observed Wycliffe. "The others love too well the luxury of Avignon. He has chosen as papal residence the Vatican distict around St. Peter's."

"I suppose its nearness to the fortress of St. Angelo influenced his choice," said Purvey.

"Doubtless," said Wycliffe. "Rome is wild and dangerous. Even a pope may need a place of refuge."

As soon as he had published the final section of *Civil Dominion*, which caused no little stir, Wycliffe turned immediately to further efforts with the Poor Priests.

"I want to gather a larger group and start them on a mission of broader coverage. The first brave efforts were intermittent. It is time now to find men to undertake this work on a permanent basis, ordained priests who are willing to hold no benefice."

Having carefully selected those he felt could qualify, he instructed them as he had the first group. They were to live simply and were forbidden to beg. They were to preach the Word of God in simplicity and truth, adapting the message to the comprehension of their hearers. He adjusted his earlier instructions to the extent that, should no one offer food or lodging, they might use private means for their needs. He would arrange somehow to subsidize those who had little or nothing.

"O marvelous power of the divine Seed!" he cried. "It overturns strong warriors, softens hearts as hard as stone, and renews in the divine image men brutalized by sin and infinitely far from God. Plainly so mighty a wonder can never be wrought by the word of a priest if the heat of the Spirit of Life and the Eternal Word does not above all things work with it."

"Will we run into trouble," asked one, "for being unbeneficed priests with no license from a bishop to preach?"

"I think you need not fear," said Wycliffe. "You will hardly be noticed by the bishop in the places you will preach. A license from one bishop would be valid only in that bishop's diocese, whereas you will be traveling from one diocese to another. In the last analysis, since you *are* priests, you have leave of Christ to preach the Gospel. What higher license can you ask?"

Off they went, two by two, in their russet robes, their bare feet, staves in one hand, Scriptures and sermon notes in their pouches, with a small amount of money for any emergency.

"Of greatest importance," said Wycliffe, "they go with the love of God in their hearts and the Word of God on their lips."

17. June-September 1377—King Richard II

News of the death of Edward III in late June found Wycliffe at Lutterworth deep in a few weeks of pastoral work. The king's condition had been deteriorating, but the end came rather unexpectedly.

"Dead on June 21," exclaimed Wycliffe. "three days after restoring to William of Wykeham the temporalities of the see of Winchester. One wonders whether he knew the end was near and that this would be his last political action."

"They say not one of his bishops was with him," said Purvey. "His confession was heard by a lone priest, and broken by a sob. With his last breath he cried, 'Jesu, have mercy!'"

The old king was buried in Westminster Abbey on the Confessor's mound, a spot reserved for him among the Plantagenet kings. "He had lost his people's love by the time of his death," said Wycliffe sadly. "There is no great outcry of mourning across the land. Instead, I fear there is foreboding as to the future when a boy is to be king."

After a period of mourning, the coronation took place. On July 15 the young king made a triumphal entry into the city, received with enthusiasm by the Londoners. Leading the procession, just before the king, rode the duke of Lancaster and the lord marshal.

"Quite a contrast," observed Wycliffe "in their behavior today with that of February. With all modesty and courtesy they are asking the crowds to make room. Changing times bring changing manners."

Next morning the procession moved from the Tower, where the party had spent the night, to Westminster Abbey. Hearts beat rapidly with stirrings of joy in beholding the beautiful eleven-year-old lad, clad in a white robe embroidered with gold, sitting so straight upon his handsome white steed, head held high.

Again Lancaster and Percy led the procession. Before the king walked his other uncles and the earl of March, while behind came the archbishop of Canterbury. A blare of trumpets sounded. The houses had been decked with cloth of gold and silver and bright colors. The path itself was laid with scarlet cloth.

Inside the abbey, the king solemnly took the coronation oath, swearing to keep the faith and the laws, to do justice and to have mercy. Then the archbishop asked the traditional question of the people, whether they would have Richard as their king.

Anthems, psalms, and prayers interspersed the long ceremony. Led to the high altar, the king knelt as *Veni creator spiritus* was sung. Then came blessing and anointing by the archbishop. The crown was placed upon his head, the coronation ring upon his finger, and the sceptre in his hand.

After the coronation the peers came forward and touched the crown, signifying their agreement to aid the king. Now the king was led to the throne, and the coronation mass celebrated.

Such a lengthy ceremony wearied even the adults, but it was almost too much for the boy. His tutor, Sir Simon Burley, carried him on his shoulders to the palace for a short rest.

All bishops, earls, and barons attended a great banquet in Westminster Hall in the evening. As was customary, any who wished could enter the hall as onlookers. So great was the crowd that the duke as seneschal and Percy as marshal had to ride up and down the great hall on their horses to make room for the servants bearing dishes. In the palace grounds a fountain ran with wine, to which the king's subjects might come and drink.

A report as to the new council chosen for the king came as a shock to Wycliffe. "Lancaster has been excluded!" he cried. "After all he has done in holding things together while the old king was dying, mistaken though some of his actions were! The king will need the support of the uncle who brought him safely to the throne.

"The real power of this new council lies with the earl of March and Bishop Courtenay, both of whom have a consuming hatred for the duke. The Queen Mother exerts great influence over her son. That may count for something, but Richard II will have difficulty bucking those other two."

"Even the Queen Mother is known to have no great love for the duke of Lancaster," observed Purvey.

"John of Gaunt has retired into private life at Kenilworth for the present. He told the king that he could, at need, bring a large army to his support. When called, he may come, but, if I know Lancaster, it will be on his own terms."

"It seems a hasty and unwise action to drive him away just now," said Purvey. "France is taking advantage of the turmoil of changing kings in England to attack along the southern coast."

"The Scots are muttering threats, as well. The message my Poor Priests are spreading is needed. God grant them success."

18. October-December 1377—At Parliament

Richard II opened his first Parliament on October 13 at Westminster. All those in attendance were aware that the new government faced formidable problems. The French and Spanish fleets sailed up and down the Channel with no opposition. Rye, Plymouth, Dartmouth and other towns had been taken. Fear gripped the nation that a large force would march into the heart of the country.

In view of the desperate need for money to support the war, the old complaints were loudly voiced about the drainage of enormous amounts from the realm into the papal coffers and to French clergy. A recent pamphlet by Wycliffe on the subject had been widely read. Consequently, Wycliffe received a summons.

"Just think, Purvey," he said, "this call did not come at Lancaster's instigation, but from those who excluded him from the new government. This means I'm looked upon with favor in spite of my connection with him."

He hastened to Westminster. The formal wording of the request ran through his mind and was like honey on his tongue. He was to answer in writing the question: "May England for its own defense, in case of need, detain the wealth of the kingdom, so that it be not carried away in foreign parts, even though the pope himself demands it under pain of censure and by virtue of the obedience owing to him?"

His simple answer to the question would be a resounding affirmative, but he determined to do a thorough job.

His reply must take the form of a state paper. He set to work putting his thoughts in written form.

He came before the combined houses of Parliament, shoulders back, head held high. After making the appropriate courteous acknowledgements and salutations to the king, council, and members of Parliament, he launched into his reply.

He appealed to three laws in making his point. "First," he said, "I take my stand upon the law of natural reason, by which the kingdom of England possesses the inherent right of self-defense." After developing this point adequately, he moved on.

"Secondly, I appeal to the law of Christ as revealed in the Gospels, by which almsgiving should in case of necessity cease to be a binding duty, yielding to the law of love. Endowments in all forms constitute almsgiving. Alms, as all know, are given in case of need and in love. England's need and her subjects' love for her must take precedence over any lesser need outside the realm." He appealed finally to the law of conscience. "Our fathers made endowments not to the church at large, but to the church in England. It would work against their intentions to allow what they contributed to be otherwise used. Enemies of England would laugh at the stupidity of allowing her own gold to be withdrawn and used against her."

He was prepared to go further, but at this point the king ordered him silenced, since he had answered the question given him. With a shrug of resignation, he took his seat. Lancaster arrived and was permitted to make a speech defending himself against the earlier accusations that he was a traitor.

His passionate oration produced a dramatic effect. The lords and prelates rose, surrounded the duke, and repeated assurances that no man could regard the calumnies of which he had spoken as other than calumnies. The Commons proclaimed their loyalty and support.

The decision to follow Wycliffe's advice as to the papal demands met with little objection. To ensure against money leaving the country, stronger safeguards were set up.

Wycliffe remained until Parliament was dissolved, finding opportunity for discussions with prominent people he would not meet elsewhere. One evening Brunton, bishop of Rochester, joined the group of which he was a part. This surprised Wycliffe, for he knew that Brunton, a Benedictine monk, had no love for him or his opinions.

The bishop said nothing for a time. Then he burst forth with, "Your Conclusions, Wycliffe, have been condemned by the papal court. I myself, as bishop, have received formal evidence of this from the notary of that body."

Not only Wycliffe, but those with him, took great offense at this. One cried, "I count what you have said a slander on the curia. Should such action have taken place we would know it."

"Not only that," said another, "but it is an insult to our king, who has such respect for the learning of Dr. Wycliffe that he called him here to render an opinion on a difficult question. If such accusation has been made, suspicion falls upon your brethren among the Benedictines, or yourself, as its author."

By the next day the rumor that bulls from the pope had been issued against Wycliffe ran through the whole assembly, causing considerable excitement. Archbishop Sudbury and Bishop Courtenay said nothing, but appeared uncomfortable. Within a short time the content of the said bulls leaked out and became the topic of discussion everywhere. Sudbury's and Courtenay's discomfort grew, but they maintained silence.

With the rumor that the pope had ordered his arrest, Wycliffe exploded with indignation. "Such a bull would oppose English law in ordering the arrest of a subject without conviction of heresy. It would imply that the king may not punish delinquent clerks by withholding their endowments, which he might certainly do, should he find my teachings in error."

On November 28 when Parliament was dissolved, Wycliffe hastened to Oxford to confer with his friends. Hardly had he arrived when rumors confronted him regarding the supposed bulls. Any knowledge was still hearsay, since no official publication had been made.

Wycliffe picked up his pen. *I call upon the soldiers of Christ*, he wrote, *seculars, clerics, and especially professors of evangelical poverty, the defenders unto death of the law of God, to rouse themselves against the claim of the papacy to bind and loose at will. By such a claim the pope becomes the enemy of the church of Christ, and the worst antichrist...*

Friends urged restraint, but he was unwilling to moderate. *I remain polite to the pope as an individual*, he pointed out. *My claim is that a pope must be judged by conformity to the rule of Scripture, that he must live soberly, justly, and piously in evangelical poverty.*

The full storm soon broke. On December 18 Archbishop Sudbury published the pope's bulls.

19. December 1377—Papal Bulls

As soon as possible Wycliffe obtained a copy of the five bulls. Thrusting all else aside, he attacked the documents with excitement and some foreboding. His hasty excursion through the pages did nothing to alleviate either feeling, but only to kindle a spark into indignation. Still, he acknowledged some relief in knowing exactly what the pope had said and what the outlook was.

"So Brunton was right in what he first told you," said Aston, as he and Hereford burst excitedly into Wycliffe's study. "But he couldn't have been the one who initially reported to the pope, or he would have informed him of your summons before Convocation, abortive as it was. No mention of that."

"The Benedictines are at the bottom of it," growled Wycliffe, "but not Brunton. Litlington, abbot of Westminster, told me last month at Westminster of a request he received some months ago from Adam Easton. You know who Easton is, I suppose?"

"He's that renowned scholar of Hebrew, who went to Avignon and seems to have taken up residence there," said Aston.

"Before he left Oxford, I had a friendly relationship with him. Since I know no Hebrew, he used to assist me by translating certain words or phrases I had occasion to use."

Wycliffe rose from his chair, his anger mounting. "That friendly relationship has died a violent death. He wrote Litlington for some of my writings which, from his description, were the published portions of both *Divine* and *Civil Dominion*.

"Before going to Westminster, Easton had fiercely attacked certain of my views. That did not surprise me. I expect opposition from the monks, in view of my stress upon the need for disendowment. But, after hearing of his request to Litlington and learning the content of the pope's bulls, no doubt remains that this black dog and his whelps are responsible for the pope's activity against me."

"That seems likely," said Hereford, "but how can you be sure Easton and his fellow-monks are the guilty parties?"

"There cannot be the slightest doubt! The articles the pope chooses to take exception to are quoted almost word for word from my books, out of context, but still my words. From what Easton sent, the pope has chosen nineteen articles for the archbishop to inspect and investigate."

"The date of the bulls is May 22. Why were they so long in reaching England?" asked Aston.

"They must have reached Sudbury before Parliament convened," replied Wycliffe. "On May 22 the old king was still alive. By the time they reached England, he was dead. Since one had been addressed to Edward III, it would have to be returned for insertion of the name of Richard II.

"I have an idea Courtenay sat smugly through the entire session of Parliament, knowing the bulls were in the hands of the archbishop. He must have writhed with indignation when I was actually called to give an opinion."

"I still don't see why he waited so long to publish the bulls," said Hereford. "Why wouldn't the occasion of Parliament, with Wycliffe there in their midst, have provided a dramatic opportunity for bringing them forth?"

"That's just the point," put in Aston, excitedly. "You forget the stature of our friend. He is known throughout the land as Oxford's most eminent scholar. His popularity, and especially the fact that he had been summoned by the king to advise the nation on a most important question, would have made Courtenay refrain from producing the bulls just then. Sudbury would have been reluctant at any time, but Courtenay, bold as he is, would never have urged publication during the session of Parliament."

Hereford nodded thoughtfully. "True! I, too, see it now. They knew Wycliffe could expect the support of powerful friends. Only after the great men and minds had dispersed to the far corners of the realm and

Wycliffe was again at Oxford would they dare. Still, I hardly see how they had the courage, except that they fear the pope more than opposition of Wycliffe's friends."

"What happens next?" asked Wycliffe. "Will the university follow the pope's bidding in the bull addressed to them and imprison me? You, too, are in danger. The bull calls for imprisonment of my 'obstinate followers'."

"Not likely," said Aston. "The university never bows to papal interference. Certainly it will not when its fairest flower is threatened. Does the pope not know *who* Wycliffe is?

"As for 'obstinate followers,' where would the search begin? They will ignore that part whatever they decide about you."

"When the bull for the university reached the chancellor's hand," said Hereford, "there was debate as to whether it should be honorably received. Some advised a disdainful rejection. Then it was reluctantly received, but with utter coldness."

"Note carefully the wording of the bull addressed to the chancellor of Oxford," said Wycliffe. "He is to follow the pope's instructions on pain of the university losing its privileges. That puts him in a dilemma."

"He'll find a way out of it," said Hereford. "He *must*."

"You've helped restore me to a degree of calm," said Wycliffe, rising from his chair. "I'm more grateful than you can know. I must set about preparing a defense of my theses. To whom I shall eventually make this defense remains uncertain."

A smile passed between Aston and Hereford as they took Wycliffe's broad hint that he wished to be alone, and made their departure.

Apparently he would not have to defend his theses immediately. Three of the bulls had been directed to

Archbishop Sudbury and Bishop Courtenay as commissioners, the fourth to the king, the fifth to the chancellor and University of Oxford. With this fifth bull Sudbury enclosed a mandate signed by himself and Courtenay. High interest kept anything from remaining secret.

Wycliffe's friends did not leave him alone long. As soon as they learned of the contents of the mandate, Aston, Hereford, Repyngton, Purvey, and Brut crowded into his small study to discuss the situation.

"Obviously," said Aston, "Courtenay does not expect the chancellor to throw you into chains, as the bull demands."

"Certainly not!" cried Brut. "Courtenay knows the illegality of arresting a subject of the king on the demand of the pope. It looks as if the pope means to start an Inquisition in England by this attack. Even Courtenay would object to that."

"The mandate instructs the chancellor to turn the questionable theses over to his best theological scholars for examination as to erroneous or heretical content. He is to send their findings in a sealed letter. I doubt the possibility of keeping secret the opinions of the examiners."

"A second requirement of the mandate has been dealt with," said Wycliffe. "The chancellor notified me that I am to appear before the commissioners within thirty days at St. Paul's to answer concerning the theses."

"Apparently, fifty conclusions attributed to you were submitted to the curia, from which the pope chose nineteen," said Purvey, who generally spoke little in the presence of the others.

"Yes, fifty chosen by the Benedictines—black monks—Easton and his brood. Incredible that they could consider that many statements even slightly questionable," snarled Wycliffe.

"Of the nineteen," said Brut, "none deals directly with church doctrine or any theological point. There is no heresy."

"Yet," said Aston, "taken out of context, and out of logical order as Wycliffe taught, they may well be twisted to say what he had no intention of saying. The foe is wily."

Soon after, Adam de Tonworth, chancellor of the university, called a meeting of the entire membership of the university, including Wycliffe. The chancellor evidently hoped to work out his difficulties through this meeting.

"In accord with the archbishop's instructions," he said, "I sent to our most esteemed and trusted regent masters of theology copies of the theses in question. They have studied these as to orthodoxy and have given their opinion. Let us hear the report."

The scribe read the unanimous response of the doctors: "The theses are true, though they may sound badly to the ear."

Aston, sitting next to Wycliffe, whispered, "He may send a sealed letter to the archbishop, but the *secret* is no secret! How could we have hoped for anything better?"

Wycliffe himself muttered in a clearly audible voice, "To condemn truth because it sounds ill to sinners and ignoramuses would render all Holy Writ liable to condemnation."

Aston asked in a scarcely less audible tone, "In which of those classes do you put the pope and his cardinals?"

The increasingly nervous chancellor continued. "There is one other matter. I shall ask the vice-chancellor to speak now."

The vice-chancellor, a monk, rose and pompously addressed the assembly. "The Holy Father demands that we arrest Doctor Wycliffe and lay him in chains. To do so would be against the laws of our land, and such an order is an invasion of our university's privileges. It demands that we act against a man who has long championed those rights and whom we count as the glory of this fair institution. Yet the pope threatens to take away our privileges unless we comply."

A general roar of dissent swept across the room. "No pope may order the arrest of a subject of the king! Let no hand be laid upon our beloved *Doctor Evangelicus!*"

The vice-chancellor, with difficulty restoring order, continued: "We have thought of a possible solution, which could in a sense fulfil the letter of the law without damage to our renowned doctor. No hand shall be laid upon him, but if Doctor Wycliffe will consent to put himself under house arrest in one of the halls of the university, such a gesture should suffice."

Some discussion followed. Most of Wycliffe's friends saw the move as an insult. Wycliffe rose to his feet. "For the sake of the university," he said, "I agree to this plan. It would not be fitting for the university to lose its special privileges as a free and independent institution on my account."

Voices were raised to deplore the action, but in the end Wycliffe, feeling it the part of wisdom, insisted. He would take up residence in Black Hall, a property of Osney Abbey, a logical location, since the vice-chancellor himself was a monk.

The vice-chancellor escorted Wycliffe to his prison, where he found reasonably comfortable quarters. His servant would bring his personal possessions from his rooms at Queens.

Just before leaving, the vice-chancellor cleared his throat and shifted about nervously, then said, "That this may have the appearance of a real imprisonment, I must order you to remain here without going out. This is for your own protection, as well, lest someone else undertake to arrest you."

Wycliffe had sought to console his friends, who appeared more distressed than he. "Merely a change of location. I shall suffer no hardship. I have no desire to go abroad in this wintry season, in any case, so I shall be content to labor at my defense and certain of the writing projects which continually engage me."

20. January-February 1378
Under House Arrest

Once alone, Wycliffe shed the optimistic attitude he had donned like a garment for the sake of his friends and let his true feelings surface. Now he must deal with the assortment of emotions within him—anger, discouragement, weariness, frustration, indignation, despair. Each must be dispelled, but by what means he was uncertain. Unless he acted quickly, he would slip into depression, and he had no time for that.

He settled himself as comfortably as possible into the unfamiliar surroundings and undertook to read again the bulls before dealing with the nineteen propositions. He found it useful to comment aloud as he worked.

"Here he attacks me by name," said Wycliffe. "The propositions I have fearlessly taught are 'false and erroneous.' They are 'contrary to the faith' and 'tend to weaken and subvert the whole church.'

"He's right in part. I have not feared to teach, but what I teach is neither false nor erroneous nor contrary to the faith. Rather than weaken, it will strengthen and reform the church."

He rose and paced the room. "This *is* a prison," he said, "for all that the window has no bars and no key is turned in the lock. Prison is what is next mentioned. I am to be 'kept in chains and carefully guarded' until further instructions.

"He fears that I may take flight to avoid imprisonment. Does the pope think I would skulk away in a cowardly attempt to escape his clutches?

"The cowardly action is on the part of the commissioners. They made no attempt to seize me while Parliament was in session and I was present. When I was back at Oxford, they left it to the chancellor to do the dirty work."

The fourth bull warned the king, the royal family, the nobility and councillors of the "dangerous errors" being spread abroad and urged them not to hesitate to lend their aid in suppressing them.

Wycliffe passed this by with a shrug. "Little does the pope realize the strong support I have at court."

With a sigh he read the fifth bull and cast it aside. "He deplores the signs of religious declension at Oxford! Urging the authorities to obedience, he threatens to deprive the university of all privileges granted by the holy see. This 'obedience' includes the prevention of the teaching attributed to me, and the taking into custody of Wycliffe and all who embrace his errors!

"A larger order than he might bargain for. If all who 'embrace my errors' are to be imprisoned, I daresay the prisons would be inadequate to hold them."

He sat back to consider all that he had read. His work was cut out for him in preparing a paper to defend the propositions in which the pope saw not only error but possible heresy.

"There is sometimes only a fine line between the two," he said. "My defense will go to the pope for judgment, but my first business is to convince the prelates. I must make it clear that there is no heresy, no error, but only *truth* in what I proclaim."

To this task he now turned. "I must consider that the propositions fall into groups, but first, an introduction."

Picking up his pen, he wrote, *First of all, I publicly protest, as I have often done, that I will and purpose from the bottom of my heart, by the grace of God, to be a sincere Christian and to profess and defend the law of Christ so far as I am able. If, through ignorance, or other cause, I shall fail, I ask pardon of God, and do from henceforth revoke and retract it, humbly submitting myself to the correction of Mother Church.*

He laid down his pen and picked up the page. Seldom did he stop to edit as he wrote, but seldom did he write anything so important as this. Satisfied, he continued.

And as for the opinion of 'children and weak people' concerning the faith I have taught in the schools and elsewhere, that Christians may not be scandalised on my account, I am willing to set down my sense in writing, since I am prosecuted for the same.

These same opinions I am willing to defend even unto death, as I believe all Christians ought to do, and especially the pope of Rome and the rest of the priests of the church. I understand the conclusions according to the sense of Scripture and the holy doctors. If it be proved that the conclusions are contrary to the faith, I am willing very readily to retract them.

He looked at the first group of five propositions. "It seems obvious what is intended here," he said. "They wish to give the statesmen and nobles the impression that I hold revolutionary views with regard to political and municipal affairs, and that I call in question the rights of private property and hereditary succession. Such an understanding—or misunderstanding—might easily come about, if one reads the bare statements, plucked out of their context without explanation."

His pen flew over the pages, and he lost all track of time. Then one morning his solitude was broken. The vice-chancellor appeared and delivered a brief message.

"Due to the insistent demands of your friends, a decision has been made to end your imprisonment. You are free to return to your rooms at Queen's."

How this had come about Wycliffe did not know. The request of his friends alone could not have availed. There must be something more. He called his servant to gather his belongings. As he stepped outside, he looked about him with a sigh of relief. Breathing deeply the crisp, cold air of the February day, he set off toward his own rooms.

Nothing further had been heard of the mid-January appearance before the commissioners at St. Paul's. The time was now long past. Depression still threatened when he gave himself time to think of what lay ahead. The delay had given him ample time for preparing his defense. The day would come when he must stand before the prelates. The uncertainty as to when disturbed him.

21. February-March 1378—A Strong Defense

In the last week in February a letter bearing the archbishop's seal reached Wycliffe. He was to present himself before the commissioners ten days later, not at St. Paul's, but at Lambeth Palace Chapel.

"Why the change to Lambeth Palace?" asked Aston.

"Who knows? Perhaps because it is more private than busy St. Paul's," said Wycliffe. "I think I like it better this way. My memories of a trial at St. Paul's are not pleasant."

"There'd be no repetition of *that* scene. This is entirely different."

Wycliffe found it good to be surrounded by his friends once more. "Aren't you afraid to be found associating with me? You remember that any who hold to my doctrines are implicated the same as I!"

"If we thought you were serious, we would be insulted," said Hereford. "We hold your teaching not because it's yours but because it is truth."

The group gathered in his rooms almost nightly in the last week before he was to go to London. They insisted that Wycliffe take an evening to read to them his defense. He completed the introduction and paused. Obtaining murmurs of approval, he proceeded to his treatment of the first propositions.

"This group of five deals with such legal and municipal matters as property, rights of possession, and inheritances. They have nothing to do with the church."

"Yet," objected Brut, "the quotation in the first one mentions that political dominion is not given to 'Peter and all his family.' Does that not touch the pope's pretended powers?"

"In choosing that statement," replied Wycliffe, "the pope either unconsciously or knowingly threw in the possibility of a misunderstanding of the words. I often use such names as Peter or Caius or Titus in a general way as examples. No reference to the pope is intended. The words read, *'Petrus et omne genus suum.'* One does not speak of the *genus* of the pope, but of his *successores*, not of his offspring, but of his successors."

"That had escaped me for the moment," said Brut.

"The principle in this first group," continued Wycliffe, "is that rights of inheritance and of ownership of property are never to be taken for granted or considered as innately unconditioned and absolute, but as dependent upon God's will and grace."

"Which," said Aston, "includes rights of inheritance and property now under the control of the ecclesiastical hierarchy, and so applies to the question of the status of endowments. But I tend to run ahead of you. That comes up later."

Wycliffe nodded in agreement. Then he read to them four more related statements.

"Here I state that, should the church fall into error, or churchmen persistently abuse the property of the church, kings and temporal rulers are entitled, both legally and morally, to withdraw, in a legal and moral manner, the temporal property. I do not state whether I consider the church to be in condition of error, but leave that to be determined by the temporal lords."

"You do lay the burden squarely upon them to act," said Repyngton, "once they determine such a condition to exist, upon penalty of damnation. That last is pretty strong."

"It's meant to be strong. It's quoted directly from *Civil Dominion*. The related theses assert the power of kings and temporal lords to take away lordships and manors from churchmen who habitually abuse them to ends of pride and luxury, and to the utter neglect of the condition implied with the donation of such property. God forbid that anyone should assume it my meaning that secular lords may lawfully take them away whenever they please, by their bare authority. They should only do it by the authority of the church in cases limited by law."

"What do you mean," asked Brut, "by 'the authority of the church'? Surely not the hierarchy."

"Not the hierarchy," replied Wycliffe, "but the community of true believers. I have some notes, soon to be expanded, as to the nature of the church. There I shall make my meaning quite clear."

He turned now to the last proposition. "This one should be considered here. Every churchman, including the pope of Rome, is our peccable brother, liable to sin, and may be corrected by the law of brotherly correction. Matthew makes this clear: *If any one sin in any thing, the stander-by ought to correct him when he has an opportunity.* When there is obstinate defense of heresy or any other sin tending to the spiritual damage of the church, it ought to be complained of to the superiors, that by its correction, damage to the church may be prevented. Even Peter was reproved by Paul, as we read in Galatians.

"To say that the pope ought not to be corrected by man, but by God alone, no matter how greatly he may sin, seems to imply that he is above the church, the spouse of Christ, and, like antichrist, represented as lifting himself above Christ."

"That's strong stuff," said Brut, "yet every word is true. Dangerous, but you often remind us that proclaiming truth is notably dangerous."

Wycliffe continued through the propositions. As he read the concluding statements, he said, "These guard against the abuse of the power of the keys, in 'binding and loosing,' especially as to how far church discipline and excommunication should be used. This power is often used to secure revenues to the church.

"I contest the pretended absoluteness of the pope's power of the keys. Its effective power is dependent upon its being used in conformity with the gospel. For him to 'bind' and 'loose' purely at his own whim and according to his own will is ineffective. It is not possible to excommunicate a man unless he has already excommunicated himself. Only what God has already done can be confirmed by pope, prelate, or any priest."

"It is well," said Aston, "that you emphasize that church censures, especially excommunication, should only be used in cases pertaining to offenses against God, not in cases concerning temporal goods or for personal reasons, such as for revenge."

Brut spoke up. "There is, for example, the case of John of Gaunt insisting that the bishops excommunicate the individuals who had ridiculed him and injured his pride."

"Quite a wrong usage," agreed Wycliffe. "The thesis that is sure to sting most bitterly is that every lawfully ordained priest has the power to dispense every sacrament. Although it is plain that the priestly power is sufficient in its essence, yet as things now stand the powers of lower priests are restrained, except in cases of necessity."

With a frown, Brut said, "Will they give you time to present all this? Patience is not Courtenay's strong point."

"They *must* give me time. I don't know who else will be there besides Sudbury and Courtenay, but I count on a fair hearing. I believe the archbishop will insist upon that."

"It seems," said Brut, "that I am always the one who must be warning you to moderation. You were prepared to exercise it at St. Paul's last year and did not get a chance. May I be so bold as to urge you to a double portion of that virtue at this time? This is different from what you've faced before. These men report to the pope. Much is at stake."

Hereford had been moving about restlessly. "I have a strange feeling that the outcome of this battle will affect the future for all of us in some tremendous way. It's a dangerous road we travel, yet it is the way God leads, and we are bound to take it. The thing is, it doesn't reach an end, but goes on and on. We don't know where it leads, but *you*, Wycliffe, see more clearly and understand the truth more fully. Lead on! We follow!"

22. March 1378—The Trial

The gray morning with blasts of cold wind whipping his cloak about him did little to encourage an optimistic outlook. An inner uncertainty gripped Wycliffe as he stood shivering on the bank of the Thames, waiting for the boat which would take him across to the Lambeth Palace wharf on the south bank. The boatman held him steady as he stepped into the small craft, followed by his servant, carrying his books and papers.

His instructions were to present himself at the crypt chapel of the palace. He had some difficulty keeping his footing on the slippery mud of the path up to the palace grounds. The boatman had told him that the river frequently rose into the palace grounds and had been known to flood the chapel, which lay somewhat below ground level.

Locating the entrance to the crypt, he descended the short flight of steps. The assembled prelates, in the midst of a discussion, were not ready for him. They bade him seat himself in the rear until called.

This gave him opportunity to compose himself. *I am alone this time,* he thought. *No duke or marshal, no doctors to support me. St. Paul stood alone at his first trial, yet he remembered that he was not alone, but that the Lord stood at his side and gave him strength. I must remember that as well.*

Besides the archbishop and Courtenay, there were other prelates and abbots, most of whom he recognized. As he looked about, he was impressed with the architecture of the chapel. Almost a miniature cathedral, it consisted of four double bays, and down its center ran a row of purbeck marble columns, capped by molded capitals, supporting chamfred arches and ribs.

He sighed. "One might, in proper circumstances, find peace here. But not in my present situation."

He opened the book which contained his defense. To it he had given the title *Protestatio,* since the word was used in the first sentence, and inasmuch as it was his protestation against the charges made by the pope and which he faced today.

An apprehensive tremor ran through him as he came forward to face his judges. Preliminary statements over, purpose of his being called made clear, he was ordered to present his defense.

His confidence returned as the words of the introduction rolled off his tongue in his usual authoritative style. "First of all, I publicly protest, as I have often done before, that I will and purpose from the bottom of my heart, by the grace of God, to be a sincere Christian..."

At this point down the steps and into the chapel strode Sir Lewis Clifford, well-known knight attached to the service of the Princess Joan. He advanced boldly to the front and stood facing the prelates. After looking at them steadily for a moment, he presented a sealed document to Archbishop Sudbury.

"I come," he said, "as an emissary of the Queen Mother, the honorable Princess Joan. You are instructed to proceed to no definitive action against Dr. Wycliffe. This is her request and her command. You will abide by it." Bowing to the shocked and speechless prelates, he turned a warm glance upon Wycliffe, and was gone.

The commissioners looked at one another in consternation. Obviously this came as a shock. Courtenay's face darkened with anger. This changed the shape of things. After a few confused whisperings, they bade Wycliffe proceed.

Heartened by this turn of events, he entered into the body of his defense. As he progressed, growing indignation marked the faces of his judges.

At a certain point, one of them could restrain himself no longer. "Can it be," he demanded, "that we, the clergy, the divinely-appointed teachers of the laity, are to be subject as to property and character to the judgment of the laity? Have things come to such a pass that temporal lords are to determine when we make proper use and when we abuse our temporalities? Is it for them to say when we should be deprived of them?"

He would have said more, but the archbishop called him to order. Wycliffe had proceeded but briefly when a noise came at the door. Clattering down the steps, a large group of men entered the room. At their head was John of Northampton, former mayor of London, known as a stanch admirer of Wycliffe.

In a loud voice he declared, "We come as citizens of London to take the part of the man you hold before you. We purpose to stand by and see that no harm comes to him." With that, the men calmly seated themselves.

Wycliffe stood with his book in his hand, waiting. The confused and exasperated prelates seemed uncertain how to continue. Finally, they told Wycliffe to read on. He completed the reading without further interruption, closed the book and handed it to the archbishop.

Sending him to the rear of the chapel, the judges deliberated at some length. When called again, he was told, "You are prohibited from further use of the theses in question, either in sermons or lectures." Then he was dismissed.

He was stunned by their mildness. He could hardly believe it. They had not even declared the theses erroneous! Could he have convinced them? Or was it fear instilled by the warnings, one from a high source, one from a lower? In allowing him to go free, they had certainly failed to comply with the direction of the pope's bull.

In the company of his noisy friends from London he crossed the river. John of Northampton insisted upon a celebration of the victory, which he felt he and his men had helped bring about. Wycliffe must join them at a dinner in his honor. How could he refuse?

Their loyalty and support touched him. It was an evening of light-hearted enjoyment. The hour grew late and the party a bit rowdy before Wycliffe could make his departure.

23. March 1378—Strong Support

Back at Oxford his friends demanded a full report. They were amazed to hear of the support he had received and at the outcome.

"I assume," said Aston, "that the hand of John of Gaunt was behind the message from the Queen Mother. In his present position and his standing with Courtenay, he would not have sent the message himself. He remains on good terms with the princess. She is reported to be attracted to Wycliffe's teaching, as are several of her courtiers, notably Sir Lewis Clifford."

"In other words," said Hereford, "Wycliffe has the support of the royal family, in spite of the pope's bulls."

Wycliffe listened quietly. "This talk of support is all very well, but remember that my *Protestatio* goes to the curia. The judgment rendered there will not resemble the action of the bishops. The book is on its way, with the written report of the commissioners. Sudbury will wait for the decision from Rome."

"The bishops required no oath from you that you would follow the prohibition against further use of the propositions," said Repyngton. "It was more a request than a command."

Soon enough the monks at St. Albans voiced sharp criticism of the weakness of the bishops. Walsingham, that outstanding chronicler, vented his indignation as to the proceedings.

The archbishop and bishop, as the pope's commissioners, he wrote, *had declared, in the fulness of their courage, that by no entreaties of men, by no threats or bribes would they allow themselves to be drawn aside from the line of strict justice in this affair, even if this should involve peril to their lives.*

But on the day of hearing,....their words became smoother than oil, to the humiliation of their own dignity and detriment of the church. Men who had vowed not to bend to princes and peers of the realm till they had punished the arch-heretic...were seized with such terror at the sight of Sir Lewis Clifford,... they became as one that heareth not, and in whose mouth are no reproofs....Thus that slippery John Wycliffe deluded his inquisitors, mocked the bishops, and escaped by the favor of the Londoners, although his propositions are heretical and depraved.

Wycliffe sat back and smiled appreciatively at these statements. "He forgets that there was no intention that the bishops declare the theses heretical. He can rage at the weakness of the bishops, while he sits safe in his cell at St. Albans. He might see things differently, had he been there."

Purvey went to Lincoln for his ordination to the priesthood. Upon his return he said to Wycliffe, "I have longed to go out with the Poor Priests. Now that I have been ordained, when may I go?"

"Perhaps in the long vacation," said Wycliffe. "I have no desire to dampen your enthusiasm, for you are an able preacher. Still, you realize that I need your help in the writing. You have this term to complete here at the university, as well."

"I would never desert you. Preaching can be worked in. The bishop wanted to find a benefice for me, but I put him off. I could hardly tell him that I prefer to be a Poor Priest. I said I was not ready for a benefice just yet. The help I give to your writing takes first priority."

Wycliffe touched him affectionately on the arm. "Pick up your pen, then. I have a tract to write in response to what a certain doctor, one I call a *mixtim the-*

ologus, or motley divine, has dared declare in opposition to my views."

From a sheet on his desk he read, *If anyone be pope, he is then incapable of sinning, at least mortally, and by consequence, if he wills or ordains anything, it is therefore just.*

He dictated: *If that be true, the pope may take away any book from the canon of Scripture and add any new one. He may alter the whole Bible, and make all the Scripture heresy, and establish as catholic, Scripture that is opposite to the faith....* He used one example after another to describe what the pope might do with no restraint, if he were unable to sin.

Purvey asked in alarm, "Do you really mean to publish this?"

"Certainly. Why should I not publish it?"

"Do you realize how inflammatory these words are? At this time, every word from your pen, every syllable you utter is reported to the pope. At any moment he may excommunicate you. Should this not be a time of at least moderate restraint?"

"Purvey, I do not fear the pope's excommunication. He has already branded me a heretic, even though not in an official document to the archbishop. He has no power over my soul, and, as I have said before, I shall defend the truth even unto death."

Purvey was not entirely convinced, but he knew better than to push the point.

"You were otherwise occupied," said Wycliffe, "when I was preparing my defense, so you have not read my *Protestatio.* It must be put in publishable form, and I mean to produce a shorter version with fewer technical terms, one the ordinary man may understand. I should like it read before Parliament, but no Parliament is anticipated immediately. I have in mind an even shorter tract along the same lines which must be readied for publication. You see that we shall be busy for some time."

Hereford burst in at this point, crying, "There's trouble. Last week a courtier from Woodstock was insulted by a group of students. It was a rowdy bunch, headed by three monks who have the reputation of being ringleaders in such brawls. They stood outside the courtier's lodging and sang a rhyme in English that contained words dishonoring to the king. They ended their frolic with the shooting of arrows at the house."

"Nothing unusual in that," said Wycliffe. "It happens all the time. Where's the trouble?"

"It's just this: The courtier complained at Westminster, and not only the monks but the chancellor and vice-chancellor of Oxford must appear before Houghton, the chancellor of England. It was the words of the song they sang. They had no business implying dishonor to the king."

A student, an eyewitness to the hearing at Westminster, brought a report: "Houghton fixed his attention on our chancellor. He said, 'If you at Oxford cannot deal with those who insult the king, it is clear that Oxford cannot be governed by clerks. The king must withdraw its privileges. We depose you from your office.'"

"I was right," said Hereford, "in esteeming that words that dishonor the king constitute a grave offense."

"But wait!" cried the student. "Our chancellor replied, 'I hold my office from both pope and king. The king can take away the part he has conferred, but not rights given by the pope.'"

"Such a reply indicates courage on his part, but perhaps not great wisdom," said Wycliffe.

"No, for Houghton replied, 'Very well, we deprive you of the king's part. See what you will make of the pope's part. The king can remove both you and the university from Oxford.' He had no choice but to lay his resignation before the council."

"What of the vice-chancellor?" asked Hereford. "Surely they could not demand his resignation as well."

"That is the amazing part. They threw him into prison on the charge of imprisoning Dr. Wycliffe at the mandate of the pope."

"Hardly fair," said Wycliffe. "I agreed to the scheme. But it shows the council's attitude toward the pope's demands."

"Besides," said Hereford, "it shows the council's attitude toward you. All England is *for* you. Little can the pope do."

A few days later it was obvious that Pope Gregory XI could do nothing against Wycliffe or anyone else. On March 27 he died.

Wycliffe, upon hearing of his death, found relief from the frustrations built up through what he had suffered by expressing in most violent language his feelings. Some of his friends were shocked at his terms, but powerless to restrain him.

"He was a horrible devil," he cried. "an abiding heretic. He died showing no penitence for his crimes, his nepotism, his slaughter of thousands in his attempt to regain his temporal dominions. He had a grudge against me and hoped to use me as an opening to force Inquisition here in England."

24. April-July 1378—Pope Urban VI

Speculation as to the next pope occupied many minds in England. Would the papacy remain at Rome or return to Avignon?

"The Romans will demand an Italian pope," said Wycliffe. "As most of the cardinals are French, there may be difficulty."

"Gregory knew he was dying," said Aston. "It seems he issued a bull with a provision that a two-thirds majority only would be required for the election of the pope."

"Then I assume the conclave won't have to wait for the cardinals who remained at Avignon to arrive," said Repyngton.

"We can only pray that things go well and the man God chooses is elected," said Hereford.

They had not long to wait. Bartolomeo Prignano, archbishop of Bari, received the papal crown as Urban VI.

"And who is Bartolomeo Prignano?" asked Wycliffe.

"He served as assistant to the vice-chancellor of the curia. Naples is his home. Not much else is known about him."

More information filtered through. He had served for years as assistant to the vice-chancellor to the pope. Thus he had observed all that went on at the papal court. On the day after his coronation he sent letters to all archbishops asking for their prayers. He was deemed a man of piety, justice, and ability, a diligent Bible student who hated simony and worldliness.

"I rejoice!" cried Wycliffe. "It seems God has given us a good pope who may bring true reformation to the church."

He sent for Purvey. "Gregory is dead and probably gone to hell," he said, "but the citation he issued for me to appear at Rome still hangs over my head. I shall write a letter to this new pope, explaining my position. I mean to include with it a draft of the *Protestatio* and the tract I am calling *Thirty-three Conclusions on the Poverty of Christ*. My faith is orthodox, and all complaints against me are void."

As Wycliffe began to dictate, the words flowed easily. "I rejoice to declare my faith unto the bishop of Rome, who, if he finds it sound, will confirm it, if erroneous, amend it. The gospel of Christ is the heart of God's law, and the bishop of Rome, as the supreme vicar of Christ on earth, is most bound to that law of the gospel. Scripture teaches that Christ for the time of his pilgrimage here was poor, abjecting all worldly rule and honor. Therefore, the pope ought to follow this example, leaving unto the laity all temporal dominion.

"If I have erred at any point, I will humbly submit myself unto correction even by death, if necessity demand. If I could labor according to my will in my own person, I would present myself before the bishop of Rome. But the Lord hath visited me to the contrary and taught me to obey him rather than men."

He concluded with a personal appeal: "Since God has given our pope evangelical instincts, we pray that these be not extinguished by crafty counsel, and that pope and cardinals not do anything contrary to God's law. We pray that God will so stir our pope that he with his clergy may follow the Lord Jesus Christ in life and manners and may teach the people effectually. We specially pray that our pope be preserved from all malign counsel, for a man's foes are they of his household."

The letter was sincere, though he could not resist throwing in a bit of sarcasm. Purvey declared it a masterpiece.

Wycliffe completed the shortened version of the *Protestatio* and turned to the tract called the *Thirty-three Conclusions*. He wrote in Latin and in English using short statements suited to the popular mind. He set out proof for each statement from Scripture, the Fathers, and canon law.

He took up several of the points condemned by Gregory. He protested against excommunication for the sake of money or temporal goods. Laymen might lawfully judge prelates. Priests should not be occupied in secular business. In the conclusion he urged kings to the defense and keeping of the evangelical law.

"Now," he cried, "we must find a means to send the letter and the tracts to Rome."

"Perhaps Bishop Rede will know of someone. He is here at present inspecting his nearly-completed library at Merton."

"It should be clear," said Wycliffe, "that I make no secet of my teaching, or I would not seek to scatter these theses over a great part of England and Christendom. Truly, Rede may know someone about to head toward Rome."

It turned out that Rede himself was contemplating a journey to Rome and readily agreed to take Wycliffe's documents.

"I'll do my utmost," said Rede, "to get them in the right hands. This time in Oxford has been very rushed with no time to spare. I promise to return soon when we'll have time together."

With a sense of relief Wycliffe turned to the next task. He must see all these most recent works delivered to the scriveners. As the finished pieces became available to the public, he learned that the *Thirty-three Conclusions*, in particular, quickly became a popular item.

Content with the present state of affairs, he paused to congratulate himself as he prepared to set forth his view of the duty of kings in a work entitled *de Officio Regis*. *All goes well. The royal house is with me, members of the nobility support me, the Commons stand for the things I strive for—and against those that I oppose. A new pope gives promise of working for reformation in the church. Victory is assured!*

His old antagonist, that inner voice, broke in. *Remember that adversaries are not lacking. Don't fly too high!*

The self-congratulatory mood vanished. *You're right. The battle has just begun. I must keep my feet on the ground. Without God, no victory can be achieved. I confess to a feeling of weakness, of unutterable weariness. Unless God be with me, I cannot continue.*

PART 4

Moving Into Deeper Waters
(1378–1380)
"Truth is of more weight than custom."

1. August-September 1378
Murder in the Abbey

In August when Wycliffe again sent out the Poor Priests, Purvey was among them. His joy appeared boundless. Wycliffe reproached himself for begrudging the loss of the help he sorely needed with his writing. He had come to depend on Purvey.

"Ah, well," he said, "I shall betake myself to Lutterworth and concentrate on my own preaching. Horne must need a rest."

Time spent among his people refreshed him. It was a change of pace, and he had developed a deep and warm love for his parishioners. To know they returned his affection brought joy to his heart. After a happy fortnight he felt almost reluctant to leave, but the pull back to Oxford was strong.

As the familiar spires came into sight, nostalgic feelings took over. *Nothing is like my devotion to this place in which I have spent the greater part of my life. I can scarcely recall the unhappiness I suffered upon my first arrival, the claustrophobic sense of being shut in by the buildings.*

How I love the tall spires of St. Mary's and St. Frideswide's! Even the bare lecture halls are dear to me, where I heard such wisdom expounded and in which I now seek to pass on to others a measure of what I have learned!

I am grateful for the pulpits from which I preach the gospel of our Lord Jesus Christ, imploring my listeners to live by God's Law and to combat the wrongs in the church and in the land. I think of walks along the banks of the Cherwell and the Thames, of shaded paths through the forests. My heart is bound to this spot. No place on earth can match it.

He was soon jolted out of his musings by fragments of conversation he overheard as he rode past a group of people. "...terrible uproar in London and Westminster...murder in Westminster Abbey...a fugitive brutally slain near the altar."

He summoned Purvey, now returned from his preaching tour. "What is all this I hear about murder at the Abbey?"

"It's true, Master," said Purvey. "Two men escaped from the Tower and took sanctuary in the Abbey. The keeper of the Tower came with soldiers and retook one prisoner. The other was attending mass. The soldiers burst in and, after a scuffle, killed him beside the altar and dragged the bloody body out. There was a terrible uproar at such a breach of sanctuary."

Wycliffe was horrified. "Who were the prisoners? Why was the keeper of the Tower called? Most unusual for violence to be used against men who have taken sanctuary."

"The names were Shakyl and Haulay. It was the court, who had an interest in the prisoners, who called for the Tower to act."

"Ah, yes! That case came up at Parliament last November. A hostage was taken by these two men while with the Black Prince in Spain years ago. They accepted the man's son as hostage in his place while he returned to Spain to find the money for the ransom. The court had an interest in the ransom, as the man was of royal blood. When time came for payment, the government demanded that the hostage be turned over to them to use in making an exchange for English knights held prisoner in Spain.

"Rather than lose their ransom, Shakyl and Haulay hid the hostage and refused to surrender him. At Parliament they were committed to the Tower for contumacy and for turning their home into a prison. So they escaped—and then this! Shocking, indeed!"

Wycliffe soon learned of the terrible struggle between church and state which followed. Archbishop Sudbury had, after three days, excommunicated the guilty parties, but only as a general condemnation, as the actual perpetrators were unknown.

Courtenay published the condemnation at Paul's Cross, specifically excommunicating Buxhill, keeper of the Tower, and those associated with him. The court had given the order which resulted in the tragic action, but Courtenay carefully exempted from the force of the mandate the king, the Queen Mother, and the duke of Lancaster.

"The pointed exclusion of Lancaster by name," cried Wycliffe, "is a low attempt by Courtenay to suggest that he may have been involved. The duke was not even there at the time!"

Wycliffe roared over what came next. "The king ordered the reading of the excommunication stopped, but Courtenay paid no attention. Imagine defying an order of the king! When Richard II demanded that the church, defiled by the bloody crime, be reconsecrated, the abbot at Westminster had the audacity to refuse! Of course no services can be held in the polluted building. He also declined an order to appear before the king.

"What are things coming to when an order of the sovereign can be so blatantly ignored? Courtenay even ignored a call to come before the council at Windsor."

He paused to chuckle. "Even the most serious matters have their amusing side. I would like to have seen Courtenay's face when it was reported to him that John of Gaunt threatened to 'drag him there in spite of the ribald knaves of London.'"

With London still seething with violence, a call went out summoning Parliament to convene on October 20, not at Westminster but at Gloucester.

2. September-October 1378—The Church

Wycliffe was terribly upset. He felt that he must take some action. Brut appeared, and Brut could always help him think things through.

"I regret the murder," said Wycliffe, "but I am more troubled over the excommunication of the king's servants. Murder is a crime, but unjust excommunication is worse. The men were not entitled to sanctuary. The king was within his right to order their arrest."

"According to the law of centuries past, they did have a right to sanctuary," replied Brut. "The king could work toward changing the law, but he was wrong to breach the existing law."

"I'm writing a treatise called *de Ecclesia* in which I show clearly that this law of sanctuary is unscriptural. I won't take time now to go into all the points I make. What I want, Brut, is to go to Gloucester and have a chance to speak."

"I have an idea the duke will see that you are called. Otherwise you would be unwise to go. Why not just wait?"

"I suppose that's best. When I heard that Parliament was to meet at Gloucester, I thought it odd, but I can see the wisdom."

"With things in turmoil, Westminster would be difficult. Besides, the Abbey has not been reconsecrated. That would hamper proceedings and be a constant reminder of the controversy."

Purvey's account of his experiences as a Poor Priest had set Wycliffe to thinking anew about the needs of the people. Having Scripture portions in English, Purvey had reported, was a wonderful help. "Hearing the pure Word of God is a new experience for many. The priests, when they *do* preach, give the content in their own words with addition of other matter. The friars use the

218

same method, with the result that the people don't know what is the Word of God and what is myth or fantasy."

"Not only must the people hear the Word read and preached purely," cried Wycliffe, "but they must have it to read for themselves. Then they can test what they hear as to whether it's truth or error."

In writing *de Ecclesia*, his treatise on the church, he dealt in a deeper way with the question of disendowment. In *Civil Dominion* he had written of it as a speculative possibility. Now he saw it as a present necessity.

"When men speak of holy church," he said to Purvey, "they mean prelates and priests, monks, canons, and friars, men who have tonsures, no matter how wickedly they live, while they do not hold laymen to belong to holy church, even though they live truly after God's law."

"You speak too rapidly, Master," said Purvey. "I'm sure you mean me to write that down, even though you haven't said so."

"By all means, write." He gave Purvey time before continuing. "I write not only from my own knowledge; I quote Augustine, Bradwardine, and Holy Scripture as defining the church as the body of the elect."

He went on to distinguish between those he called the "predestinate" and the "foreknown." The former were those who, from all eternity, were chosen by God for salvation and for glory by the grace of final perseverance. The rest were foreknown to eternal punishment because of persistent impenitence. No one, he stated, could know for certain whether he were of the elect. He boldly suggested that even a pope might not be of that number.

"Surely," said Purvey, staying his pen, "there are some signs by which to ascertain one's position. You mention 'the grace of final perseverance.' May not the degree of one's apparent perseverance be an indication?"

"Just so you keep in mind that *apparent* is not necessarily *absolute*. I hold that the church of the predestinate, the true church, exists in three parts. The church militant, made up of those now living on earth; the church resting, those now in purgatory; the church triumphant, those in glory."

As he prepared his works for publication, Wycliffe lectured upon the same themes. Many of those who thronged his lecture hall were admirers who absorbed all they heard. A few critics edged their way in, seeking to find him in error.

Among this latter group were those who criticized him for his reliance upon scriptural authority alone. They condemned him for placing Scripture above the accumulated wisdom of the church. In his work on *Truth of Holy Scripture* he argued vehemently against such critics. He maintained and defended the literal inspiration and absolute authority of the Bible. Scripture is God's Law, and upon this he based all his conclusions.

"The real heretics," he insisted, "are those who claim there are inconsistencies and obscurities in the Bible which no layman can understand without official interpretation."

With a feeling of sadness, he considered a recent attack made by his friend William Barton, with whom he had enjoyed a close association at Merton more than twenty years earlier.

He voiced his reply in a lecture. "I have been addressed by a doctor whom I believed to be my friend and an outstanding defender of catholic truth. I will patiently bear personal injuries in accordance with the rule of Scripture, but for the honor of God and the profit of the church, I must take from her the scandal I would give if I kept silence. I must reply to the arguments by which the doctor teaches that I and my supporters are heretics, traitors to the kingdom of God."

He turned to his old hero, Armachanus, for support. "Fitzralph has shown us how to deal with such claims. He reached a point in his life when he repudiated the techniques and ambitions of the schools and affirmed the absolute and divinely revealed truth of Scripture. At one time parts of Scripture seemed contradictory, but he came to know it to be concrete truth. When a text seems unintelligible or unacceptable in the Vulgate Scriptures which we use, he bids us refer to the original Greek or Hebrew texts, which can always dispel our doubts."

Wycliffe contended, "All Christians, and lay lords in particular, ought to know Holy Writ and defend it. No man is so rude a scholar but that he may understand the words of the Gospel according to his simplicity."

"You see what that leads to, Master?" asked Purvey. "Is the whole Bible to be put into English?"

"All in good time, Purvey. I'm pondering that question."

Another matter claimed his attention. "Pope Urban VI does not know how to handle his new power. He has offended and insulted both friends and foes by the roughness of his speech and action. Now the French cardinals, already hostile, have elected another pope, Clement VII. Two popes! And such a man as this!"

A French cardinal, Robert of Geneva, was known to be devoid of all spiritual principle. His contemporaries called him "a man of blood." In the previous year his extreme cruelty had shocked even the mercenaries under his command when he dealt with the citizens of Cesena who had revolted against their legate. He ordered several thousand men, women, and children butchered. The bishop of Florence compared him with Herod and Nero.

As this news came in the first week of October, the court gave permission to Arnold Garnier to collect moneys accustomed to be paid to the church of Rome.

In disgust Wycliffe cried, "An effort to prevent trouble with the papacy over the violation of sanctuary! So much for my advice! Even the strong resolutions adopted are disregarded."

With renewed vigor he pursued his lecturing and writing on the church. "The accumulation of temporal possessions produces in the church a lust for lordship," he thundered. "This leads to entanglement with affairs of this life. Avarice and neglect of preaching the Gospel follow. When riches become an occasion for contention and quarrels, to the disturbance of the church, then the only route to follow is to take them away."

He offered a radical solution which went much further than he had gone before: "The church must return to the state of poverty in which she began. The clergy must live on the gifts of the people, renouncing tithes and settled property. This is the only way to recapture the purity of the early days.

"I hold that the state possesses the authority to perform the act of disendowment. The lords temporal can legitimately and meritoriously deprive an offending church of its wealth."

He knew he could expect repercussions.

3. October-November 1378—Gloucester

Parliament opened on October 20. Later the same week he had cause to lay down his pen. At his door stood two of the king's knights. They were to bring Master Wycliffe to Gloucester to defend the royal cause with regard to sanctuary.

Just what he had hoped for! He realized he was turning his back for the moment on one inflammatory cause to champion another. It took him little time to gather up the notes he had previously prepared on the subject and be on his way.

He learned that Litlington, abbot of Westminster Abbey, had been summoned before Parliament to answer for his contempt in refusing to reconsecrate the abbey at the king's order. To the court's surprise, he was able at Gloucester to gain the support of the Commons to such an extent that it seemed wise to call noted clerics to defend the king's position.

A number of doctors of theology and civil law had been called. It was their duty to present argument and proof against the prelates regarding the court's right to act as they had in the matter of Shakyl and Haulay.

As the speeches were about to begin, the chancellor, Adam Houghton, tendered his resignation. He would not be party to an attack on the privileges of the church. The court replied that the king had the right to make the arrest, and pointed out that abuse of sanctuary caused untold injury to the public welfare.

When the doctors took up the defense of the king, Wycliffe, in his turn, presented his proofs with all assurance. "Law must be supreme; Shakyl and Haulay offended against the law of God and the church. The crown has absolute right, under God, to obedience. Scripture nowhere indicates that God offers refuge for debtors or thieves or other criminals. In the Old Testament, sanctuary was offered only for one who had killed accidentally.

"The practice of sanctuary for any and every crime is illegal; it provides a license for sin. It is not only wrong, but false and vicious. To turn the church into a haven from justice is not conducive to rest in the Lord, which holy monks need." A twinge of conscience bothered him at this last statement, considering his view of monk-possessioners.

"The argument that earlier charters granted sanctuary is of no value. Such charters were not founded on Scripture nor according to canon law. Truth is of more weight than custom."

During hours when Parliament was not in session, Wycliffe took the opportunity to visit the abbey and find out all he could about its operation. The cloisters were being rebuilt on a magnificent scale. Inquiry revealed that there were forty-four monks, and that they required 200 servants to minister to them!

He could not deny the magnificence of the stately buildings, but the display of luxurious living distressed him. In the newly-finished hall he observed with astonishment a huge tank for fish, so that there never need be any shortage at mealtime.

The income for this abbey amounted to 1,700 marks, much of which came from seventeen wealthy livings appropriated to it. Wycliffe shook his head in consternation. Could this be a proper use in the best interests of the church for so large a sum? He found his prejudice against possessioners increasing, and he began to consider points he could add to his book on the church.

Seeming to feel that he was not sufficiently impressed with their institution, one monk said, "Are you aware that the shrine of Edward II is a special treasure of our abbey? Our Abbot Thoky in 1327 daringly rode to Berkeley and brought back the body of the murdered king. Many miracles take place at his shrine."

They brought forth for his admiration a book entitled *Book of Miracles of Edward, late king of England.* He felt their keen disappointment at his lack of enthusiasm. From his earliest childhood he had known that Edward II was no saint. To publicize the tomb as a shrine and to collect money for expected miracles was nothing short of fraud. His heart grew sick.

On a day when proceedings in Parliament promised to interest him little, he undertook to see something of the city. The monks had showed him their hospital of St. Bartholomew, but a group of men on the street supplied him with further information.

"Corrodies the hospital has, which means the poor get care at no charge," said one old fellow. "Only lately there was a big scandal, when they were caught selling what's meant to be offered free."

"Even after that," said another, "it's the same. They're back at it, still collecting bed money from the poor that has almost nothing."

Another added, "When one of them poor dies, they take what little he has, even his clothes, except for one upper garment. Pigs and other animals runs through the wards any time of day."

As he wandered back toward the abbey, Wycliffe sought to analyze his feelings. He could weep, but anger mounted that such things should be tolerated. "Yet those sitting this moment in Parliament refuse to see what goes on, turn a deaf ear to the cry that disendowment must come, and *now*. Nor would they listen a whit more to any plea against these private religions, these orders which make themselves a separate church. I am losing my confidence even in the mendicant orders on that account. Not a hint is there in Scripture of such a thing as a separate order."

He groaned. "I could tear out my hair and beard, as Ezra did at the ungodliness of those supposed to be God's people, but what would that accomplish? Better to be like Nehemiah and tear out the hair of the culprits. That would make me feel better, but it would not right the situation. To keep speaking and writing is the only course. And prayer, always prayer."

The only matter of interest to Wycliffe in the remainder of Parliament was the appearance of envoys from *both* popes. Without much discussion, an Act was passed that England would support Urban VI. Anyone who supported Clement VII was guilty of treason. All English benefices held by French cardinals or other clergy siding with Clement, the antipope, were to be confiscated.

To Wycliffe's disgust action concerning the sanctuary issue was postponed until the next Parliament. He hurried back to Oxford, picked up his pen and finished the sentence which the call to Gloucester had interrupted. His head was full of material he must insert before he could publish *de Ecclesia.*

4. November-December 1378—The Scriptures

Purvey had little free time, striving to finish work for his degree. He came when he had an hour or two, but Wycliffe proceeded largely on his own. He meant to get the two volumes on which he worked ready for publication before the year ended.

"I shall finish work on *de Ecclesia* first," he told Purvey. "I must incorporate into it much from my presentation before Parliament concerning sanctuary. The whole argument must appear. It's the best way I know to keep the issue alive. Parliament took no action. The next Parliament *must* make changes."

He started to read over the material already written, but soon put it aside. "I don't have time for that. What if I repeat myself? If readers get a double dose of some of the points, there's more chance of their remembering."

He noted the special privilege claimed by Westminster Abbey with regard to sanctuary. Wrongdoers unable to take sanctuary elsewhere were welcome there, as its rules were broader. He reiterated that such practice provided a license to sin.

If this privilege is made universal, he wrote, *it could lead to the ruin of the realm. A hostile army could invade England, take refuge in the abbey, and make preparations for further actions to plunder and lay waste. Such a thing is by no means impossible. Consider the three conquests of our land by Britons, Saxons, and Normans.*

He concluded the section as he had closed his argument at Parliament with the words, *Truth is of more weight than custom.*

His word-weapons next centered upon the "possessioners," the monks who piled up so many possessions. Fresh in his mind was what he had seen at Gloucester. Disendowment applied to these institutions as much or more than to the wealthy bishoprics.

He digressed slightly to focus briefly on the question of private religions. This applied to monks and friars, for both were under orders that set them apart from other Christians. The church must be one, as Paul had emphasized in his epistle to the Corinthians. No saying, "I am of Benedict" or "I am of Dominic" or "I am of Francis."

With satisfaction he rushed *de Ecclesia* and *de Veritate Sacrae Scripturae,* his defense of the Scriptures, off to the scriveners. These works must be ready for distribution by the end of the year.

Hardly had this work left his hands when the announcement arrived that Urban VI had issued a bull excommunicating the antipope and was talking of proclaiming a crusade against him.

Wycliffe's mind was in turmoil as he considered this. A papal schism was bad enough. A "crusade" could only mean a bloody war between two "vicars of Christ." Unthinkable! An abomination!

5. January-March 1379—On King and Pope

"I hear," said Purvey, "that in your lectures you are beginning to make strong objections to what you term 'private religion.' Must this be?"

"Purvey, what I have to do saddens me. But, yes, that issue must be faced." With a sigh he pushed aside the pages of lecture notes on which he had been working. "But that unhappy subject must wait. We must work on something else now."

Purvey picked up his pen. "You are never lacking a new subject, Master. It almost makes my head whirl."

"This concerns the duties and responsibilities of the king and will be called *de Officio Regis*. It will take into consideration the relative importance of church and state."

Closing his eyes in concentration, he began to dictate: "The king bears the image of Christ's Godhead as the priest bears the image of his manhood. Even bad kings bear this image and must be obeyed, as we read in Peter's first epistle, 'Servants, be in subjection to your masters.'

"It is desirable and expected that the king be a man of virtue and justice and in all things set an example to his subjects. His subjects have no choice but to obey the laws. The king must obey them voluntarily and be committed to ruling in conformity with God's laws.

"The church should be under the supervision of the secular power. She has shown that she cannot reform herself, and bishops, cardinals, and popes refuse to abolish notorious abuses. Therefore, the state must assume the task of disciplining the church and cleansing her of those evils."

These statements startled Purvey. "I should be accustomed by now to your bold claims," he said, shaking his head.

"The king, because of the image he bears, must exercise superiority over church and clergy in temporal matters. This involves disendowment, the forfeited revenues to be used for employing good lay ministers. It is the king's responsibility to ensure that in his realm civil possessions are in secular hands.

"The king must keep his eye on the bishops and insist that they oversee the morals and attainments of those who hold benefices. Tithes should be withheld from non-resident clergy. Only qualified theologians should hold benefices."

In this treatise he cited Urban's call to the secular arm to punish Clement as an example of the misuse of ecclesiastical power. In keeping with his thesis as to the king's responsibility, only the king could authorize such a move.

"That's enough on the connection of the church with secular rule, Purvey. Put that aside and prepare to start again. I'm ready now to consider the spiritual ruler of the church. I shall assume, as I write on the power of the pope, that those who read this work have already read *de Ecclesia* and *de Officio Regis* and are familiar with the ideas there expressed."

Purvey looked at his master questioningly. "You have expressed differing opinions as to the pope and his power. Have you settled your own thinking as to his true power and position?"

"I admit to conflicts and contradictions. These spring from the actions of individual popes. My opinion of one pope is not necessarily my belief about the papacy in general."

"Earlier," said Purvey, "you wrote with confidence about our new pope Urban VI, noting that he is a deep Bible scholar."

"True, but he does not use his wisdom in the best way. His rudeness and insolence have offended both

229

friend and foe. He openly condemned the morals of his cardinals, not a tactful move. They deserted him and chose an antipope. Some have applied to Urban the proverb, 'None is so insolent as a low man raised suddenly to power.' Maybe he will yet listen to wise advice."

"You have voiced some pretty strong opinions about certain other popes."

"Purvey, you sound like the inner voice which often accuses me of excesses in thought and language. The Roman primacy has value, but one must obey a pope only as he follows Christ and acts in accordance with Scripture. A dogma which declares right all things decreed by the Roman pontiff is sheer blasphemy.

"Our time is limited. Let's not waste it. Begin your writing with what I have just said."

Wycliffe planned to demonstrate that historically and doctrinally the power claimed by the papacy lacked foundation. He pointed out the contrasts between the primitive church and that of the present day. The institutions had changed, even the doctrines. He would condone no departure from primitive custom.

He was still, in his own mind, uncertain about Urban VI. The pope must be the shepherd of the flock, the preacher who brings men to Christ. Would Urban's life measure up? Certainly he must abandon the idea of a crusade.

"I admit," he said to Purvey, "that Urban's insistence on evangelical poverty is commendable. He decreed that his cardinals have only one dish served at meals, a practice he himself follows. This will go hard with some of the greedy cardinals."

The writing continued: "All went well for the first three centuries. The trouble began with the gift of the Emperor Constantine to the church, the so-called 'donation of Constantine.' There began the craving of church and pope for temporal goods, wealth, and power. The only remedy is a return to evangelical poverty, in which the pope must lead the way."

In considering the qualities a pope must have, Wycliffe emphasized grace and character. "As Peter became Christ's vicar through his great love, his humility, and his resemblance to his Master in life and doctrine, so it must be with his successors. As for the method of choosing a pope, I suggest drawing lots. The system of election by cardinals, a sect unknown in Scripture, I consider a scandal.

"If the pope would embrace the poverty of Christ and renounce interference in all temporal matters, God might bestow upon him more perfect gifts and the power of working miracles."

His next point aimed a blow directly at the heart of the system. "We cannot tell whether any pope is a predestined member of holy church. Only through deeds of holiness can we believe in his predestination, and by the conformity of his acts and writings with Scripture."

He paused to give Purvey a brief rest and to stretch his own legs. Then he moved on to answer a hypothetical question, "Who then *is* Christ's vicar?"

"He who imitates Christ in his poverty, who chooses poor, simple men for disciples, who grasps not at jurisdiction, who dwells not in a rich palace but preaches the Gospel where Christ's name is not known, who protects the privilege of the clergy to live the higher life, who gives his life for the fallen ones, and who leads his flock into a fold built of strong stones."

Purvey looked up from his writing and asked, "Can there be such a man? Certainly you describe no pope of our times!"

Sighing deeply, Wycliffe said, "I remind you that simply to be the bishop of Rome does not make a man Peter's successor. This completes one more work for publication. I should be ashamed to show myself at Oxford if I upheld in the schools or elsewhere any other doctrine."

"Now you should rest a bit, Master," said Purvey.

"Rest? No time for that! Always the lectures! One term ends, another begins. Writing fills every spare moment. Don't speak of *rest*! Work stares us both in the face, for I cannot do it alone."

With tenderness, Purvey responded, "You can count upon me.

Soon, when that degree is mine, *all* my time will be yours."

6. March-April 1379—On Private Religions

Hereford found Wycliffe troubled over the problem of "private religions." "I can't leave the subject alone, Hereford," he cried. "These orders are nothing less than sects. They divide the church, the Body of Christ. Christ did not institute these sects, nor did Paul make mention of such a thing. Monks and friars take vows to which they give their highest loyalty. Mendicants are, in effect, the pope's private army."

Hereford sat in thoughtful silence. "You have good friends and followers among the mendicants," he said. "When you speak against their orders, you will offend and alienate them."

"Yes, and that saddens me. I have admired their finest qualities for years," replied Wycliffe. "Most of them uphold me in my attack on the possessioners. Among them are many true scholars. I often lecture in their houses here at Oxford."

"You patterned your program for the Poor Priests somewhat on theirs, with certain differences. We do not beg, or accept pay for our preaching, or hear confession, or grant absolution."

"Just so!" said Wycliffe. "The differences are important. You mention the negatives. I dwell on the positive in my assessment. The ideal of St. Francis held to the highest principles. Unfortunately the ideal has become tarnished."

"I recall that Grosseteste approved in glowing terms their activities in his day," said Hereford.

"In his day priests were negligent of their preaching, as many are today. He applauded the preaching of the friars for filling a need in getting the Gospel of Christ to the people."

"Apparently their preaching was more along scriptural lines at that time."

"Time moves on and things change. Armachanus complained that friars crept in and worked against parish priests in ways that did damage to the people. Acting as confessors, they granted absolution for money. Easy absolution encourages sin."

"Of course, if there is no true repentance," said Hereford, "the words of absolution count for nothing."

"Fitzralph's objection to their preaching is still valid. They preach in an extravagant style, mixing Scripture, fables, myths, and unseemly anecdotes. They draw the people away from the parish priest, yet offer not the Bread of life."

"I see the need for opposing these wrongs. Let's hope that your friends among the mendicants may be led to see as well."

"It's good, Hereford, to know that you understand. I hope you understand, as well, that when I lash out in strong—even violent—terms against an individual or an institution, it is not because of any innate vindictive spirit. Where I see pervasive evil sending countless souls to hell, I cannot but speak out as I do. If there is to be any reformation of the church, men must hear, and soft words make no impression."

Hereford gave his friend a look of compassion and said with almost a sob in his voice, "Do what you have to do. It seems God has called you to be a Jeremiah, and you know what his lot was."

"*'To uproot and tear down, to destroy and overthrow, to build and plant.'* The destructive actions had to come before building and planting. I fear I may never get beyond tearing down and destroying, leaving it to others to build and plant. Not a happy lot. Yes, I feel a kinship with the prophet Jeremiah."

So Wycliffe took the next step—a small one at first-along the path in which he was being inexorably led by the Word of God and the God of the Word. He lectured and wrote against the religious orders as being divisive of the church. As for the sins of the mendicants he must point out, he earnestly strove to be gentle but knew that he failed. Can sin ever be handled gently?

With his lectures on this subject he lost the support of many of the friars. These joined with the monks who had attacked him earlier, and the attacks increased. A few friars seemed puzzled, but stuck with him, trusting that they might understand, and perhaps accept, this new turn in his teaching.

He prepared a shortened form of *de Potestate Papae*, one suited for the general reader. It developed into a reasoned inquiry as to whether the papacy is necessary. He felt a special urgency for this message to be heard beyond the walls of Oxford, for another matter troubled him and cried out for expression, a teaching which would be even harder for his hearers to accept.

7. April 1379—Rede's Library

At last Rede's library at Merton was finished, and Rede himself came to call Wycliffe to inspect his creation. "This dream took a long time to come true, Wycliffe. Your encouragement helped keep it alive in my heart when I might have despaired of its ever becoming a reality."

Rede seized his arm and steered him through the Merton archway into the quadrangle. "Behold!" he said. "The work of eight years, finished at last."

With pride he led Wycliffe through the lower floors, up the stairway to the south wing. "When you were urging me on toward making my dream a reality, perhaps you recall telling me to have plenty of shelves for lots and lots of books. Here they are!"

Wycliffe stared in amazement. A narrow aisle stretched through the center of the room. To the right and left bookcases ranged from aisle to wall, row after row, with space between for a stool beside a shelf upon which the reader's book would lie.

"The more valuable books are chained to the shelves, lest eager students be tempted to make off with them. They must work in daylight hours, for no candles or lamps are permitted. Too much danger of fire. They must pray for bright, sunny days!"

"You and I have come a long way in our personal lives since we studied here at Merton," said Wycliffe. "You've been a bishop all these years and have given this gift to Merton, while I..."

Rede broke in. "While you have become the 'flower of Oxford,' known throughout the land and abroad as the *Doctor Evangelicus*, outstanding philosopher and theologian of our time."

As they parted, Wycliffe said, "You return to your diocese, I to my desk. Though our paths, and perhaps

235

even our thinking, diverge, our friendship remains. Knowing that, I leave with a glad heart, an exultation of spirit which will buoy me up for days to come."

When Parliament convened at Westminster that same month, Wycliffe was concerned over what they would do with the question of sanctuary. To his disappointment only a mild action was taken. Fraudulent debtors would be denied the right of protection, and sanctuary would be limited to cases of felony.

"Such a statute changes nothing," cried Wycliffe. "Debtors will still take sanctuary at Westminster. The wording, 'cases of felony,' leaves open the door of all places of sanctuary to murderers, rapists, robbers, and every other sort of criminal."

"Shakyl still holds his hostage," said Purvey. "The crown is reportedly seeking to negotiate, but as yet Shakyl keeps him hidden. Meanwhile, who considers the prisoner? More years may pass before he sees his homeland again. It seems an evil thing."

"War is an evil thing," thundered Wycliffe. "None of this would have happened except for the greediness of our lords and the king himself. This war with France, and the more senseless one with Spain, should have ceased long ago."

Wycliffe's latest works reached the bookstalls and found an eager readership. *De Potestate Papae* produced opposition, but the tract which included his attack on the religious orders and on certain practices of the mendicants caused the greatest uproar.

Some friars continued to attend Wycliffe's lectures, perplexed and uncertain, but unready to abandon their master. Others bombarded him with letters and public denunciation of his propositions.

8. May-June 1379—Illness

Without warning illness struck Wycliffe. Purvey said it was the result of long hours of writing, combined with the struggle against opposing forces and the weight of the wrongs in church and nation about which few seemed concerned.

A raging fever left him barely conscious. The doctor attending him rendered what treatment he could, but nothing helped. His condition worsened. One or another of his friends sat constantly beside him. A hush fell over Oxford as word spread that the *Doctor Evangelicus* lay dying.

One evening a group of friars appeared and demanded to be admitted. They were four doctors, one from each of the mendicant orders. Wycliffe realized who they were as they began to speak, but he lay with closed eyes. Each expressed a wish for his return to health. Such hypocrisy angered him, but he did not speak.

After standing irresolute for some minutes, one of them spoke again. "We remind you of the grievous wrongs you have heaped upon our orders by your lectures, sermons, and writings. As the hour of death approaches, it would be well to repent of what you have said against us and revoke your disparaging words."

Wycliffe continued to lie still, as if he had not heard them. As he pondered what to reply, a verse from the Psalms came to him: *Non moriar sed viviam et narrabo opera Domini.*

Opening his eyes, he motioned to his servant to raise him up in bed. Fixing his eyes upon the startled friars, he spoke with great passion in a voice suddenly grown strong, *I shall not die, but I shall live and declare the works of the Lord.*

With that he fell back, and his visitors made a hasty departure. Their visit, however, seemed to jar him out of the depths of illness, and he began to mend. He later laughed and asked Purvey whether he should thank the mendicants. He was soon back at his desk, in spite of Purvey's remonstrances.

One day while he was semi-convalescent, Aston put his head in the door. Seeing Wycliffe at his desk, he was about to leave without entering, but Wycliffe restrained him, saying, "I need to rest for a while, and your coming gives me an excuse. I find it difficult to remain long at writing."

Aston expressed concern at his continued weakness of body. "Could you not manage to give yourself time to regain your strength before pushing so hard? It might pay in the long run."

"And again it might not. Who knows how much longer I have? God granted me an extension of time in restoring me when all, including myself, thought I would die. I must not waste the time when much is still to be done."

"Your remaining friends among the friars showed concern about your illness. They remain attached to you, but are unhappy over what they consider your turning against them. The stress you put upon the sinfulness of membership in their orders distresses them most. The thought of revoking their vows and leaving their orders horrifies them."

"I know," said Wycliffe. "I wish I could make it easier. At present I'm at work on a series of lectures on the subject *de Apostasia*. I want them to see that withdrawing from their orders is not apostasy. The real apostasy lies elsewhere."

"I suppose you mean to deliver those lectures when the new term opens. By then you should be physically stronger. I only hope the mendicants find what you say convincing."

"I hate to think of being deserted by the friars. It seems the crown has already deserted me."

"What? Only last year you were called to give advice at Parliament. What reason is there for a break with the court?"

"Oh, I don't mean there's been an open break, but I sense an unspoken consent for our relationship to lapse. Lancaster's decline in power since Edward III's death has meant less influence to support me."

"He certainly gave his full support when you were called before convocation at St. Paul's. Even at Lambeth his backing continued, though it came nominally through the Queen Mother."

"At Richard II's first Parliament, when I gave an opinion on the question of paying money to the pope, I spoke too on disendowment. Though members of Convocation opposed this, the Commons and the nobility seemed to be behind me. Yet, when it came to action, my advice was ignored."

"Lancaster supported you at that time, but actually he has no great quarrel with endowments. It's been his habit even up to the present to make large gifts to monasteries and abbeys."

"Then my advice about sanctuary laws was disregarded. The crown has no desire to ruffle the feathers of the ecclesiastical brethren. Money is needed, and only with the vote of Convocation can it be obtained. So my ideas have become an embarrassment."

"That's probably not the whole story," said Aston. "When Pope Gregory was alive, they were glad to go along with your antipapal views. With the election of Urban, it looked as if things were about to take a new turn. Parliament voted to give allegiance to Urban when a second pope was elected. Antipapal feeling has declined."

"What it really amounts to is that the crown no longer needs me. In a sense, it's a relief. If they chose to maintain my services, it would restrict me in what I have to say, and I cannot be muzzled. It's better this way. No open break."

"I imagine you still have Gaunt's goodwill and friendship. In a pinch he would again come to your defense, as I know you would to his."

"I hope you're right. Personal friendship is reassuring, even if official support is not possible. It's somewhat the same with Rede. Our deep friendship endures, even when we are not in perfect agreement on certain theological questions."

"Since you don't discuss these matters with Rede, you don't know his position. You may not be as far apart as you imagine. Rede's a pretty steady Christian."

"You comfort me. Sometimes, when I move on as I must, I wonder whether any of you will stay by me. Opposition will get rougher. For me, to live and be silent is impossible."

"The weakness from your illness depresses you. Otherwise you would not doubt the steadfastness of your friends. I leave you to your work on apostasy. I look forward to reading it." With a touch on the shoulder and a warm smile, he was gone.

Wycliffe moved back to his desk and picked up his pen, but he did not begin writing. *Dear Aston! He will remain true whatever comes. What of the others—Brut, Hereford, Repyngton, Purvey? In the present circumstances it's hard to know who is weak and who is strong, who has depth of belief and who goes only part way. Persecution will come. That will be the decisive point. Personally, I feel that I can say, 'Let the blow fall.' Each man must speak for himself.*

9. July-October 1379—On the Eucharist

Slowly his strength returned. Brut came one summer evening to coax him out for a walk. They did not go as far as in the old days, but being out in the open did Wycliffe good. Most of all, being with Brut did him good.

He still struggled with the treatise *de Apostasia*. The title was almost a blind, for he intended to incorporate it into a larger work to be called *de Eucharistia*. He was getting into deep water. It burdened him, but he saw no escape.

"I mean to be as restrained as possible as I deal with the question of apostasy," he said to Purvey. "I'm anxious to convince the friars who continue with me that they may without apostasy abandon their private religions."

"They'll not find that easy."

"The secular clergy should see that the status of bishop, a truly scriptural office, is higher than any private religion, of which no mention is made in Scripture. Yet I would point them to a higher ideal, that of Christ's life, without property. I would urge the friars to abandon their ships on the seas, their jewels and money, their palaces and extravagant churches."

With some reorganizing he fitted these thoughts into a preamble which satisfied him. Moving to the subject of the Eucharist, he recalled that when he and Woodford had debated on this, Woodford had accused him of changing his opinion several times.

"He was right," he said to Purvey. "I was struggling to find the truth. I decided to let the subject alone for a time. I can do that no longer. It burns in my heart and in my mind. I must speak, for it is a matter on which I'm convinced the teaching of the church is heretical. It leads men to idolatry and worse."

"As is your custom," said Purvey, "when you lay hold of a truth, you must proclaim it."

Transubstantiation, he could assure his readers, was a relatively new dogma in the church. It dated only to the previous century. Up to the reign of Innocent III the church had not known such a doctrine. According to this doctrine, the bread and wine, at the touch of the glorious Substance which takes possession of them, cease to exist. Only the appearances remain, indicating the presence of something else. A two-fold movement supposedly takes place—the bread ceasing to be and the creation of the Body.

Such a possibility Wycliffe denied, in the first place, on the basis of his philosophical view that nothing can be annihilated, and that there can be no accidents, or appearances, without subject. The bread and wine remain after consecration.

Scripture upheld this. It was *bread* Jesus broke and gave to the disciples, and of this same bread he said, *"This is my body."* Paul says, *"As often as ye shall eat this bread and drink this cup, ye shall show the Lord's death till he comes."*

Wycliffe stated that he had no doubt of the Real Presence of the body of Christ in the host. There was in the bread both the reality of a sign and also the reality of the body of Christ. The bread and wine were no mere symbols of the body and blood.

"Yet I dare not say that the body of Christ is essentially, substantially, corporeally or identically that bread. There is no corporal presence at the altar, and they are idolators who believe the bread of the sacrament to be identical with their God. The body is not present as the body of Christ in heaven. Rather it is present not corporeally but spiritually."

He struggled to express adequately and exactly what he meant. If he insisted too much on the Real Presence, it would be understood as physical and lead to idolatry.

Yet if he laid too much stress on the figurative interpretation, it might be taken to mean the absence of Christ in any *real* sense.

He sought analogies. To what could the bread and wine and the presence of Christ be compared? He found a quote from John of Damasacus: "As the live coal is not mere wood but wood united with fire, so the bread is not mere bread but bread united with deity." As Christ is two substances, earthly and divine, so this sacrament is the body of sensible bread and the body of Christ.

This difficult work completed, he was ready to publish *On Apostasy* in a short form and at the same time *On the Eucharist*, including in it the same material but with fuller and stronger arguments. With this accomplished, he felt wrung dry.

Since his physical strength had in large measure returned, he preached several times on these subjects. Immediately an undercurrent of disapproval broke out, growing into open and furious denunciation of his teaching. In October his new books appeared, adding fuel to the flames of indignation.

Students returning for the new term, unaware of the breaking storm, were enthusiastic about a new series of lectures from the *Doctor Evangelicus*. He felt optimistic about these young men, for among them were a number of friars.

As the lectures proceeded, he carried the students along with him. This was new thinking, and they had to get used to it. Some found it shocking but continued to listen, willing to weigh the evidence. A few dropped out.

As members of the community read his books and animosity surfaced, he had to deal with attacks made against him by friars who had long stood by him, as well as monks and others he had counted among his friends.

"Brut tells me I have always loved a fight," he said to Purvey. "I can't say I look forward to this one. It promises to be the fiercest yet. I abhor bloody warfare, but words can be sharper weapons than swords."

Most of the seculars stood by him, either from sympathy with his teaching, or for loyalty to Oxford's most outstanding and honored doctor. It was not a good sign, however, when a minority among the seculars assisted in a reaction that caused William Barton to be elected chancellor of the university.

10. November-December 1379
Rising Opposition

Ever since Wycliffe's addresses at the time he received his doctorate, William Remington, a Cistercian monk and former chancellor, had worked against him. He was known as "a great assertor of the Eucharist," so Wycliffe was not surprised when he wrote a defense in opposition to his view. Wycliffe dealt in vigorous language and at great length with this attack.

A Benedictine monk, John Wells, became a persistent opponent, zealously defending the monastic life and the Eucharist against Wycliffe's stand. Wycliffe published a reply to him and made reference to him in sermons as "a certain black dog of the order of Benedict."

Among the friars, Kenningham continued his controversy. To him Wycliffe expressed concern that transubstantiation could so easily lead to idolatry. "As the fathers of the old law warned against worshiping images," he said, "so ought Christians to be warned not to worship what the moderns call accidents and the earlier church called bread and wine, as if they were the true body and blood of Jesus Christ."

Former friends and supporters continued to turn against him, but one opponent who remained a friend was Ralph Strode. He and Wycliffe had become close friends when they studied at Merton. The two had carried on controversies for years, but without destroying the friendship.

Strode attacked Wycliffe's plea for disendowment and a return to the simplicity of the early church, claiming that this would destroy the church's rites and organization. Peace of the church should be maintained even at the cost of possible abuses. Too, bishops should have endowments so that they might provide hospitality and carry out works of mercy.

While agreeing to the latter claim, provided all was used for such purposes, Wycliffe reiterated his views as to the pressing need for disendowment and the necessity for all "dominion" to be held by laymen. The whole church was in need of reform, and he set forth a plan for its accomplishment.

In reply to Strode's objection to his attack on the orders, Wycliffe used stronger and bolder words. "The 'new orders,' which I call 'sects,' should come to an end. It would be well that there be neither pope nor Caesarean prelate. The need at present is for men to speak out with courage. Not by silence or by the wisdom of the serpent will the church be delivered from the tyranny of the devil, but by following the example of the martyrs."

In consideration of his friendship with Strode, he softened. "You are right to urge with Augustine that evil not be punished at the cost of the peace of the church. I confess that I myself have often sinned in this matter from presumption and arrogance. Reformation should not be sudden but carried out with prudence. We trust God for the results, but faithful soldiers of Christ must do all possible to defend God's Law in the church militant, and to reduce the burden of taxation for the commons."

He noticed Purvey smiling as he finished this last bit. "Are you wondering, Purvey, whether my humility and my confession of sin to Strode will have any lasting effect? I shall try to abstain from presumption and arrogance, but you know my nature."

"I was thinking rather," said Purvey, "that it seems odd to hear you urge in the same breath the defense of God's Law and the reduction of taxes."

"Have you not read in the Scriptures, Purvey, that God's Law extends to affairs of daily life such as oppression of the poor?"

With other opponents Wycliffe did not deal so kindly as with Strode. "Who is this pseudofriar, this idiot, this ignoramus," he cried, "who objects as Strode did to my plea for disendowment on the basis that it would rob the church of power to offer hospitality? I shall answer that friars never show hospitality."

All Oxford seemed fiercely divided into warring camps. His bitterness toward those who attacked him grew, and he knew no way to control it. "I tried to tread gently, but that failed. Now it's fight to the finish, with no let-up, no turning back."

The battle concerning his Eucharistic views was beginning in earnest.

11. January-March 1380—English Bible

In January, Archbishop Sudbury became chancellor of England. "A further indication," said Wycliffe, "of my fall into disfavor at court. My protests against Caesarean clergy are ignored."

Translating passages of Scripture for the Poor Priests occupied what time he could spare during February. As he worked one bright morning on the parable of the prodigal son, he suddenly stopped in mid-sentence.

"Why have I not seen it before?" he asked himself. Calling his servant, he sent him to search for Hereford. "Ask him to come as soon as he conveniently can—or even inconveniently."

Hereford appeared promptly. "More opposition?" he asked.

Wycliffe laughed. "Doubtless we have that, but such is not my reason for calling you. Why have I been so slow to see the necessity for something we should have done before this?"

"I don't know what you refer to, but I hardly see how you could have worked on anything more. You stay fully occupied."

"That's what I mean. My time is too full. I intend to assign you an enormous task. Let's see...you are in more or less the final stages of your struggle for your doctorate. What I have in mind may slow you down a bit."

"Perhaps you could speak plainly, inasmuch as I cannot read your mind. You have aroused my curiosity. Whatever it is, do remember that I've worked toward my doctorate for a long time."

"I speak of something of far greater importance than your degree, Hereford. As I sat painstakingly translating a passage of Scripture, I realized that Poor Priests are not the only ones needing such help. Yet, I have time to produce so little."

"I begin to catch a glimmer of what you mean to propose," said Hereford, "but please continue."

"Hereford, the whole Bible must be put into English. It's far too difficult for a priest to translate each passage he needs. Great sections of Scripture are being neglected, while ignorant or lazy priests use over and over the brief portions they find available or which they are able to translate. I do not have time for this undertaking. *You* are the man to do it."

Hereford seemed stunned. "I see the wisdom of such a move, but what makes you think *I* am the one to do it?"

"I know your scholarship, your love for the Scriptures, your facility with words, whether English or Latin. Of most importance, I know *you*. I have heard you preach in English. Your ideas as to the method of translation agree with my own."

"I hardly know how to reply. I fail to comprehend why this task falls to me. There must be someone better fitted."

"I ignore that last statement. As for the task, it is tremendous and unbelievably weighty. It is not God's way to assign easy tasks. You may call on others to help, but it is upon you that the responsibility must fall for getting the work done. Begin with Genesis and work through the Old Testament."

Hereford closed his eyes and groaned. "It's unthinkable that I should refuse. With God's help, I'll do what you ask."

"Without God's help you would be foolish to begin," replied Wycliffe, laying his hand upon Hereford's slumped shoulders.

Hereford sat in silence for some moments. Wycliffe spoke again in a softer tone. "I think you must discard all thoughts of a doctorate this year. In good time you'll have it, but it's less urgent than this new goal toward which you will be striving."

Wycliffe's friends, excited over the undertaking, admitted the need, but wondered about ecclesiastical approval. "I fear Courtenay will not be pleased to think of the Scriptures in the vernacular getting into the hands of the laity," said Repyngton.

"The Bible has been translated into French," said Wycliffe. "Some of the nobles possess and read it.

248

Eleanor, wife of Thomas of Woodstock, possesses the Norman Scriptures in two volumes."

"If men and women of the nobility may read the Bible in French," said Aston. "why not in our own language, which is replacing French? Certainly the clergy need such help."

Wycliffe turned over one of his rooms for the translation. The work must proceed as quickly and as quietly as possible. A too-early publicizing of the venture seemed unwise. The necessary manuscripts could remain in one place, along with the finished pages. Space was adequate for helpers Hereford might call in.

Hereford began at once. He tried to continue his university work as well, but soon gave it up. "This is too important. The sooner it's completed, the better. Translation and correction will require much time, and when one copy is complete, there is the gigantic task for the scriveners. Who will pay for this?"

"That question need not concern us at the moment," said Brut. "God will raise up men and women of wealth who will be interested in the project and willing to finance it."

Hereford worked diligently. At first he worked alone, but soon established a more efficient method. He did the translation and dictated to another who wrote. A third read and made corrections. He enlisted several capable helpers.

12. April-July 1380—Barton Acts

One April day as Wycliffe and Purvey were at their usual occupation in one room, while Bible translation proceeded in the next, Aston burst in with a concerned look on his face.

"I dislike to interrupt," he said, "but there's something you must know. Chancellor Barton is selecting a committee for the purpose of considering your doctrine on the Eucharist."

Wycliffe rose to his feet. "I wondered how long it would be before he took action."

"It's supposed to be a secret, but you know how word gets around. Apparently he intends to name twelve men. I know of four seculars. The others will probably be monks and friars."

Hereford, hearing excited voices, joined them. "Why did Barton wait so long?" he asked.

"Later, Hereford," said Wycliffe. "I must know who the seculars are. Aston...?"

"All are doctors. Robert Rygge is the most important, the one upon whom you can count with certainty. I know less about the others—John Laundryn, John Mowbray, and John Gascoigne."

"Ah, Rygge," said Wycliffe. "A good man. The others I think I can count on, though I do not know them well. Laundryn is doctor of medicine as well as of divinity. Mowbray is doctor of civil and canon law, while Gascoigne is a canonist doctor. Barton is crafty in his selection. He could not choose all regulars, for the university would not have stood for such one-sidedness. He can't expect a unanimous decision, but he'll make sure he has a majority voting as he intends."

"Upon what basis will they judge?" asked Hereford. "The *de Eucharistia* is a large volume, too long to digest quickly."

"It seems Barton has garnered twelve points from Wycliffe's teaching. He may ask them to base their judgment upon those."

"Hardly fair," said Purvey, "but to be expected. The usual ploy of lifting sentences out of context so that the writer's meaning is obscured. They should study the whole book."

"If they did, they might find the truth." said Hereford. "The arguments are highly convincing."

"I understand," said Aston, "that Barton will not rush the men. He evidently means to take his time in making a report."

"Back to your question, Hereford, as to why he waited so long," said Wycliffe. "I think it safe to say he waited to see which way the wind blows. You may be sure he has listened not only to the content of my teaching, but to the reaction to it. When he saw the friars falling away and aligning themselves with their old enemies the monks, he felt it safe to act."

"He has a certain freedom to act," said Aston, "since the renewal of the *writ significavit* last year. By it the chancellor of the university may excommunicate a person and send his name to the chancellor of England, who, if the accused remains unyielding for forty days, may consign him to the king's prison without further trial. That gives added strength to his position."

Wycliffe tried to shake off concern about this new development by applying himself to lecturing and writing. As the term ended, he had heard nothing more about Barton's council. Distributing sermon outlines to his Poor Priests, he sent them out again. Several new men had joined them, each of whom he assigned to a more experienced man.

Purvey remained behind. Wycliffe could not help but notice his longing look as the others set out. With a sigh, he said, "I know, Purvey, you would like to be among them, but I need you. In a short time I plan to go to Lutterworth, and then you may join them. I'll suggest to Hereford that he, too, go for a short time. He's making remarkable progress with the translation, but he needs a change. You two should make an excellent team."

13. July-August 1380—Lutterworth

He intended to throw himself wholeheartedly into the work of his parish. He would put all thoughts of Barton out of his mind. Needs at Lutterworth would more than consume his time—and thoughts. It occurred to him that Hereford was not the only one who needed a change.

"I intend you to have some days of leave while I'm here," he told Horne, "but not immediately. I want to hear you preach, and I want *you* to hear *me* preach. After that we shall see."

He prepared a schedule for visiting his flock. He could be sure of finding some Feildings, Thomas Baker and his wife Jane, and William Milner and his family. These were the parishioners with whom he was better acquainted, but he must get to know the others. He never limited his visits to the prominent families, but spent time with the lesser members of the community, paying special attention to the serfs, of whom there were but few.

"I must ride over to Groby one day," he said to Horne, "to pay a visit to the Lady Isabel and young Sir Henry de Ferrers. I see them at church on Sundays, but I have never been to Groby."

He spent many hours with Horne, explaining the views he was teaching with regard to the religious orders and on the Sacrament of the altar. Horne wanted to know about various other matters upon which Wycliffe constantly lectured and wrote. The time was never long enough for all they needed to discuss.

Horne preached, and Wycliffe was not altogether displeased. He recommended ways of strengthening some points and suggested things he might omit and others that he might add in order to stick more closely to Scripture. This seemed an opportune time to present him with the sermon outlines in English which he had brought with him for that purpose. Horne gratefully received the help. Wycliffe felt they had a good relationship.

One afternoon Wycliffe set out to enjoy a long walk to the outskirts of the parish. He followed Ely Lane past the farms with their modest dwellings and little crofts, or farm plots. On either side behind the houses lay fields and pastures. Then the houses were left behind, and only flocks of sheep lay within the hedgerows of hawthorn and blackthorn on one side, with a heavily wooded area on the other.

He was tempted to enter the woods and wander in the shade of the tall oaks. But the lateness of the hour and the thought of how far he had come caused him to turn back. Overexertion could lead to aching back and legs tomorrow!

He retraced his steps until he came to a path to the left. Yielding to temptation, he entered it. It would lead eventually, he supposed, into Snellgate lane. Beyond the first field, he came to a hedgerow he must cross by a stile. With a grimace, he made the strenuous effort necessary to climb over the stile and down into the next field. From here the path soon led into Snellgate.

This was a beautiful little lane with a row of cottages on the left, with fields running down to the river. On the right were the backs of fields belonging to the cottages he had passed on Ely Lane. He reached the High Street and soon the rectory.

Horne was surprised to hear the distance he had traversed. "This was just a walk," he asked, "with no other object?"

Wycliffe laughed. "Do you never take such a walk, Horne? Walter Brut taught me the value of that many years ago. I seldom go the distance I did today, for the years are slowing me down. It's not a waste of time, for it puts the brain, the heart, and the body in better condition. It's a habit you should cultivate."

Wycliffe smiled at Horne's doubtful expression. He slept unusually well that night.

"Last Sunday, Horne, you preached and I listened. This Sunday we shall reverse the process. You may be as critical of my sermon as I was of yours."

"Oh, Sir, I hardly think I shall make any criticism. It will offer me a pattern which I may seek to follow."

"You may find a point or two with which to disagree," said Wycliffe with a twinkle in his eye. "After you have done your duty in that line, you deserve a vacation. You may take the next two weeks. Getting away occasionally from one's labors is another means of bringing refreshment to body, mind, and spirit."

In a more serious tone he added, "Be sure you remember that you are God's man wherever you go. Let your life bring honor to the name of your Lord and set an example for all you meet. A Christian takes no vacation from holy living."

Wycliffe experienced a rather exuberant joy in activities so different from his life at Oxford. As his people came to know him, they sought his counsel on their problems, some of a spiritual nature, some of a more mundane character.

He always preached the Gospel, but he did not hesitate to speak of his other great concerns—of disendowment, warnings against practices of the friars, a proper understanding of the Sacrament of the altar. He held that reformation of the church would have to come from the laity. They should be informed on these matters. Few here would have a say-so in making changes, but they should recognize right moves when the time came.

14. September-October 1380—Silenced

September found Wycliffe back at Oxford, driven by an urgency to be at his writing. The Poor Priests had returned with news both encouraging and discouraging. A discouraging item was that one bishop had reminded Hereford and Purvey that they had no license to preach in his diocese and had threatened action against them if they continued.

"I knew this would come," said Wycliffe. "What did you do?"

"We moved on to a more remote area," said Hereford. "We left by night, so the bishop could not know the direction we took. When we reached a likely spot, we preached again, then moved on."

"We found most of the people eager to hear," said Purvey, "and out among the hamlets no one would think of reporting us to the bishop. A priest showed up at one place and took a deep interest. We reached some areas where there was no parish priest within miles."

"Unless I am mistaken," said Wycliffe, "this is a beginning of what will become real persecution. I am pleased at your reports. This work is needed, and we can expect God to bless it, no matter how difficult it becomes."

Hereford returned to the translation, but he decided to have Repyngton and one or two others replace him at times. This made it possible for him to continue his studies. Perhaps within the next year he could complete work for his doctorate, even while spending a large part of the time on translation.

Aston had more to report on members of Barton's council. "The two monks are Crump and Wells," he reported.

"They would enter the council with their decision already made," said Wycliffe. "Both have opposed me. Crump began his attacks after reading *Civil Dominion*, objecting to my statement that a worldly pope is a heresiarch and should be deprived. He reacted violently to *de Eucharistia*. Who are the friars?"

"Three are Dominicans of no particular distinction."

Wycliffe snorted. "Barton showed wisdom in choosing three Dominicans. They are opposed to me and have been for some time."

"The other three are an Austin friar, a Carmelite, and a Franciscan."

"The council must have finished its work by now. When will Barton make public his report? Why the delay?"

"I have a feeling," said Aston, "that he means to wait until the term opens and all the students are here. There is, however, the possibility that the decision did not go as he had hoped. In that case he will be reluctant to publicize the results."

Wycliffe had agreed to deliver a series of lectures in the schools of the Augustinians in the new term. He was pleased at the opportunity to present the doctrines which had turned some of the friars against him. The Austins were at least willing to give him a hearing. Some might be convinced of the truth.

As he entered the lecture hall in the first week of the term, he found the benches crowded with eager students. They gave him a courteous hearing, asked intelligent questions, and appeared to consider seriously his views.

The second week began. "As the words of Scripture tell us that this sacrament *is* the body of Christ, not that it *will be*, or that it is sacramentally a *figure* of the body of Christ, so we must admit without reserve that the bread, which is the sacrament, is truly the body of Christ. But the simplest layman will see that it follows that, inasmuch as this bread is the body of Christ, it is therefore *bread*, and remains bread—being at once both bread *and* the body of Christ."

His students listened intently, for this was a point on which they had been taught to the contrary. He experienced a growing excitement. They were with him!

"An illustration may be helpful. When a man is raised to the dignity of lordship or prelacy, does he cease to be the same man? Certainly not. As to his substance he continues in all respects the same, though in a certain sense elevated. So, by the consecration of the priest, the bread becomes truly the body of Christ, but the bread no more ceases to be bread than the man ceases to be the same man in my illustration. The bread has come to be *sacramentally* the body of Christ, while it is still bread substantially."

At that moment the door was flung open and an emissary of the chancellor entered. In a loud voice he read from an official paper a condemnation of the doctrine Wycliffe was then expounding. By a unanimous vote the council had singled out two articles which they proclaimed "execrable even to listen to." The first was the assertion that bread and wine remain after consecration. The other was his statement that in the sacrament Christ was present only "figuratively, not truly in his own corporal person."

"The true doctrine," read the emissary, "is that of Duns, that only the appearance of bread and wine remain. This view must be believed, taught, and defended against all gainsayers.

"As for the condemned views, it is forbidden that anyone shall publicly hold, teach, or defend the same in this university, either in the schools or outside, under pain of imprisonment, suspension from all scholastic functions and the greater excommunication. All scholars are to flee such teachers as they would a snake spitting out baleful poison."

Being taken by surprise, Wycliffe felt utterly confused for the moment. The matter of the condemnation was not unexpected, but the place and manner of its delivery was shocking. Regaining mastery of himself, he looked the messenger in the eye and stated firmly, "Neither the chancellor nor any of his accomplices can alter my convictions in the slightest."

Naturally this marked the end of his lectures to the Augustinians. He discovered that the vote had been seven to five against him. He could but wonder which of the friars had, with the four seculars, stood by him. The chancellor called the decision unanimous, but it was obviously one of those fictional unanimities often employed. When they saw that they were outnumbered, his supporters may have reluctantly assented to allowing the chancellor to call it a unanimous decision.

His friends were quick to offer advice. "You must appeal to the Congregation of Regent Masters." said Aston.

"That is certainly the proper course," said Hereford. "Should they uphold the decision of Barton's council, you should then appeal to the Great Congregation of the whole university. You stand a good chance of having the decision reversed by following this route."

After due consideration Wycliffe declared, "No, I shall appeal directly to the king." Nothing could shake him from this decision.

"I cease lecturing temporarily," he said, "but they cannot still my pen." He wrote furiously and constantly. Hereford and his helpers, busy at translation, marveled at the steadfastness with which he sat at his desk and wielded his pen. He only paused to send his servant out for more pens, ink, and parchment.

15. November-December 1380
Special Concerns

He produced a tract written in English, *A Short Rule of Life*, intended for lords and laborers alike. Since Ludgershall, when he had first come into close contact with serfs, he had felt deep sympathy for the poor and indignation at the treatment they often received. The memory of the sick old man lying helpless in the mud of his wretched hovel remained with him.

He had expressed himself rather fully upon this subject in *Civil Dominion*, stating that both rule and service are necessary in our fallen state. He insisted that serfdom should not be hereditary nor perpetual. Free tenants are better off than serfs, but both must be patient under suffering, though this in no way lessens the sin of cruel lords. All should live under the law of love, the lord forgiving debts which serfs could not pay and reducing charges to poor tenants.

"The people I now address," he said to Purvey, "are unlikely to be familiar with *Civil Dominion*. I write in a popular style, as if addressing them personally."

To the lords he wrote, *You are to govern your tenants well, showing mercy in their rents and not suffering their officers to do them wrong by extortions.* He inserted relevant Scripture passages for both lords and servants, pointing out to them their duty as Christians.

To the humblest class he wrote, *If you are a laborer, live in meekness, and do your work willingly. Then if your lord or master is not a Christian, he, by your loving and true service, may not have a grudge against you or your God, but rather be constrained to come to Christ.*

If your lord is a Christian, do not serve him with grudging or only in his presence, but truly and willingly in his absence. Do this not only for worldly fear or worldly reward, but for the fear of God, and conscience, and a reward in heaven.

This piece done, he turned to his shelf of published books. "Purvey," he said, "I shall begin now to produce a shortened version of each of these. Some readers do not have the scholarly depth to read the lengthy primary version."

"I presume you will put these into English."

"No, not at first. Later I mean to prepare a briefer English tract from each one, still carrying the message of the original."

"By all means," said Purvey. "Tracts in English can reach a multitude of people who are not able to read Latin."

16. December 1380—Rumblings of Trouble

Parliament convened at Northampton in November. Soon after its close Brut came riding into Oxford with a report. He came from Westminster, where he had encountered Bishop Rede traveling back from Northampton and had obtained from him a fairly full account of proceedings.

"Rede was not in a happy frame of mind," said Brut, as he drew close to Wycliffe's charcoal brazier to warm his frozen hands. "The weather was abominable and the roads all but impassable. Days passed before a sufficient number straggled in to make it possible to attend to business. Accommodations were poor, causing no end of grumbling among the lords, who travel with great trains of attendants."

"You speak of the nobility," said Wycliffe, "but the bishops rarely fall behind in number of attendants. I hope Rede is more modest than most in that respect."

"Sudbury, as chancellor, related the usual tale as to finances. The king's garrisons on the French coast have not been paid, and the troops threaten to desert. The king is in debt; his jewels have been pawned and are in danger of being forfeited.

"The speaker demanded to know the exact amount necessary, reduced to the lowest possible figure. The people, he declared, are very poor and hardly able to bear any more burdens."

"He is right on that score," said Wycliffe. "The members of Parliament may grumble about poor accommodations, but the poor of the land grumble about empty stomachs."

"The king's ministers replied that 160,000 pounds would be needed."

"Outrageous! How could they expect to obtain such a sum?"

"After heated arguments on all sides, it was agreed that the clergy would undertake to provide one third of the amount, the rest to be raised by a poll tax."

"The church possesses at least a third of the land of England," said Wycliffe, "so it is only right that they should provide a third of the tax. However, to collect 100,000 pounds from the laity will be found easier said than done."

"Feeling against the church ran high," continued Brut. "The Commons dared to petition for the instant dissolution of all foreign monasteries and the expulsion of all foreign monks."

"An excellent move," cried Wycliffe, "but I have no doubt it was turned down."

"I'm afraid so. As Parliament dispersed, its members desired to hurry home as quickly as possible. Word of the new poll tax preceded them, and Rede was concerned about the insolence of the people in the villages along the road. In places he noticed a crowd gathered about a speaker delivering an oration of some sort. Rede was glad to be headed back to Chichester."

"There's bound to be trouble over the poll tax," said Wycliffe. "Those responsible for collecting it will be fortunate if they meet with nothing worse than insolence."

"I suppose you've had no response from your appeal to the king," said Brut.

"Not a word. I can't help but wonder how much longer I may have to wait."

The year ended with no answer. When at last it came, it was not from the king.

PART 5

Point of no Return
(1381–1382)
"I Will Walk a Lonely Path."

1. February 1381—Fateful Decision

On an afternoon not many weeks into the new year as Wycliffe sat at his desk, pen in hand, his servant entered, wide-eyed with excitement. "You have a visitor, Master..."

Before he could say more, into the room strode the duke of Lancaster. With a backward look of concern at his master, the servant made his escape.

Wycliffe, in surprise, rose to greet his visitor. "This is an unexpected pleasure, my lord. I welcome you to my humble abode and offer you such hospitality as is at my disposal."

The duke seated himself with a weary slump in the chair Wycliffe offered. "Wycliffe, I have ridden hard today and am travel-worn. I did not pause to rest or refresh myself upon arriving at Oxford, so great did I feel the urgency of seeing you. I would have come sooner, but when Parliament was over various matters detained me in the north, then at Westminster."

Wycliffe bade his servant bring refreshment for his guest. He then turned full attention to what the duke would say.

"I scarcely know how to begin, Wycliffe. I am deeply concerned over this latest turn of your teaching. Your appeal from Barton's mandate reached the king, and I asked that he turn the matter over to me. So, while I am here in an official capacity, I prefer to come as a friend.

"For that reason I am unwilling to command you to withdraw your objectionable views. Rather I would plead with you, urge you to silence. I have stood to your defense when your views were declared erroneous, but Wycliffe—I cannot take your part when you proclaim heresy."

Wycliffe looked into the troubled face of the duke for a long moment. Then with a deep sigh he replied, "What

I teach is no heresy, but truth. I hold the church's position to be heretical. I believe that of all the heresies which infect the church, no other deceives the people in such serious ways. It renders them idolators, it denies the doctrine of Scripture, and, through this infidelity, it moves Christ himself to wrath."

"It alarms me to hear you speak thus," cried Lancaster.

"The truth sometimes alarms. You might feel differently if I could give you a full explanation. The church is aware that this so-called miracle of the mass is closely connected with the hold of the clergy over the lay world. If this stone is pulled from the unwieldy structure, composed as it is of accumulated tradition and superstition, the whole will soon collapse."

They talked at length, Wycliffe trying to make clear his position. "Even should you convince me," said the duke, "which I consider unlikely, in the eyes of the church your teaching is heresy. I would save you from the fate of heretics. You have much to give. Why throw it away? You could still turn back."

Reluctantly, Wycliffe agreed to consider the matter and give his answer the next day. The duke urged him to weigh carefully the consequences of his decision. They parted for the night.

Wycliffe gave no thought to sleep. He considered sending for Aston or Hereford or Purvey, but discarded the thought. *The decision must be mine. I dare not lean on any person—except the Person of my Lord Christ. I will lay the facts out before me, weigh them, as the duke advised, and come to a final conclusion. I owe him that much.*

He put his head in his hands and prayed to God for guidance. He realized that the answer would not come in some great burst of light but through the careful sorting of his own thoughts, using the wisdom God gave.

It comes down to this: I once believed what the church teaches; I do so no longer. Long before I admitted that I disbelieved what the church teaches, I knew that matter could not be annihilated, that accidents could not exist without substance.

I never found it easy to consider particles of matter as sacred. This meant that the orthodox view of the Eucharist led to idolatry. People too often looked upon the host as their God.

He paced the dark room again and again, ignoring the pain in his back and refusing to light a candle.

I have become increasingly aware that priests, including friars, use transubstantiation to gain the veneration and obedience of the people. What a horror to consider the idea that every priest who celebrates the mass makes the body of Christ!

I know the truth from Scripture, even as I sought to unfold it on that last day in the hall of the Austins. I have no doubt as to the truth of my position. The question is, what will I do with it—voice it or take refuge in silence and a lie?

Then a strange stillness came upon him, like the calm one finds in the eye of the storm. The tempest was not over; the full blast might yet come.

John of Gaunt is my friend. He stood by to protect me from the wrath of the bishops at St. Paul's and at Lambeth. I owe him my loyalty. He has fallen from his high position. Is his loss of power reason for alienating him by refusing to do as he advises?

By denying a principle, I would be free from further annoyance by the church. I could remain at Oxford without threat of being cast out. But I would be in virtual slavery to the duke. I would have let my friends down, lowered my own position.

He walked to his desk and lit a candle. He stamped his foot, struck the desk a resounding blow with his fist, and cried,"No! No! I cannot do it! I cannot deny the truth or remain silent. This is the path I must take, regardless of consequences."

At the duke's return in the morning, a haggard Wycliffe met him with his firm reply, knowing that he was sacrificing an alliance which had served him well, that he was alienating powerful support, that he was possibly losing a valued friend.

John of Gaunt, with unutterable sadness, said, "I see that further argument is useless. You are determined to stand by your heresy, which will mean, I believe, your ruin. It was my hope to save you from that."

They stood and looked at each other in silence. Wycliffe saw tears in Gaunt's eyes, even as there were in his own. In a quick move, the duke stepped toward Wycliffe, threw his arms about him in a firm embrace, turned, and departed.

Wycliffe sank into his chair. Having entered the path from which he would not turn, he would consider consequences. He had sacrificed his alliance with Lancaster. He could no longer expect protection from the government. He would be at the mercy of the bishops. How long would he even be allowed to remain at Oxford? Already his position was shrinking. Would he forfeit the loyalty of the men who had been his friends? The hopes, the dreams of years—would they all vanish? He sat thus for a long time.

Then he lifted his head. He had refused to obey the duke. He had entered irrevocably upon a path in which until now, he had drifted. He was now purposefully committed to a course for the rest of his life.

"Truth!" he murmured. "My search for it leads into unexpected paths. The truth of which I have now become convinced will prove unacceptable in my day. I will walk a lonely path, but I will build for the future. Such is my destiny. A fighter I have always been; so shall I be to the end! Truth is worth fighting for. Peace is sweet, but not at any price."

His course set, he rose, squared his shoulders, opened his door, and walked out with a triumphant air into the sunshine.

2. March 1381—Ominous Rumblings

The news of John of Gaunt's visit spread rapidly. Its purpose was easily surmised. It produced an immediate effect upon various clerics who had for some time had only the bitterest words with which to describe the character of the duke.

"You will be interested," said Aston to Wycliffe, "in the new description of the duke of Lancaster since his visit to you. He is now 'the noble and eminent duke, valiant soldier, and wise counselor, faithful son of holy church.' Strange how assessment of one's character can change overnight."

"It would amuse him to know this," replied Wycliffe, "and I am sure someone will see to it that it reaches his ears."

"I'm just back from Cambridge," said Brut, "where I saw a change in estimate of your character in the opposite direction."

"Not unusual of late," said Wycliffe. "What did you find?"

"I visited with a young Austin friar. As we conversed about his studies, I examined one of his notebooks. In it he had copied one of your more violent anti-papal broadsides. He had written in the margin, 'by the venerable doctor, Master John Wycliffe.' Subsequent to that entry, he had crossed out the words 'venerable doctor' and substituted 'execrable seducer.' He made no comment, knowing of my close relationship to you."

"Some of the young are quick to change their opinions," said Wycliffe. "The change may come in either direction."

"Fear may have caused him to alter the wording," said Aston. "Barton's mandate makes it dangerous to hold certain opinions of yours. Some may believe this applies to *any* opinion of yours. Changing his notebook need not mean changing his mind."

"Yet it's obvious that my influence is waning."

"Not noticeably among the younger masters of arts," said Aston. "They stand by you in large numbers, though they are careful what they say. It is the same with the undergraduates. Battles rage among the older members of the university, but I would wager fully one-half the younger members share your views."

"One thing is certain," said Brut. "The university is not ready to have its fairest flower cut down. Squabbles may take place here, but let the bishops interfere, and many will side with you. Outside interference is always resented."

"As to squabbles," said Aston, "not all are on the subject of the Eucharist. Oxford is seething with unrest. Fighting goes on in the streets, and houses are burned. The authorities are unable to maintain control."

"From what I hear," said Wycliffe, "the unrest is by no means restricted to Oxford. Brut spoke of the signs Rede saw through the country last winter. A John Ball, who calls himself a priest, is stirring up the lower classes. He waits outside a church and, as the people come out, preaches to them on the injustice of some being wealthy and some so poor. He has been arrested but when released, he moves on to new territory and continues as before. Such a man can do great damage."

"Yes," said Aston, "he started that jingle that we hear in every village we enter. The children chant it in their games.

'When Adam delved and Eve span, who was then the gentleman?'"

"Sounds innocent enough," said Brut, "but you can see what he's driving at: All men should be equal!"

"Sad to say," said Aston, "he could be wrongly identified as one of the Poor Priests, thus giving us a bad name."

"As I have pointed out before," said Wycliffe, "the poll tax will make great trouble. The poor can stand for just so much."

The bitterness in his soul found expression in the harshness with which he now spoke. "They see the lords ride by with great trains of followers, clad in the finest fabrics, with even the saddles of the horses trimmed with gold and silver and sparkling gems. The clergy are close behind in ostentation. These are able to pay their assessed share of the tax without missing it, while the poor go hungry and ill-clad if forced to pay."

3. April-May 1381—Effects of *Confessio*

Wycliffe considered returning to the lecture hall, but decided against it. He could not in good conscience lecture without expressing himself freely on the forbidden subject. He had publicly declared that neither the chancellor nor anyone else could alter his opinions. His young students knew where he stood, but it went hard with him not to appear before them in person.

"I'll *write* what I mean to say to them," he decided. "I'll call it a *Confession*. This is a subject for academic dispute, and I shall keep within those limits. I'll defend my conclusions so that no one may have any doubt as to my views."

He would be clear on the points Barton's committee had condemned. "I acknowledge that the sacrament of the altar is very God's body in form of bread, but it is in another manner God's body than is in heaven. When a man looks at an image, he does not trouble his mind as

271

to whether the image is made of oak or ash, but he thinks of the one whom the image represents. Even so a man should not fix his thoughts upon the bread, but upon Christ. In fixing his thoughts upon Christ with all cleanness, devotion, and charity, he may worship Christ and receive God spiritually."

He struggled to make it clear that he believed in the Real Presence, but not in a corporal sense such as was commonly held. This work included the essentials from *de Eucharistia*, but in more easily understandable terms.

Translation of the Scriptures continued in the next room, but he left the task in the hands of Hereford and his helpers.

He had long intended to combine his theological works into one great *summa*. He was ready now for the production of a three-fold work on heresy. *On Apostasy* was already written. The companion-pieces would be *On Simony* and *On Blasphemy*.

"Simony! That subject will occupy me for some time. It is one of the worst of the heresies. I'll wield the pen myself until Purvey has time to take over as I dictate."

The common practice of simony infuriated him. No appointment, no benefice, no smallest position could be obtained without payment. Cardinal, bishop, even pope, he doubted not, was guilty of this practice. Who could blame a parish priest for demanding payment for a baptism or a burial? Even this he considered simony, for it was payment for spiritual blessings. The most abused and most damnable form throughout the land was that of payment for absolution.

As he put his ideas into words, he waxed warmer. No vilifying terms seemed too strong to apply to those guilty of this practice, and especially those who used it as a means of obtaining more and more benefices.

In May his *Confessio* appeared in the bookstalls. It produced an immediate outcry. Several friars and monks took up the pen or raised their voices against Wycliffe. One declared the *Confessio* "a confession of Judas Iscariot."

Wycliffe fumed over the opposition, but could have expected no less. He had the satisfaction, even in the midst of the reverberations from the lecture rooms of his enemies, of knowing that friends and followers were reading and understanding what he had written. They might be unable to speak out, but they were finding the truth and holding it in their hearts.

His close associates insisted that his position was not as weak as would appear from the attacks made. Barton as chancellor did not speak for the seculars. A ray of hope burst through in May when the university chose as chancellor for the next two years Robert Rygge. While not an outspoken supporter of Wycliffe, he would be more favorable than his predecessor.

4. June 1381—Peasants' Revolt

Brut clattered into Oxford in frantic haste, his horse in a lather from the wild ride. Pausing only to see that his horse was cared for, Brut made for Wycliffe's rooms.

"Disturbing news," he cried hoarsely as he struggled to get his breath.

"What is it, Brut?" asked Wycliffe in alarm.

Brut sat back in his chair and closed his eyes until his rapid breathing slowed. "You were right in predicting trouble over the poll tax. In Essex a spark fell and a flame kindled that will not be easily extinguished."

Wycliffe waited patiently for Brut to recover himself and to give him the details.

"Thomas Bampton arrived in Essex," he continued at last, "and, with a high-handed approach, called the

273

villagers before him, demanding that they pay the poll tax. The villagers refused. When he ordered his soldiers to make arrests, the enraged people chased them away. In alarm Bampton galloped off to Westminster.

"When jurors were sent to Essex to restore order, the angry crowd beheaded them and carried the heads on pikes before them, as they joined forces with men from other villages."

"This is incredible!" cried Wycliffe. "Worse than I dreamed it would be."

"There's more," said Brut. "John Leg, head tax-commissioner, met insurrection in Kent. At Maidstone a mob broke open houses and seized property. Rioters burst into Canterbury cathedral and broke up a mass in progress. They forced the mayor and bailiffs to take an oath of fealty to 'King Richard and the Commons.'

"Leaving a guard, the maddened throng of peasants and laborers, many of them serfs, rushed off for London, toward which peasants from other areas were converging. The ground has been well prepared, the seed carefully sown throughout the realm."

Wycliffe shook his head in dismay. "They have a single aim: to gain freedom from bonds of servitude. What about that John Ball? Is he in the midst of all this?"

"He's the leader. The rioters released him from the archbishop's prison at Maidstone, where he had been confined for his railings against the ecclesiastical establishment. He galloped off at once toward London. It seems word has gone out for people to gather at Blackheath Moor, five miles from London."

Brut's figure of an inextinguishable flame was apt. Confused rumors continued to come in, but it was some time before the whole horrible story reached the ears of those at Oxford.

John Ball, upon reaching Blackheath Moor, had taken control. He had preached a stirring sermon, taking as his text the familiar and by now famous couplet about Adam and Eve. All men are created equal. The condition of serfdom is the work of sinful men and ought to be abolished. The sermon had its desired effect in consolidating the people firmly behind him.

His plan was to lead his forces into London and deliver a swift blow while the upper classes were still in a state of panic. The multitude surrounding him had grown to 30,000 or more by this time and was increasing hourly.

Inside the city the king's council and others met to consider the situation. They saw themselves shut up like rats in a trap, cut off from all communication with the outside.

From the south side of the river London Bridge was the only means of entry into the city. The fate of the city depended upon holding the bridge. Surging toward the river into Southwark, the mob threatened to burn everything south of the river unless they were permitted to cross. They broke down the gates of Marshalsea and King's Bench prisons and freed the inmates. Through treachery on the part of one of the aldermen the drawbridge was lowered, permitting a riotous sea of humanity to roar across.

About the hour the bridge was lowered, someone at the north opened Aldgate, and the Essex men entered the city. Men of London joined the rebels from Kent and Essex. With the resounding cry, "To the Savoy!" the mob pushed out the west gate and along the river. Into Lancaster's palace they burst and began to throw rich furniture and priceless art treasures out the windows and doors.

While flames engulfed the ruined palace, voices

cried, "On to Highbury!" This next goal lay a few miles to the north, the magnificent manor house of Robert Hales, treasurer of the realm. Next to Lancaster and Sudbury, Hales ranked as the greatest enemy, for to him they attributed the bad government of the past few years. His mansion suffered the same treatment as the Savoy.

Fleet and Westminster prisons were broken open and the inmates freed, adding a worse element to the frenzied mob. Next were the Inns of Court and the Temple, heart of the system of law which strangled the rights of men. The buildings were leveled, records and documents hauled out and fed into a great bonfire. The royal account books from Milk Street enhanced the blaze.

A shout went up, "Let all lawyers be beheaded!" The reign of terror now began in earnest, as victims were dragged from their hiding places into Cheapside, where a block was set up and heads began to roll.

The only haven of safety was the Tower, now the king's headquarters for two days. With him were the Queen Mother, Treasurer Hales, Chancellor Sudbury, his uncle Buckingham, John of Gaunt's son Henry, and a number of others. John of Gaunt was absent and would have reason to be thankful. He was in the north arranging a truce with the Scots.

That night thousands of rebels camped outside the Tower, loudly demanding the heads of the ministers who were sheltered within. From a turret window the king, with dazed mind and sinking heart, watched the flames rising from the Savoy and mansions in the city. All night the horrid cries of the bloodthirsty mob just beneath the castle wall penetrated to the ears of those within.

The earl of Salisbury offered what seemed wise advice. "Sire," he said to the king, "if you can appease them by fair words and grant what they wish, it will be much better. Should we attempt to subdue them, we would almost surely fail. It will be all over with us and our heirs, and England will be a desert."

King Richard himself made the final decision. "Send word to the rebels that their king desires to meet with them tomorrow at Mile End. That will draw the mob away, giving the archbishop and Hales an opportunity to escape."

The rebels accepted the plan. A jostling throng moved off toward the meeting place, but a good number remained behind to guard the exits of the Tower and to continue the work of destruction in the city.

The king, surrounded by his nobles, rode out of the Tower gate to the meeting place. A spokesman for the rebels stepped forward and read from a prepared list. "These demands must be met. Serfage must be completely abolished throughout the land. As free men, we'll no longer perform the servile duties forced upon us. We'll pay rent for our land at four pence an acre. A general pardon must be granted to all who've taken part with us."

The king agreed to these demands. Thirty clerks set to work preparing the charters of liberation and pardon. Not only each shire but every village and manor would receive one. With their king, the peasants returned to the city, shouting the glad news.

During the conference at Mile End a gruesome series of events had taken place at the Tower. About five hundred rebels had forced their way in, and in an orgy of violence surged down the halls and into every room. They ripped up the king's bed, to make sure no one was hiding there. Leg, the head collector of the poll tax, was brutally murdered.

With a premonition of what was to come, the archbishop had during the night entered the chapel, taking

Hales with him. At dawn he said, "I have spent the night in prayer. We have little time. Let me confess you; then we will take the Sacrament."

A short time later the mob burst into the chapel and with a shout seized both men. With victorious cries they rushed them across to Tower Hill, where the waiting axeman did his work.

A cry rang out, "Mount the heads of the arch-enemies on stakes! Set them up on London Bridge for the crowds still entering to see."

Sudbury had met his death more because he was chancellor than because he was archbishop. To him was attributed the blame for misgovernment and for the hated poll tax.

By the time the king arrived, his mother had been taken up the river to the Garde Robe near St. Paul's. Here the king, too, took up residence, but there was no rest. The manumissions and pardons must be prepared. Upon receipt of the precious documents, many of the rebels hurried away on Friday evening.

John Ball had vanished, but at dawn on Saturday Wat Tyler assumed the place of leadership of the thousands who remained. At his instigation complaints began to arise as to social grievances. Voices demanded disendowment of the church for the benefit of the peasants. Tenants on estates should have freedom to hunt and fish in woods and streams. Laws which declared so many to be outlaws must be abolished.

Again the king agreed to meet with the rebels, this time at Smithfield, a market square located outside the city. Wat Tyler and his men lined up on one side of the market. The king and his men rode into the opposite side.

Tyler advanced toward the king, and some words passed between them. Mayor Walworth, misunderstanding

Tyler's motives, drew a knife and rashly struck the man, mortally wounding him.

At this the young king, in an act of tremendous bravery, rode out alone toward the crowd, crying, "I am your leader!" This captured the heart of the mob, who had lost their leader and had no plan of their own.

In a hastily made plan, the king led the rebels out into the country north of Smithfield, while his men returned to the city to raise forces. In London many citizens were armed and ready to join Sir Robert Knolles and his private regiment of soldiers. They marched out and without difficulty surrounded the rebels.

Knowing that uprisings in other parts of the country remained to be dealt with, the authorities took no strenuous measures against the rebels, but dismissed them to return home.

5. June-August 1381—Deep Distress

News continued to filter in to Oxford. Wycliffe found himself physically ill with deep heartsickness.

"This horror," he cried, "is far more widespread and with more terrible consequences than I could have imagined. The poll tax was not the sole cause, but only the last unbearable stroke. I recognized the symptoms of underlying causes long ago."

"The king and a well-equipped army go from place to place," said Purvey, "showing no mercy in putting down any remaining spark of rebellion. The job will not be easily completed."

"This latest report is appalling," said Wycliffe. "A deputation of peasants sought an interview with the king to plead the charters of liberation which he himself had granted. Throwing off all pretense, the king replied, 'Serfs you are, and serfs you will remain!' When they returned to their main body to report the treachery, soldiers followed and, by a great slaughter, broke up the camp."

"Nor is the end yet," cried Purvey. "At the assize at St. Albans a horrible revenge was taken in the slaughter of the serfs of the abbey who had tried to break the bond of servitude."

"I am convinced," said Wycliffe, "that the state has made a serious mistake in the unwonted bloodshed and cruelty, especially since the rulers showed bad faith in ruthlessly breaking their promises to the people, for the peasants had left London not only with charters of manumission but of pardon."

Three years earlier he had published his views on serfdom in a tract, *de Servitute Civili*, in which he urged the speeding up of a system being worked in some areas, but too slowly. It could help to alleviate the growing distress between serf and lord.

"Rule and service are needful in our fallen state," he had written. *"Some men lacking in intellect but with sturdy bodies suitable for manual labor are fitted for servitude and nothing better.*

"Serfdom, however, should be limited to a man's own lifetime, never hereditary. Considering the natural gifts that God often bestows upon the sons of serfs, it is unreasonable for the condition to extend from one generation to the next.

"Free tenants bring in a greater return than serfs. The remedy would be for serfdom to be gradually discontinued in such a way as to prevent revolution. In the meantime serfs should remain patient even under suffering."

He had never meant to relieve cruel lords of their burden of sin. Always he had urged a relationship of love between serfs and masters. Lords should deal fairly and generously.

"Had they heeded my advice much of this might have been avoided," he said. With difficulty he sought to translate his thoughts and feelings into writing. In view of the horrible events transpiring across the land, it seemed impossible.

Then the shocking realization came to Wycliffe that he was being accused of instigating the rebellion. He was said to have preached doctrines which encouraged the lower classes to rise against their masters and to have sent his Poor Priests to sow seeds of such teaching in their preaching across the countryside.

None of these charges could be proved, but rumors tend to be believed and repeated. One preposterous claim was that John Ball was a disciple of Wycliffe, but Ball had been roaming the land sowing seeds of sedition more than twenty years before Wycliffe began to be heard. A number of priests did take part in the rebellion, but none could be proved to be followers of Wycliffe. Enemies would have hastened to bring such information to light.

"No matter what their fiendish claims," he said, "I have no intention of changing my opinions. I wrote in *A Short Rule of Life* that lords should rule their tenants well, maintaining their rights, being merciful in their rents, not allowing their officers to wrong them by extortions. I added that laborers should serve with meekness. In spite of the evils we have so recently witnessed, I continue to offer that advice."

Pulpits in Oxford were still open to Wycliffe. "I am barred from the lecture hall," he said, "but I can preach."

From the pulpit he made points which could be easily grasped and remembered: Servants must be loyal. The idea recently spread abroad and acted upon, that no one should serve, he declared to be from the Fiend. Lords should protect poor men. Prelates should not waste goods of the poor in gluttony. Priests must not demand much money for the performance of spiritual duties.

In spite of the enthusiasm with which his sermons were received Wycliffe knew he was losing ground. The false rumors had not failed to damage his reputation. Some who had before been his friends began to show a marked coolness toward him.

Anger seized him when he thought of his enemies and the destructive means they employed against him. He poured out streams of invective upon their heads in the tracts he produced in great number.

Then tenderness would replace anger as he thought of the lives he had touched, of what he had accomplished that could not be destroyed. He again resolved that he would not be defeated but would build for the future. Those of a later generation would take full cognizance of the truth he proclaimed.

6. August 1381—Difficult Decision

He stayed more to himself, not avoiding his friends, but not seeking their company. The burden of his lost influence weighed heavily upon him. He visited more often the chapel at Merton College. Here he could feel God's presence most closely; here he could unburden his troubled soul. He could cry, "Why? Why? What more could I have done?" He received no answer, but felt God did not hold the lament against him.

One August morning as he came from the chapel into the bright sunshine of the quadrangle, he lifted his eyes to Rede's library across the way. He walked across, entered the door, and wandered through the silent building. In the long vacation few students were about. With an effort which seemed to require all his strength he climbed the stairs to the upper floor.

A lone student pored over a heavy tome in one of the alcoves. As Wycliffe passed, a look of recognition passed over the young man's face. He half-rose, but Wycliffe passed on.

Reaching the far end, he gazed at a familiar old book chest, then at the spacious room he had traversed. "Rede moved from this humble chest to the production of a beautiful and solid edifice which will house countless volumes and be a blessing to untold numbers who study here and go out to bless others."

He stepped into the last alcove and sat down. With his elbows on the shelf before him, he put his head in his hands and sighed. "Rede's work will stand for centuries," he said with almost a sob. "Why must mine be torn apart and destroyed?"

Leaving Merton, he took a lonely walk through the streets of Oxford, pausing here and there to gaze upon some favorite spot. He entered the churches in which he had preached, the halls in which he had lectured, remembering. Passing out the North Gate, he crossed the ditch and stood before Balliol. Then he sought the banks of the Cherwell for a last walk along the wooded path.

His thoughts flew back to the last day he had spent on the banks of the Tees before coming to Oxford. *I felt I could not leave the scenes which were so much a part of me,* he recalled. *I felt certain that nothing could be so dear to me. I've spent twice as many years at Oxford as that lad had spent in Yorkshire. A throbbing love for this place has grown wilder and stronger. I'll find it even more difficult to leave forever these scenes.*

7. August 1381—Bitter Moment

On a late August afternoon he assembled the friends who were closest to him. A solemn group crowded into his room at Queen's. He looked from one face to another—Brut, Purvey, Hereford, Aston, Bedeman, Repyngton, Alington, and a few others.

Wycliffe, usually so ready with words, struggled to speak. What he was about to do broke his heart, and the emotion stirring him was difficult to control. Finally in a voice which was not quite steady he said, "The time has come for me to leave Oxford. Thirty-five years ago I entered the gates of this fair city, an untried youth looking to the future with high hopes."

Attempting a smile, he turned toward the younger men. "Some of you were not yet born, and it is well that you have come at a later date. You will labor on after others of us end our days.

"I came seeking with all eagerness for truth. I thought I would find it in Aristotle, and his works did satisfy me for a time. Yet I felt a lack. I seemed to hunger and thirst for something more. After drinking from other fountains and turning away unsatisfied from each, I found the source which wiped away the need for all others. I found Truth. I found it in a Book, and the book led me to a Person, who is himself Truth. The Truth of the Holy Scriptures is ultimate truth. It is this upon which I have based my life and which I have fearlessly proclaimed."

He sat for a few moments with bowed head. "I have sent you out to preach that truth, the truth of the gospel which brings the message of salvation to sinners wandering in darkness. I hope to send others as I find those with hearts for Jesus Christ and the courage to proclaim the message. As you know, I consider preaching the most important work of the Christian ministry."

He fell silent. In a soft voice Hereford asked, "What of the translation work?"

"Translation of the Scriptures into our native tongue must proceed, that truth be made available to all. You, Hereford, and those who help, will continue with the Old Testament as you are able. Purvey and others will do the New Testament, parts of which I have completed in connection with various labors. Some of you will follow me to Lutterworth, others will remain here, but lines of communication must be kept open. When finished, copies must be made and distributed."

"Who will accompany you?" asked Brut.

"Couldn't we all go?" asked Aston.

Wycliffe gave him a tender smile. "You must not all go. Oxford must not be deserted by those still able to take a stand for truth. Others who are still wavering may yet be persuaded by your sermons and your lives. Stay as long as you are able. You may be forced to remain silent or leave for other fields, even as I have. It is my earnest hope that you will not choose silence.

"Purvey will accompany me to Lutterworth, for he is necessary to me. An overwhelming amount of work remains. Writing on new subjects, revising what is already written, preparing and sending out more Poor Priests, and caring for my parishioners—all these duties present me with a challenge hitherto unknown and will strain me to the uttermost. One or two others may be more useful at Lutterworth than here, especially in training new members of the Poor Priests."

After a pause, he said, "Tomorrow I shall pass from this beautiful garden which is the University of Oxford. May it yet send forth across the land a fragrance pleasing to God and profitable to man. Some of you will have a part in that. I depart the field not willingly but of necessity."

8. September-December 1381 Archbishop Courtenay

The move was not without its difficulties. Conveying books and unbound manuscript pages presented problems. Work not yet completed had to be kept in order.

He would need writing materials to last until he could obtain supplies from Leicester.

Wycliffe struggled to keep from dwelling upon what lay behind, applying himself to the multiple labors facing him at Lutterworth. His parishioners welcomed him warmly. He and Purvey joined John Horne, who remained as curate. It pleased him that the rectory would provide ample space for translation and copying work, as well as adequate lodging for those who arrived to help with this and for the Poor Priests as they came and went.

"How good, Purvey," he said, "to have you to set things in order. I can trust you to put everything where it was before. When I want something, it will be where I expect to find it."

They settled into a regular schedule. Purvey expressed amazement at the hours Wycliffe spent at his desk and the unbelievable quantities of material he produced. Nor did he neglect his pastoral activity, preaching on Sunday and giving a number of hours each week to visiting and encouraging his flock.

He tried to keep abreast of what was happening in other parts of the country. "The rebellion has not been quelled, Purvey," he said. "Like a forest fire, when brought under control in one area, it breaks out in another. I fear the undue severity of the authorities will continue to provoke other risings."

"You're right," said Purvey. "Only today news has come of the peasantry around Salisbury seizing the marketplace. And the men of Kent have risen again."

"That last is understandable," said Wycliffe, "in view of the king's turning savagely against them after the promises he had made. Since they consider John of Gaunt the natural rival of the king and chief candidate for the throne, they are crying that they will make him king. They'll suffer for that."

Another not-unexpected event took place when a papal bull translated Courtenay from the see of London to the archbishopric of Canterbury. In October, with the temporalities transferred, Wycliffe said, "We may now expect action against us. He has been biding his time, and it has arrived. How and where he will first seek to deliver his blows remains to be seen."

Courtenay, however, refused to act officially until he received the pall from Rome. "He has more patience than I would have given him credit for," commented Wycliffe.

"I hear the search for a bride for our young king has come to a conclusion," said Purvey. "A marriage has been arranged with Anne of Bohemia, sister of the reigning monarch, Wenceslaus."

"That should prove satisfactory," replied Wycliffe. "Bohemia has remained faithful to the Roman pontiff, so he will approve this match. There will be excitement across the land. A royal wedding will demand elaborate preparations!"

Parliament met at Westminster in November with a primary aim of ending the rebellions. An act was passed granting pardon to rebels, with certain exceptions. Grace did not extend to any who took part in the murders of the late chancellor, treasurer, and chief justice. Inhabitants of Canterbury and certain other towns were excepted from pardon, along with two hundred eighty-seven others. Most of these were outlaws in hiding.

The chief impulse which had incited the rebellion had been the determination to obtain personal freedom. Parliament firmly crushed this demand, confirming the king's repeal of the liberating charters. A unanimous vote contradicted rumors that Parliament was seriously considering emancipation of all serfs.

"For the record," said Wycliffe, "the Rising has failed. May it be a permanent failure so far as violence is concerned. I abhor the murders of Sudbury and the others, but to some extent they brought it upon themselves. As to the demands of the peasantry, their fulfilment may be delayed, but they must be met. The lords may have learned a lesson and will move more rapidly toward just dealing with those under them."

9. January-March 1382—News from Oxford

On January 14 Anne of Bohemia was married to Richard II in the chapel at Westminster Palace amid great stir and celebration. Anne's Bohemian attendants attracted much attention. Richard retained many of the Czech courtiers to stay permanently with him. Court life took on an exciting new turn with the addition of a foreign element.

Wycliffe gave little thought to the affairs at Westminster. His ears remained tuned to Oxford, from whence Hereford kept him informed. His followers had made good use of the opportunity offered by the election of Rygge as chancellor. Preaching went on apace. Strife between regulars and seculars escalated, the regulars insistently naming Wycliffe the author of the Rising.

The seculars retaliated by asserting that the four orders of mendicants had been the cause. To this accusation the friars were not slow to act. In February the four orders appealed to John of Gaunt. Stephen Patrington, a Carmelite whose eloquence had put him in the forefront of Wycliffe's opponents, acted as agent in delivering the letter, naming Nicholas Hereford as chief accuser. They did not, however, seek to lay blame upon Wycliffe and the Poor Priests as instigators of the Rebellion.

Wycliffe ranted over this appeal, especially over the mendicants naming Hereford as author of the accusations against them. He had no kind word for the friars, and was delighted to learn that the duke ignored the appeal.

At his first opportunity Hereford preached at St. Mary's before the university a sermon against the religious orders. He claimed that no monk or friar should graduate from the university, a secular body. To do so would cause him to break the vows of his order.

The seculars applauded the claim, joined by the proctors, who were regents in arts. Members of the religious orders had for years tried to evade following the required arts program of the university, saying they needed only theological training.

Wycliffe received with appreciation news of the steadfastness of friends remaining at Oxford. Knowledge of their continued action helped dispel some of the bitterness he felt. He put as a first priority now the completion of the treatise *de Blasphemia*, which would be the twelfth and final volume of the theological *Summa*, upon which he had labored for several years.

This was an exceedingly bitter attack on the established order of the church. He described the "Twelve Tormentors" of the church. No order of officials escaped him. He claimed that if Christ came back to earth, they would burn him as a heretic.

First he considered the pope the root of blasphemy. "It would be better for the church if there were neither pope nor bishops, but, throwing aside the whole Caesarean tradition, poor priests only to teach in nakedness the law of Christ."

He held the cardinals responsible for the present state of the church. Bishops and archdeacons he faulted for pride, luxury, and abuse of excommunications.

Rural deans, like incarnate fiends, encouraged harlots by accepting payment of fines for sins. He passed on to the four orders of friars, to door keepers who diluted holy water, to minor clergy who were employed in secular roles. In final place came the *questors* who went about selling indulgences. Among them these devil-leeches sucked out of the realm 100,000 pounds every year.

Aston arrived at Lutterworth on his way to Leicester, where he was to preach on Palm Sunday. "Your latest work has reached the bookstalls at the university," he said to Wycliffe, "and you can imagine the intense excitement produced even in the first few days. Copies have already reached London."

"Copies should soon be at Leicester," said Wycliffe. "It will stir new controversy, but should convince many of the truth it contains. You always encourage me, Aston, and give me strength. I would detain you, but it is more important that you preach. You are the most gifted of the Poor Priests and by far the most energetic."

Wycliffe's ideas had early taken root in Leicester under the leadership of William Smith and William Swinderby. Through the preaching of these men many of the people had come to know and accept Wycliffe's doctrines.

Swinderby, a strange character known as William the Hermit, was a most effective preacher. Bishop Buckingham heard of this and ordered him to cease preaching until called before episcopal officials.

"You will find Swinderby in your congregation, Aston," said Wycliffe. Look into his affair. His preaching may be a bit more incendiary than necessary. Give him what counsel you can. It is impossible to predict the outcome of this action Buckingham is taking."

10. April-May 1382—Bold Preaching

Aston preached to a large and receptive crowd on Palm Sunday at Leicester. A canon from Leicester Abbey, however, came with notebook in hand, and claimed to have recorded eleven points made by Aston in defense of Wycliffe's doctrine. He complained that Aston went about on foot, making friends with the peasants at their meals, and pouring out his "poison."

As Wycliffe had predicted, Aston found Swinderby inclined to take lightly the bishop's order not to preach. Aston warned him against excessive zeal. However, in that same week he followed Aston's sermon with two incendiary messages of his own.

About the same time, Repyngton stirred up excitement by preaching a sermon at Brackley in Northamptonshire strongly defending Wycliffe's doctrine of the Eucharist. It was a particularly daring move to preach on this subject in such a place, for the church at Brackley was connected with Leicester Abbey where Repyngton had been an Austin canon. News of this sermon would soon reach the ears of Wycliffe's opponents there.

Preaching at Oxford Repyngton had to be more careful. He was completing work on his doctorate in theology. When in early May it came time for him to deliver one of the set addresses required toward inception, he exercised restraint.

"I am willing," he said, "to defend Wycliffe's doctrine in relation to ethics, but will hold my peace as to the Eucharist until God is willing to illuminate the hearts of the clergy."

It was difficult for his opponents to find fault with this. They might have their doubts as to the "peace" the speaker held, and as to which clergy's hearts he expected to be illuminated and of what that illumination would consist.

When Parliament convened in May, Wycliffe determined to appeal directly, since the king had given no official response to his appeal. Parliament might be more anticlerical than the crown. He prepared a *Petition* in Latin and a *Complaint* in English.

In the *Petition* he made four points. First, England should obey prelates only when such obedience agreed with Christ's Law. Second, no money should be sent to Rome unless it could be proved right from Scripture. Third, no man should hold any English benefice without residence. Finally, no one should be imprisoned because of excommunication. He felt strongly on this last point, knowing that he or his disciples might well face excommunication, since his doctrine of the Eucharist had been censured.

He addressed the English *Complaint* to King Richard, to the duke of Lancaster, and to seculars and men of holy Church. He appealed to them to hear, assent to, and maintain the Articles he presented. "Members of religous orders must be free to leave them. King and council have the right to take away temporal goods of the church. When curates fail in their office, payment of tithes should cease. Christ's pure doctrine of the Eucharist ought to be openly taught in the churches."

"Surely I may expect some response," he said to Purvey, as he examined the finished pieces one last time.

Purvey was doubtful. "Considering the importance of the content and the source from which the plea comes, it *should* come before the Lords as well as the Commons. But some would block consideration and cause it to be thrown out without a hearing."

"Yet," said Wycliffe, "some would insist that the petition receive a hearing and fair consideration. I must seek the best channels through which to approach the matter."

On May 6 Courtenay received the pall from Rome and could now act officially as archbishop. Parliament convened the next day at Westminster. Wycliffe arrived early, hoping to find a means of having his complaint laid before Parliament. He found little encouragement and left with scant hope of its being presented.

One bit of news alleviated his disappointment somewhat. The vicar at Odiham, a former Oxford man, had invited Hereford, Aston, Bedeman, and Alington to his parish for a preaching tour. Odiham was in the northeast of Hampshire and provided an easy center from which to reach into Berkshire as well. They would preach the matters Wycliffe pushed at Westminster.

Wykeham, bishop of Winchester, heard of this preaching in his diocese and immediately sent a mandate to the vicar of Odiham, prohibiting further preaching in the area by these men.

He was not the only bishop taking action against unlicensed preachers. Bishop Buckingham heard that Swinderby had defied his earlier order. Three friars from Leicester approached him at Westminster and laid before him sixteen points against Swinderby, points echoing some of Wycliffe's most objectionable statements. Buckingham ordered immediate action in the case.

Before Wykeham's message to Odiham reached its destination, Hereford was back at Oxford. Chancellor Rygge had appointed him to preach the Ascension Day sermon, the chief sermon of the year. On May 15, while Parliament was in session, he preached in the churchyard of St. Frideswide's a daring sermon. Chancellor Rygge was present, also a large number of clergy and of laity.

Some in the congregation made special note of the fact that in making the usual prayers for all secular and religious leaders, he pointedly omitted the pope.

"As Christ's work became more effective after his ascension than during his earthly life," he said, "so St. Richard's attack on the friars is of more force now than when first made." This referred to Richard Fitzralph's long-time battle with the friars.

He dwelt upon the current search for temporal rather than eternal wealth. "The monastic orders pursue temporal riches, against the intentions of their founders, involving themselves in secular lawsuits in their greed for wealth. Friars beg from rich and poor. They have become masters of vanity rather than masters of theology! England can never flourish while such men are tolerated. The answer is disendowment. All should work toward that end. If necessary, the laity must enforce it."

Courtenay had earlier appointed Dr. Peter Stokes, a Carmelite friar, to keep close track of Hereford. He followed him about, taking notes on every lecture and sermon. The man's red face stood out in contrast to the collar of his white robe in a ridiculous way. Because of his appearance, and knowing of his close tracking of Hereford, Wycliffe nicknamed him "White Dog."

Stokes had Hereford's Ascension Day sermon recorded in full. He made serious accusations against Hereford, claiming that he stirred up insurrection and excused and defended Wycliffe. Actually Hereford went beyond Wycliffe with what Stokes termed "many intolerable and unspeakable utterances."

Hereford sometimes lacked the high courage of his master, but he was not known for restraint in speaking. Hostility to the friars had long been obvious. Any sermon he preached would have caused trouble, but this sermon stirred up much opposition, even though approved by a large part of the university.

On the day on which he received the *pallium* from Rome, Courtenay summoned a committee to meet on

May 17 in the hall of the Blackfriars to pronounce judgment upon various questionable propositions being
preached. The archbishop could feel safe to act against
Wycliffe and his followers, for Wycliffe's petition to
Parliament received no reply, indicating that he could no
longer expect support from either Parliament or the
crown.

One significant if unpublicized source of support for
Wycliffe must have proved a bitter pill for Courtenay.
John of Gaunt issued a quiet but authoritative word to
the archbishop that, however he might choose to deal
with Wycliffe's teachings, he was not to touch the man
himself.

PART 6

Handing on the Torch
(1382–1385)
"In the end it will all come to pass."

1. May 1382—Blackfriars' Council

On May 17, while Parliament was still in session and just as a report of Hereford's sermon preached two days earlier reached him, Archbishop Courtenay convened his committee at the priory of the Blackfriars. He had exercised great care in the selection of those he identified as "the most famous, skilfulest men of soundest judgment in religion of all the realm."

He had called nine bishops, sixteen doctors of theology, eleven doctors of law, seven bachelors of theology, and two bachelors of law, a formidable and biased group. Wycliffe's friend Rede, bishop of Chichester, undoubtedly the most distinguished scholar on the bench, was not among those called.

The doctors of theology all were friars except one, the exception being Wells, Wycliffe's strong Benedictine opponent, known as the "Hammer of Heretics." They were chosen from the four orders of mendicants from Cambridge and Oxford. Kenningham, with whom Wycliffe had debated years earlier, was among them. Of the bachelors of theology all but one were friars.

Archbishop Courtenay sat enthroned in glory beneath a canopy, with bishops in copes and mitres on either side of him. Friars, in grey, brown, black, and white, according to their orders, sat across from the archbishop. Bachelors of theology sat on one side, with lawyers in their robes opposite them.

Courtenay opened proceedings with due ceremony and moved to the purpose of the assembly. "I hold before you twenty-four Conclusions which are erroneous and repugnant to the determination of the church and which tend to the subversion of the realm. I call this council to pronounce upon them."

He handed them to a scribe, bidding him read them slowly and distinctly so they might be discussed. Every man present was aware that these had been extracted from Wycliffe's works, but his name was not mentioned. After the reading Courtenay adjourned the meeting with a charge that they faithfully consider and be ready to declare their opinions at a later meeting.

Four days later, on May 21, the council reconvened. Again the Conclusions were read aloud, followed by discussion. Ten of the propositions were declared undoubtedly heretical:

1. Material bread and wine remain in the Sacrament after consecration.

2. No "accidents" remain without their "subjects" in the Sacrament.

3. Christ is not in the sacrament truly and really in his corporal person.

4. A bishop or priest in mortal sin does not ordain, consecrate, or baptize.

5. If a man is truly contrite, confession is superfluous and invalid.

6. That Christ ordained the mass has no foundation in the Gospel.

7. God ought to obey the devil.

8. An evil pope has no power over Christians unless the emperor gives it to him.

9. After Urban VI no man is to be pope; all should live in freedom as did the Greeks.

10. It is contrary to Scripture for clerics to own temporal possessions.

As they proceeded to a final consideration of the others, they heard a great roar and the building began to rock and tremble, upsetting tables and sending books and documents flying. The men clutched each other to avoid being thrown to the floor. It was an earthquake such as none of them had ever experienced.

The trembling of the earth stopped, but confusion reigned among the council members. Several voices were heard, declaring that this must be a sign of heaven's displeasure at their proceedings. Some wished to terminate the meeting.

Courtenay, unruffled, cried, "The earthquake predicts a purging of the realm from heresies. As there are bottled up in the bowels of the earth foul air and winds which are expelled in the earthquake, purifying the earth, but with great violence, in the same way there are many heresies shut up in the hearts of the reprobate of which the realm must be cleansed after their condemnation but not without travail and great effort."

Reassured, the council continued its work and unanimously pronounced the remaining fourteen propositions erroneous:

11. There is no excommunication unless God pronounces it first.

12. He who excommunicates otherwise, excommunicates himself.

13. Excommunication of a cleric who has appealed to the king is treason.

14. Failure to teach or hear the Word for fear of men is treason to God.

15. Any deacon or priest may preach without the authority of pope or bishop.

16. A man in deadly sin is neither bishop nor prelate in the Church of God.

17. Lords may correct bad clergy, and the commons may correct bad lords.

18. Tithes may be retained by parishioners on account of their curates' sins.

19. Special prayers by religious for one person are no better than general prayers.

20. Entering a religious order makes one less able to obey God.

21. Holy men who established private religions, monks or mendicants, erred.

22. Members of the religious orders, living in private, are not of the Christian faith.

23. Friars should live by their labors, not by begging.

24. He who gives alms to friars excommunicates himself and them.

The condemnation completed, the archbishop hurried off in search of the king, whom he persuaded to admit into the business passed during the closing session of Parliament a chapter dated on the closing day.

This chapter ordered that, with the bishops' certification, commands be issued in the king's name by the chancellor of the kingdom to sheriffs and other state officers for the arrest of all "itinerant preachers who go from town to town, in certain habits, under pretence of great holiness, preaching daily in churches and churchyards and wherever there is a great congregation of people."

The ordinance had the appearance of a law made by the joint consent of crown and Parliament. Actually it was a royal ordinance, passed, possibly with the consent of the lords who were members of the council, but in the absence of the Commons. Courtenay was on shaky ground, but must have hoped for the best.

As soon as Wycliffe's enemies at Oxford learned of the outcome of the council, they wrote to the archbishop imploring him to publish the condemnation of the Conclusions at once. Chancellor Rygge had appointed Philip Repyngton to preach the sermon of June 5, the Feast of Corpus Christi.

"The choice of this preacher," they wrote, "portends an attack on the doctrine of transubstantiation. Such a man must not be allowed, on this day above all others sacred to the holy Eucharist, to proclaim the heresy of Wycliffe."

2. May-June 1382—"Earthquake Council"

Wycliffe had heard of the archbishop's council while at Westminster struggling to get his petition presented. He had obtained the names of those chosen by Courtenay, knowing that the "erroneous and repugnant" matters to be judged were his writings.

Back at Lutterworth he waited impatiently for a report. "Parliament will almost certainly ignore my petition. I can expect no more support from that direction as things now stand. I have lost the support of the crown. Now Courtenay is about to lead the attack of the church against me. What is left?"

"You have strong support at Oxford," Purvey reminded him.

"For how long?" He picked up the list of the members of the council. "I could have selected the names for him. He has good reason for every choice. It might well be called 'Council of Friars.' In choosing bishops he would not for a moment have considered Rede."

"It's strange he has not called you before this council," said Purvey. "If they are considering certain of your views, why would he not want you there to answer for them?"

"He may yet call me. Parliament still sits, and Courtenay has Convocation. This council will not finish in a hurry."

A day or so later Brut appeared. "I have something which will interest you," he said, handing Wycliffe a folded sheet.

Wycliffe seized the missive, hardly taking time to greet Brut. He read it quickly, then, glancing up, said in a tone of controlled rage, "I suppose you have familiarized yourself with these? You and Purvey and I should go over them together."

What he held was a copy of the Conclusions Courtenay's council was considering. Wycliffe's anger burned as he read the list. "He has chosen isolated sentences completely out of context. The statements *are* my own, but standing alone they can give quite a wrong impression. In the proper setting the meaning is perfectly clear."

As serious as the matter was, Brut could not restrain a chuckle. "When they consider the bare statement, 'God ought to obey the devil,' they will be stricken with horror. Even your explanation is, as I recall, difficult for the unsubtle mind. As it stands, they can only declare it heretical."

"All would agree that God is not the author of sin. In his program for punishment of sin, God has sometimes bowed to Satan's control, allowing him to rule for a time, as when wicked tyrants persecuted God's people. His plan for salvation included Christ's subjecting himself to evil men and suffering under Satan's power in order to defeat him and to redeem lost mankind."

"Your ability to explain the statements," said Purvey, "may answer my question as to why they haven't called you to appear. They don't want an explanation; they don't want to understand."

"It suits their purposes better," cried Wycliffe, "to misunderstand, misinterpret, and condemn the bare statements."

"It comes to my attention," said Brut, "that several of the bishops on the council have reason to please the archbishop, including your own bishop, who has matters under investigation for which he cannot give a reasonable explanation. It is to his advantage to act on the Conclusions as is expected."

Brut was still at Lutterworth when the earthquake came. Soon after came word of the action of the council and of Courtenay's interpretation of the meaning of the earthquake.

The condemnation of the Conclusions came as no surprise to Wycliffe. The number called heretical was smaller than he had anticipated. Nevertheless, he stormed in virulent terms at Courtenay and the demonic powers which possessed him. Courtenay's explanation of the earthquake disgusted him.

"I consider that earth-din to have been the outcry of the world against the heretic prelates," he said. "These friars have put a heresy upon Christ and the saints in heaven. Since man's voice failed to answer for God, the very earth trembled, even as in the time of Christ's passion." He published a tract, dubbing the meeting the "Earthquake Council," a name which stuck.

Wycliffe wasted no time in idle speculation. He was involved in a work called *Trialogus* and was editing his sermons, both Latin and English, and supplying the Poor Priests with material.

3. May-June 1382—Oxford Activity

Courtenay spent the last week of May preparing a mandate to accompany the condemned items. He answered Wycliffe's opponents at Oxford with a letter to Dr. Stokes, commissioning him to read the Blackfriars' condemnation on Corpus Christi Day at St. Frideswides before Repyngton's sermon. He charged him to prevent the teaching or defense of the condemned articles within the university, in or out of the schools, publicly or privately.

Relying upon the king's ordinance and the decisons of Blackfriars, Courtenay moved to strike across the realm. He sent copies of the mandate and condemnation to Braybroke, bishop of London, with orders to dispatch them to the other bishops.

In an explanatory letter Courtenay described the propositions to Braybroke as those "*which are said to be conclusions of Wycliffe.*" Only here was Wycliffe mentioned. No official document or other correspondence named him.

Each bishop in his own cathedral and churches was to warn that no one should hold, teach, preach, or defend these heresies and errors, nor admit to preach any one that was prohibited or of whom there was any doubt. In case of any disobedience, the bishops were to act "as inquisitors of heretical pravity."

On May 30, on the archbishop's orders, the bishop of London led a procession of barefoot clergy and laity through the streets of the city. Its alleged purpose was to intercede against the plague, which was again raging. The hidden purpose came to light when the procession reached Paul's Cross. Here Wycliffe's opponent, Kenningham, preached a powerful sermon, and read the archbishop's letter to the people.

After sending his communication to Stokes, Courtenay wrote a letter to Chancellor Rygge. He did not mention Repyngton, but referred to Hereford's sermon on Ascension Day. Marveling at Rygge's choice of a preacher for the most important sermon of the year, he warned that Rygge could by showing such favor appear to put himself in the sect represented by Hereford. He informed him of the promised support of the king and chiefs of the realm.

He charged Rygge to give all assistance to Stokes in the publication of the archbishop's letters. At the next lecture in the theological schools he was to see to it that these were read in their entirety by the bedel of that faculty.

This letter set Oxford in an uproar. It was considered an attack on the liberties of the university. Rygge at once asserted, "Neither bishop nor archbishop has power over the university even in matters of heresy." Uncertain whether this claim was valid so far as the archbishop was concerned, he felt that a vigorous declaration of it might be persuasive.

On Wednesday, June 4, the eve of Corpus Christi, Stokes presented the chancellor with letters which the archbishop had instructed him to deliver, with a copy of the commission he had issued to Stokes himself. Rygge said that he would hold the documents until he could determine that they were official.

Bishops and friars, an unlikely combination, united in their opposition to Wycliffe. This brought a similarly strange alliance between "town" and "gown" in favor of Wycliffe. Oxford was in commotion on the morning of June 5. A hundred armed men escorted the chancellor with his proctors and the mayor of the city to St. Frideswide's to hear Repyngton's sermon.

His main subject was the Eucharist, as was expected on that day. Repyngton mentioned transubstantiation only briefly, saying that Wycliffe, his master, was a catholic doctor who never laid down nor taught any doctrine concerning the Sacrament of the altar which the whole church did not hold. He passed on from this to a political side issue.

After the sermon members of the university poured into St. Frideswide's, among them twenty bachelors or masters of arts with weapons concealed beneath their gowns. When the crowd departed, Stokes remained in his seat, trembling with fear, not daring to leave. Rygge waited for Repyngton in the porch, and the two went off laughing. Wycliffe's friends counted it a day of triumph.

Next day Stokes approached the chancellor with regard to the archbishop's mandate. Rygge insisted, "I have not seen sufficient evidence, with an authentic seal, that I am to assist you in publishing the mandate."

The exasperated Stokes then handed him the letters patent sealed with the archbishop's private seal.

After examining these closely, Rygge said, "I agree to help in the publication of the letters, under certain conditions. I must discuss the matter with the university, and, if they decide such a step ought to be carried out, I will lend my support."

Immediately Stokes sent off a frantic letter to the archbishop, declaring, "I know not what will happen next. I fear for my personal safety and beg that you give me help."

Next day, Saturday, June 7, Chancellor Rygge, accompanied by his proctors, set out for London. "I mean to appear before the archbishop," he said, "and explain my actions before I am called upon to do so. A second Blackfriars' synod is soon to meet, and I would hope to set my affairs straight before that time."

To Stokes' relief, he received a letter from Courtenay telling him to report to Lambeth. He set out at once and reached London the next evening. Rygge had not obtained an immediate audience, so Stokes was able to get in his account first.

The archbishop kept the chancellor of Oxford waiting four days. On June 12 Rygge and his proctors appeared before the second gathering of the Blackfriars' synod. The personnel was not the same as that of the Earthquake Council. Some faces were missing, and a number of new ones appeared.

Rygge was courteously seated as a member of the council, but he discovered to his consternation that the business of the day was his own trial for promoting heresy. Several charges were made against him. He had chosen Hereford, a disciple of Wycliffe, for an important sermon, and had neither silenced him nor allowed complaints against him. He had allowed Repyngton to preach, had failed to rebuke him, and had praised him with smiling face. Finally, he had refused to aid Stokes and had treated the archbishop's letter with contempt.

Facing this assembly of fifty eminent prelates, theologians, and lawyers, Rygge found no courage to resist. Actually he had acted not so much in sympathy with the beliefs of Wycliffe, Hereford, and Repyngton as in desiring to uphold the seculars in the university against the encroachment of the regulars. When the twenty-four Conclusions were placed before him, he yielded, accepted the condemnation as passed by the earlier Blackfriars' Council, and signed his name in agreement.

On his knees, Rygge begged the archbishop's forgiveness for contempt shown to the letters sent him. Courtenay pardoned him at the special request of Wykeham, bishop of Winchester.

The chancellor would be permitted to return to Oxford, bearing a humiliating mandate from the archbishop which began, "You Master Robert Rygge have inclined, yea, do incline to the aforesaid condemned Conclusions." It sternly admonished him not to interfere with any of Courtenay's agents. He was not to allow any to teach, maintain, preach, or defend such errors.

Hereford, Aston, Repyngton, and Bedeman, suspected of heresy, should not preach or take any part in the schools until they had purged themselves before the archbishop. Rygge would obey in all this on pain of the greater excommunication.

Further, he must publish the condemnation of the twenty-four articles in St. Mary's in Latin and English, and in the schools. Inquiries must be made in every hall, and any who favored these opinions should be required to clear themselves or recant.

Courtenay had a further question. "Why did you not assist Dr. Stokes to publish the decree?"

"I dared not," cried Rygge, "for fear of my life."

"Then," replied Courtenay, "the university is a favorer of heresy, since she will not allow catholic truth to be published."

Rygge's ordeal ended the next day, when he was called before the Privy Council. He stood in uncomfortable silence with every eye upon him. Richard Scrope, chancellor of the realm, cautioned him, "See that you follow every command of the archbishop. This will ensure that both clergy and people are warned."

He undertook to make the sixty-mile journey back to Oxford in one day. Weary as he was, he took time to call Hereford and Repyngton late Saturday night, warning them that he was required to publish the archbishop's mandate the next day, including the item of their suspension from further activity in the university.

The reading of the mandate brought about the result Rygge had anticipated. The seculars arose in hot indignation at this assault on their rights. Their cry was, "Death to the friars."

Back in familiar surroundings, Rygge's courage returned. He acted to show where his real sympathies lay. Crump, an obnoxious opponent of Wycliffe and one of Barton's council of Twelve, was now a member of the Blackfriars' synod, where he had assisted in Rygge's humiliation. He had recently called the followers of Wycliffe by the contemptuous name, Lollards. With this as a pretext, Rygge summoned Crump to appear before him. He did not respond, since, as Rygge well knew, he was still in London on Courtenay's synod.

When he failed to appear, Rygge suspended him as a disturber of the peace.

4. June-July 1382—Momentous Decisions

The day after publication of the mandate Hereford returned to the translation work. Nearing the end of the major prophets, he hoped to finish the Old Testament within the next few weeks. Preaching, locally and elsewhere, and the excitement and uproar over the condemnation of the Conclusions had set him behind.

"Nothing goes well since Wycliffe's departure," he said with a sigh. A sense of foreboding hung over him. "The condemnation of the articles is only the beginning. What next?" He grasped the pen with determination and found the place in the Latin Scriptures at the third chapter of the book of Baruch. In a few days he would move into the long and difficult book of Ezekiel.

He read, "*Iuvenes viderunt lumen et habitaverunt super terram viam autem disciplinae ignoraverunt.*" Then he translated, "*Young men have seen light, and dwelt upon the earth...*"

At that point a rapping came on the door. Impatiently he dropped his pen and rose to attend to the interruption. On the doorstep stood a man clad in the livery of the archbishop. In his hand he held a letter, which he handed to Hereford. After inquiring where he might find Master Repyngton, he departed.

Hereford hastily broke the seal. It was a summons from Courtenay to appear at Blackfriars on Wednesday, June 18, to answer for certain allegations against him. His heart sank.

He started to rush off to find Repyngton, but stopped and glanced at his desk. His first duty was to ensure the safety of the translation. He ran mentally down the list of those who had helped him recently and chose the one he felt most trustworthy. A hasty word in that direction relieved his mind. The manuscript would be safely cared for in case he did not return immediately.

Repyngton was in a state of turmoil. They agreed they must begin their journey immediately. Within an hour they rode out of Oxford in the bright sunlight of a warm summer day.

"I can't say I'm happy about making this journey," said Repyngton, "but I suppose we should have expected it."

"I confess to some feelings of apprehension," replied Hereford. "I wish we could talk to Wycliffe before going."

"Strange that his name was not mentioned in any of the papers read. I would expect Courtenay to aim directly at him."

"It's my opinion that Lancaster is still protecting him. Some felt that he was merely using Wycliffe for his purposes, but I think he has a deep admiration for him, as well as respect."

"That could be the answer. If Courtenay is frustrated in his desire to make a personal attack on Wycliffe, he'll throw all his ammunition at the rest of us. The road ahead will be rough."

"It distresses me," said Hereford, "that the call came just as translation of the Old Testament is nearing completion."

"You realize that we may not get back to Oxford at all. I'm sure you left the manuscript in safe hands."

"It's quite safe. Aston and Bedeman are both out preaching. They are sure to be summoned, and who knows how many more?"

"We're called first on account of our recent sermons."

"Courtenay's little 'White Dog' will have made a full report of those and of all else he has noted in tracking me around."

"Crump will be there, gloating over having us at last undergoing trial for our 'heresy.'"

Conversation lagged. It had been more or less "whistling in the dark" to keep up their courage. They paid scant attention to their surroundings as they traveled. Then Hereford suddenly stopped. "Look, Repyngton," he cried. In the woods and across the meadows bluebells bloomed in that glorious extravagance which blankets much of the English countryside at this season.

"Truly a sight to lift our hearts," said Repyngton. "I hope they are as profuse at Lutterworth. Wycliffe loves them so."

On Tuesday as they neared London, Repyngton asked, "What are we going to do when they try to force us to sign an agreement to the condemnation of those twenty-four articles?"

"I shall refuse to sign," cried Hereford with some heat. "Given the opportunity, I shall explain the meaning of each one."

"I doubt you get that chance. I don't intend to sign either. I can't help but wonder what approach they'll take."

"Christ told the apostles that the Holy Spirit would guide them as to what to answer when brought to trial. We must keep that in mind and pray for that guidance."

"We haven't thought of appealing to the duke of Lancaster," said Repyngton. "If he is protecting Wycliffe, he might help us. He turned down the complaint the friars made against you."

"We could try, though I doubt his willingness to involve himself openly in a struggle with Courtenay. He locks horns with him often enough without seeking an unnecessary conflict."

They completed the journey in silence, each deep in his own rather gloomy thoughts. At his Tottenham manor the duke of Lancaster received them kindly and listened to their plea for his support. They called his attention to the fact that suppressing Wycliffe's teaching would strengthen clerical power and weaken temporal dominion, both in Parliament and of the crown itself.

At first he hesitated, seeming to consider their request, but his mind was clearly on other matters. When Wycliffe's doctrine of the Eucharist was mentioned, he stood up abruptly and turned away, saying, "That doctrine is detestable. I can do nothing for you. You must obey the archbishop's summons."

As they approached Blackfriars next morning, they encountered Aston. "So the archbishop found you," said Hereford. Aston smiled. "You might have been in doubt as to where I was, but you must have known I was preaching."

They discovered as they entered that the number on the committee was not large. Most were friars. The archbishop caused them to swear to give their views as to the condemned Conclusions. When he questioned them separately, both Hereford and Repyngton asked for a day in which to deliberate. They requested permission to reply in writing and asked for a copy of the articles. Courtenay granted the request, but warned them, "See that you leave out all sophistical words and disputations."

He turned then to Aston, who stated his desire to reply immediately. Actually he hoped to avoid committing himself. Courtenay had no intention of letting him off easily. He informed him that he was notoriously suspected of heresy and had disregarded the mandate against preaching without a special license. He must appear with the others on Friday, June 20.

The three spent Thursday making plans. Hereford and Repyngton carefully wrote out their replies. Then Hereford said, "When Wycliffe appeared at St. Paul's for his earlier trial, and later at Lambeth, the citizens of London stood by him. Aston has a following here even now. Why not appeal to these citizens?"

Hereford and Aston each wrote a brief confession of faith in Latin and English and managed to have copies passed out on the streets. John of Northampton, Wycliffe's staunch friend, was mayor of London. These efforts must surely bear fruit.

On Friday they faced the full synod at Blackfriars. "White Dog" Stokes was in the group, as were Crump and Kenningham. Hereford and Repyngton handed in their written replies. In careful wording they had first admitted that to a clerical eye, the articles did seem heretical.

Some of their written comments which followed were declared of doubtful orthodoxy, others ambiguous or obscure. They were examined on their statements regarding the first three Conclusions on transubstantiation, on the seventh about God obeying the devil, and on those concerning excommunication, special prayers, and friars begging. When the two declined to go beyond the written answers, a vote was taken, and they were found guilty of heresy on four counts and of error on two.

Courtenay did his best to get them to change their minds, but to no avail. He postponed final judgment until June 27, giving them additional days for reflection.

All had proceeded in an orderly manner and in Latin until Aston's turn. A group of his lay supporters broke down a door and burst into the chamber, causing no little disturbance. The archbishop managed to have them brought under control, and the proceedings continued. Aston made an obvious play for the sympathies of these

friends. He gave his answers in English in a disrespect-
ful tone, even with a touch of insolence.

Courtenay, nervous over the presence of the London
citizenry, ordered Aston to answer in Latin. Aston continued to speak in English in an even louder tone. He
refused to go into the scholastic questions put to him,
saying, "The doctrine of transubstantiation passes my
understanding, but my desire is to believe what
Scripture and the church teach."

This innocent-sounding statement did not deceive
his hearers. All present were well aware that Wycliffe
maintained that his teaching was from Scripture and that
the church for more than a thousand years had believed
as he did as to the Eucharist.

When the archbishop tried to pin him down as to
whether material bread remained in the Sacrament after
consecration, he incautiously spoke derisively of the
word "material," saying, "You may put the word in your
pocket." His refusal to answer further was taken as guilt,
and he was condemned as a teacher of heresy. He, too,
was commanded to appear again on June 27.

Courtenay and his fellow clergy were considerably
upset over the state of things with regard to the London
citizens. They had some fear that John of Northampton
would try to interfere.

After deliberation, the archbishop announced, "This
council will convene on June 27 at the chapel of my
manor at Otford."

The pamphlets distributed by the heretics were
causing a stir. "A countermeasure is in order," cried
Courtenay. He set a group to draw up a statement of faith
of their own. "Include the information," said Courtenay,
"that Aston will not confess that the body of Christ in the
Sacrament of the altar is identically, truly, and really present in its corporeal nature."

So another flood of leaflets spread across London, to the amusement of the populace.

Courtenay took the precaution of covering another weak spot. The action inserted in the statutes of the previous Parliament authorizing imprisonment of itinerant preachers by officers of the state upon notification by a bishop would be challenged, because it subjected civil power to prelates. To remedy this he obtained from the king a patent equally effective but with a slightly different slant.

Courtenay smiled as he read the document: "Out of zeal for the Catholic faith, whereof we will be on all occasions the defender, the king conveys to the archbishop and his suffragans plenary power to imprison all defenders of the condemned theses, in their own or in other prisons, at their pleasure, until they give proofs of repentance and make recantation, or until the king and his council shall have taken other action in the matter."

A final word of caution added to Courtenay's satisfaction. "All lieges, ministers, and subjects of the king are enjoined upon their allegiance, and on pain of forfeiting their estates, not to give any favor or support to those preachers or their favorers, but, on the contrary, to assist the archbishop, his suffragans, and ministers in the execution of these presents."

The king's patent reached Courtenay on June 26, giving him confidence to face his victims on the next day. Hereford and Repyngton appeared in the chapel at Otford as instructed. Somehow the archbishop's theological and legal advisers failed to arrive, which did not seem to unduly upset him. He merely adjourned the meeting until Tuesday, July 1, at Canterbury. Aston had failed to present himself.

On the morning specified the archbishop gathered his committee in the chapter house at his chief seat of

Canterbury. Only about a dozen members arrived, the distance to Canterbury having discouraged some. Among those present were Kenningham and Barton. One could almost see them rubbing their hands in glee at the spectacle they hoped to view. A number of clergy filled the room, eager to observe the proceedings.

The bedel called the names of those to be examined, but they did not appear. After a time, he called again, with similar results. The council members shifted restlessly and murmured. Finally the meeting adjourned until after dinner.

Upon their non-appearance Courtenay pronounced Hereford and Repyngton guilty of contumacy and disobedience and excommunicated them. While waiting for an opportunity to deal with them in person, he turned his mind to other great plans.

5. July 1382—Courtenay Intensifies Attack

When Hereford and Repyngton left Otford on June 27, they had no intention of appearing at Canterbury a week later. They returned to London to decide upon a course of action. Unable to locate Aston after diligent search, they made their own plans.

"It will be best if we separate," said Repyngton. "I'll go by Lutterworth and report to Wycliffe, then to Leicester where I can remain out of sight until I see how things are going."

"He'll be eager for a firsthand account," said Hereford. "Tell him to send to Oxford for the translation manuscripts. The work must be finished, and with Courtenay on the rampage, there is small likelihood it can continue at Oxford. Wycliffe and Purvey must surely have the New Testament complete by now."

"We should stay here in London until we hear news from Canterbury," said Repyngton. "If Courtenay excommunicates us, I'm for filing an appeal to Rome against it." Accordingly, when word arrived, they nailed copies of their appeals on the doors of the church of St. Mary le Bow and St. Paul's.

"You go on as you planned," said Hereford. "Tell Wycliffe I've gone to Rome. The quickest way to reach the pope is to deliver our appeals in person. I'll seek an audience, present our appeals, and defend the Conclusions by making a full explanation of each one. That should clear us *and* Wycliffe."

Repyngton drew in his breath sharply. "I'm not sure I'd have the boldness. Are you sure that's the best way?"

"It's the best way," said Hereford, giving him a grim smile. "Nothing's going to be easy. Can you suggest a better plan?"

On that note they parted. Repyngton rode off toward Lutterworth feeling unsettled and uncertain. "He's right," he muttered. "Nothing's going to be easy."

Hereford faced a complicated course. While dodging the archbishop's men, he would have to devise a plan for getting out of the country without being recognized. He dared not return to Oxford. Obtaining money was a necessity. Wycliffe's London friends were also his friends. Resolutely he began his search.

Within a fortnight he had gathered a modest sum, but not enough. Where else could he turn? "Why not try the duke of Lancaster again? I'm sure he won't turn me over to Courtenay."

To his joy he found Lancaster willing not only to help him with money but to aid him in arranging passage across the Channel. This required time. Hereford waited patiently.

Wycliffe's excitement and joy at seeing Repyngton were touching. He poured out questions without giving Repyngton time to answer. "What of Hereford and

Aston? Are Bedeman and Alington safe? My concern for all of you has been great."

He devoured the information Repyngton brought, holding him at Lutterworth several days to make sure he missed nothing. To know that Hereford and Repyngton stood firm under the archbishop's attacks gave him great joy. He was particularly interested in knowing the contents of the archbishop's mandate.

"I hear that Braybroke has sent copies to all the bishops according to Courtenay's instructions," said Wycliffe, "but Buckingham may take his time about passing it along."

"You may know," said Repyngton, "that Buckingham ordered an investigation of articles laid against Swinderby. Last month he confronted Swinderby with sixteen articles friars at Leicester claimed he had preached, several similar to items among the twenty-four Conclusions. Swinderby denied having taught those articles. Buckingham ordered him to get the signatures of twelve priests to that effect and gave him a month in which to do this."

"You will have to go into hiding at Leicester, but you will have means of keeping abreast of what goes on. If possible, see Swinderby and encourage him to stand firm before Buckingham."

"You have no idea where Aston went?" asked Purvey.

"Not the slightest. He disappeared after the hearing of June 20. He could be still in London, for friends there rallied to his support. John of Northampton may be able to protect him."

"I think it likely," said Wycliffe, "that he moved on to the west. Aston's zeal will keep him preaching as long as possible."

"He so antagonized Courtenay by his attitude," said Repyngton, "that it will go hard with him if he is caught."

"As to the translation," said Wycliffe. "We must by all means bring the manuscripts here. Purvey and others can finish the Old Testament. The entire Bible in the English language! Think of it! A notable milestone!"

As Repyngton prepared to leave, Wycliffe asked, "Why has Courtenay called you, Hereford, and Aston before his council, but has never called me? You say my name was not mentioned in the mandate or in connection with the condemnation of the Conclusions. Why does Courtenay hold back from attacking me?"

"I believe the duke of Lancaster has something to do with it. He has thrown no stumbling blocks in Courtenay's way in his warfare on heresy. Perhaps they reached an agreement: no trouble from Lancaster provided he left you alone. Hereford and I sought his help, but he told us to submit to the archbishop."

Warm emotion flooded Wycliffe's heart. He said in a broken tone, "It would be in character. He cannot agree with me or support me openly, but he is still my friend and will do what he can. Thank you, Repyngton. I believe you may be right."

Purvey himself went to Oxford for the precious manuscripts, unwilling to trust anyone else with so important a mission. Meanwhile, Wycliffe received his copy of the archbishop's mandate. The messenger gave him the information that Swinderby had returned to the bishop at Lincoln when his month was up. The duke of Lancaster with his son, Henry of Bolingbroke, and a number of other magnates had been in the audience at his hearing.

"Had he the signatures of twelve priests attesting to his innocence regarding the accusation against him?" asked Wycliffe.

"No, but he produced a document with twelve seals from the mayor and other important men of Leicester who upheld him in his denial of having taught the articles in question. The bishop accepted this with seeming reluctance. He questioned him on eleven other beliefs several friars swore he had preached."

"And Swinderby stood firm through all this?"

"For a while. Then five friars and three priests came in, bringing wood with which to burn him. At that Swinderby collapsed, in fear of his life. He cried out that he never held those articles, but that he would confess to them and abjure."

"Did the bishop then release him?"

"Not yet. He was ordered to make a recantation on Sunday at the Lincoln Cathedral, then on succeeding Sundays in the Collegiate Church at Leicester, and in four other parishes in the diocese. After that he'll be free."

Wycliffe read the mandate with mounting anger. "So every parish priest is 'to admonish and warn that no one henceforth shall hold, teach, preach, or defend these heresies and errors, nor must he admit to preach any one of whom there is any doubt.'

"In at least one parish church the archbishop's fine words will not be read," he declared. "Yet Courtenay is unaware that he is contributing to the spread of truth. As the condemnation is read, truth is expressed, even though condemned. Hungry souls may find the grain amid the chaff, the silver amid the dross."

Purvey returned not only with the all-important parchments but with an astounding account of what was taking place. "The archbishop disregarded the appeals of Hereford and Repyngton to the pope," he reported. "On Sunday, July 13, the sentence of excommunication was read out with the solemnity of bell, book, and candle at St. Paul's Cross."

"That would be expected," muttered Wycliffe.

"Then Rygge received orders at Oxford to publish the ban at St. Mary's and in all the schools. He was to seize both culprits within a fortnight, if they could be found."

"Small chance of Rygge laying hands on Hereford or Repyngton, but surely Courtenay went further. What next?"

"He forwarded to Rygge letters patent from the council, of the same date, July 13, ordering him to make an inquisition..."

Wycliffe interrupted with a roar, "Inquisition! Right in Courtenay's line! He'll set up his torture implements next!"

Purvey continued, "It hasn't come to that, but Rygge and the proctors are to inquire among the regents in theology and law, to determine whether any of them hold the condemned articles."

"He may have serious difficulty extracting that information from some of the regents, especially the seculars."

"The royal mandate expressed in strong terms the king's determination to 'repress, punish, and restrain impugners of the faith which wickedly sow their naughty and perverse doctrine, preach damnable conclusions notoriously repugnant, perverting our people in their pernicious errors.'"

"Those words," said Wycliffe, "were most certainly put into the king's mouth by the archbishop."

"He went on to appoint Rygge 'Inquisitor general,' with all the chief divines, graduates, and lawyers as assistants. Within seven days they are to drive out of the university and the city any member who receives into his house or inn, or who has any communications or dealings with Wycliffe, Hereford, Repyngton, or any other of that party."

"Aha!" cried Wycliffe. "My name mentioned at last. My banishment from Oxford, then, is complete. The chancellor has the power of banishment as part of his ordinary criminal jurisdiction, but it is seldom put into practice."

"It goes further," said Purvey. "Your writings are banished. A search of every hall and college is to be made for books and tracts by you or Hereford. These are to be confiscated and sent to the archbishop without correction or change being made."

Again Wycliffe snorted. "He'll not succeed with that. Little does he know of the hiding places in which the books will be secreted. What more? Or has he done his worst, with that?"

"Just an added threat. Unless the instructions are carried out, the university faces loss of its liberties and privileges. The sheriff of Oxfordshire and the mayor of the city are to assist in the carrying out of the orders.

"All was in uproar over a second letter Rygge received from the king ordering him to retract his charges against Crump and restore him to his position. He was warned not to 'impeach, molest, or grieve' Stokes, Patrington, or any other because of opposition to your doctrine or that of Hereford or Repyngton."

"Which means, I suppose," said Wycliffe, "that the name with which Crump has graced my followers will stick. 'Lollard' is as good a name as any. Its meaning is disputed, so it can take on its new meaning: one who holds the teachings of John Wycliffe."

"A name of which to be proud, even though intended derisively," said Purvey. "You recall that the name 'Christian' was first applied to followers of Jesus Christ at Antioch as a term of scorn, but it became accepted as an honor."

On Sunday Wycliffe delivered a powerful sermon of protest against the current trend. He spoke of the entombment of Christ and the devices the priesthood set up to defeat the resurrection. "Even so," he exclaimed, "do our high priests seek to fetter and suppress the Gospel of Christ and keep God's Law from being made alive. They make statutes stable as a rock, obtain grace of knights to confirm them, and mark them with the witness of lords. This they do, lest the truth of God's Law, hid in the sepulchre, should break out, to the knowing of the common people."

In conclusion he voiced a fervent prayer: "O Christ! Thy Law is hidden thus. When wilt thou send thine angel to remove the stone, and show thy truth unto thy flock?"

6. August-September 1382—English Bible

Courtenay was by no means through. When, to his chagrin, Rygge reported that diligent search had failed to discover Hereford and Repyngton at Oxford, he declared, "I'll find them if it's the last thing I do. What's more, I'll clamp down on those itinerant priests, peddling their heresy about the country."

Back at Otford manor, he wrote again to Braybroke ordering extension of the publication of the excommunication of Hereford and Repyngton to all towns and villages, demanding their arrest. He was to set the friars to work, especially in London and Lincoln dioceses, hunting Wycliffe's roving priests.

"Buckingham has never been energetic," mused Courtenay. "Now that he is getting old I can expect little from him. Lincoln diocese is a veritable hotbed of this 'Lollardy.' This heretical teaching can and must be wiped out."

Surprisingly Buckingham exerted himself. In Leicester, where Swinderby, Smith, and others still presented a problem, he reported success in silencing a number of the unlicensed preachers.

Rumors came that Aston was preaching in the west country, but no one could establish his whereabouts. Sought in one area, he moved on to another. Bedeman was reported to be preaching in Cornwall, his native territory. His countrymen protected him, so it seemed impossible to lay hands on him. Courtenay ground his teeth and reinforced his efforts.

Something more solid appeared with regard to Hereford. Just as he left for Rome, two anonymous tracts began to gain wide circulation. The western dialect proved, so far as Courtenay was concerned, that they came from Hereford's pen.

The first protested the imprisonment of Poor Priests following attacks of friars upon them, warning that England would be punished severely for this. Knights and Christian men should defend these evangelists, delivering themselves out of the devil's hands.

The second tract claimed that, at the London council, the friars had deceived the bishops, lords, and commons by condemning the Conclusions which insisted on clerical poverty. Scripture supported the contention for clerical poverty. The religious orders must be emptied of funds, according to the teaching of Christ. Only then would temporal goods multiply.

Wycliffe exulted in this feat of Hereford's. "Courtenay will be unable to stop circulation of these tracts. Copies will pass from hand to hand, as is true of the tracts I produce."

Aston managed to get word to him occasionally. Itinerant preachers still came quietly to Lutterworth to report, to gain encouragement, and to obtain materials. He knew that others were still active, though they found no way to communicate with him.

Bitter resentment at the archbishop's mandate against these preachers inspired a spate of sermons and tracts, always now against the friars. "What reason is there," he asked, "in hindering true priests from preaching the Gospel freely, without alms or myths or flattery, and giving leave to these friars to preach fables and heresies and afterwards to despoil the people and sell them their false sermons?"

To the claim that a priest must not preach without a license, he answered that they preach with Christ's leave. Until he left Oxford, he had accepted only ordained priests in his band. Now when he found evangelistically-inclined Christians, grounded in the Scriptures, he sent them out, after careful instruction and testing. When possible he sent new men with experienced preachers on their first tours.

"I still marvel," he said, "that no one comes to seek heresy and heretics at Lutterworth. True, the archdeacon of Leicester, who might cast an eye on Lutterworth, is an absentee Italian cardinal, but why has Buckingham not made a move?"

Wycliffe thanked God for the freedom to continue writing without interference, to preach as he wished, and to train his preachers and have them come and go, unhampered. Through these channels his cry for reform was heard across the land. His was no muted voice smothered in the obscurity of a rural parish!

Translation of the Old Testament was complete, thanks to the efforts of Purvey. Almost the entire burden had fallen upon him. The complete Bible existed in the English language! Wycliffe's elation knew no bounds. One of his chief goals was achieved.

"We must make copies of the entire work," he cried, "but also copies of individual books of the Bible. Few can afford a whole Bible, but many can purchase a book or two."

Purvey was for taking the manuscript to Leicester at once, where professional copyists could be employed. Wycliffe insisted that at least one complete copy be made at Lutterworth first.

"It will be safer," he said. "Something could happen to the manuscript. We must retain a copy here, and continue to produce copies here as well. Those among the Poor Priests with ability to do accurate work must spend time at it between preaching tours.

"Some who come in, desirous of preaching, are not gifted in that line. You may employ their enthusiasm as copyists, fully as important a labor at this moment as preaching."

"You spoke of copies of single books," said Purvey. "Such will be more convenient to carry around, and will be easier to hide, should Courtenay's men come searching."

"To my knowledge," said Wycliffe, "no law exists against translating the Scriptures into English. Courtenay, however, will act, regardless of law, or he will see to having a law passed. If for no other reason, he will fight the English Bible because of the 'heretical' background from which it comes."

His eyes gleamed as he continued. "We must not be content with only copies of single books, Purvey. The finest scriveners in Catte Street at Oxford and in Paternoster Row in London must produce beautiful illuminated copies of the whole Bible, richly bound with firm boards and tawed leather. There will be a demand for such from those able to pay the price."

As summer moved on toward autumn, Wycliffe continued at the same furious pace with writing, getting material published and distributed, and overseeing the copying of the Bible. Purvey worried that his master's physical powers were lessening. He seemed so frail. Wycliffe scoffed at the idea.

"We cannot afford to slow down," he said. "The Fiend is on the rampage. We must use the time God grants."

He manifested anxiety about his followers. "No word from Hereford!" he cried. "He must have reached Rome by now. I'm not sure it was wise for him to go. It's unlike Brut to remain away so long. Does Repyngton remain at Leicester? Do Alington and Bedeman lie in some bishop's prison?"

With a sigh he committed them to God and buried himself more deeply in writing. The faithful disciples involved in copying the Bible progressed more slowly than professional copyists would have done, but the work moved on under Purvey's supervision.

Occasionally Wycliffe took note of the long hours of labor and sent them off to the bowling green for an hour's recreation.

7. July-October 1382—Recantations

Young Richard II began to pull away from restraints on his freedom. He felt that at sixteen years and as a married man he was capable of making his own decisions. He discharged his tutors, retaining only Sir Simon Burley, who had become one of his favorites. Michael de la Pole became his chamberlain, with Robert de Vere and John Beauchamp as other officials. He spent money wildly and lavished generous gifts upon his favorites.

When these friends realized that he was scraping the bottom of the barrel and that their source of supply might be cut off, they persuaded him that a king should be able to take any crown property for personal use. When Richard le Scrope, chancellor of the realm, remonstrated with him and counseled the curtailing of personal expenditures, the king, in a fit of temper, dismissed the chancellor.

Dismissal of his most valuable servant, an official appointed by Parliament, caused widespread sorrow and alarm. Many began to express concern about the handsome young king, who had shown such wisdom and valor during the Peasants' Rising.

The king named Braybroke, bishop of London, chancellor of the realm to replace Scrope. He ordered the archbishop to call a meeting of Convocation "at St. Paul's or elsewhere" in November. Convocation would be expected to vote a grant for meeting the expenses facing the government. With a secret smile the archbishop opted for "elsewhere" as the location for the meeting. "Why not Oxford?" he whispered.

On October 6 Parliament convened, facing its usual demands for money. In June Urban VI had issued a bull for a second and grander crusade against the French antipope Clement. Intended to rescue Ghent from the French pope's forces, this move had a strong appeal for the woolen merchants of London, who would find things difficult if the French forces continued. It appeared that England might even be in danger of an attack by the French.

The Commons refused to vote funds for any cause until they gained satisfaction on the matter of the statute the archbishop had persuaded the king to add to the actions of the previous Parliament. It had provided that bishops could issue orders in the king's name for the cooperation of state officers in the arrest of itinerant preachers and others suspected of heresy.

At the insistence of the Commons, the king approved an order that the statute be stricken from the books. As it turned out, it remained in the statute rolls, but at least for the time being, it was not put into action.

With that settled, John Gilbert, treasurer, with difficulty obtained a grant of a fifteenth and a tenth for the defense of the nation. The Council would decide how the money should be spent, and Parliament rose on October 22.

Even as Parliament sat, autumn weather had come with a vengeance. Driving rains and heavy winds set in all over the land. Bedeman had been preaching in Cornwall for some weeks. Although protected by his fellow-countrymen, he kept on the move. When he preached at Exeter, word reached Bishop Brantingham, and Bedeman fled to a more remote site. As the weather worsened, he slogged around Devonshire in deep mud and relentless cold.

At last he reached the breaking point. "I can't go on like this. I preach and then run, over and over again. Nothing the archbishop can do will be worse than such a life."

He sent a plea to the archbishop, who gave him permission to return to Oxford. On October 22 he appeared at the mansion of Wykeham, bishop of Winchester, at Southwark, across the bridge from London. Wykeham called a group of doctors of theology and law to examine Bedeman.

"You are suspected of preaching heretical doctrines in my diocese," said the bishop. He outlined the points upon which Bedeman stood accused.

Intensive questioning followed, and the frantic and exhausted man insisted, "I swear I have never held such errors."

The committee accepted his word and dismissed the charges, declaring him to be a true Catholic. He returned to his studies at the university and left off his Lollard preaching.

The weather may have played some part in Repyngton's decision. When he found it expedient to slip away from Leicester, he tramped across to the

Severn and joined Aston. Together they preached up and down the area around Hereford and along the Welsh border. As they were climbing among the hills near Great Malvern a strong cold wind from the west drove them down into a valley and draped the Malvern Hills in an impenetrable cloak of mist.

Finding no shelter and unable to see their way, they huddled with chattering teeth over a fire that seemed to give no heat. In desperation Repyngton said, "Aston, what's the future in this? Here we are, excommunicated, cut off from the church, branded as heretics, hunted like animals. Where will it end?"

Aston had felt Repyngton weakening. "Wycliffe would tell us that Courtenay's excommunication means nothing. We are not cut off from the true church. As followers of Christ, we can expect persecution. Preaching the Gospel is our task, whatever comes."

"Wycliffe is right in most things, and I've gone along with him so far. But suppose—just *suppose*, Aston—that he's wrong about excommunication. If he is, that leaves us outside the church and consigns us to hell."

Nothing Aston said had any effect. He was not surprised when, a few days later, Repyngton said, "I'm going back, Aston. Hereford may get some action on our behalf at Rome, but not likely. The best thing I can do is turn myself in to Courtenay and throw myself on his mercy."

He reached London on the same day Bedeman appeared before Wykeham, but he knew nothing of this at the time. Facing Courtenay was a humiliating business. He stood before the bishops at Blackfriars and without hesitation abjured all heresy.

He knelt before the archbishop and received absolution. "You will read your recantation at Paul's Cross," said Courtenay. "After that you may expect to be restored to your status in the schools at Oxford."

Courtenay, highly pleased at this triumph, determined to make the most of it. When Repyngton had met all the archbishop's conditions and hoped to be released, he was told, "You will make one further appearance before Convocation on November 24 at Oxford. If all goes well at that time, you will be free."

8. November 1382—Aston's Fall

Efforts to obtain from Repyngton information as to Aston's whereabouts failed. Courtenay remained optimistic. "Someone will bring him in," he said. "He must be in the west, and diligent search will find him. Or he, like Repyngton, may grow tired of running and turn himself in. I rather think, however, he is made of different stuff from Repyngton."

Recollection of the London mob's interference on Aston's behalf at Blackfriars influenced him to call Convocation at Oxford, but also he felt that his hour of triumph was at hand. The university could expect no help from the crown. With Wycliffe at Lutterworth and Hereford overseas, there were none to resist.

"The Commons had the statute against heretics revoked, but I have other plans. An archbishop has not recently dared use powers of visitation at Oxford, but I will do it. I mean to eradicate heresy if I have to crush the university in doing so."

The clergy gathered at St. Frideswide's on November 13 in obedience to the archbishop's call. The canons' welcome to these guests was somewhat cool. The priory was in serious financial straits, and entertaining Convocation would be no light matter.

John Dodford, the prior, was a clever but unscrupulous man. Discipline within the priory was at an all-time low. The members of Convocation began to hear whispers of outrageous scandals. The archbishop relieved some of the stress among the canons by heading a commission to act in settling the most outstanding disputes between St. Frideswide's and the university.

At the opening session the archbishop sat in pomp and glory among his mitred bishops. University Chancellor Rygge preached the opening sermon. Courtenay smirked as Rygge announced his text, *Congregati sunt in valle benedictionis*—Assemble now in the valley of blessing. Rygge might hope for blessing, but would not likely find it. Courtenay had little confidence in obtaining Rygge's willing cooperation, but he had means of gaining it, willing or unwilling.

At the close of the sermon the archbishop announced the first and most important reason for this meeting: to repress heresies which have sprung up in the realm.

"It is reported," said the archbishop, "that certain in this university hold the heretical and erroneous Conclusions which we have condemned. I name the following commission to act upon this report: the bishops of Sarum, Hereford, and Rochester, with Doctors Rygge, William Barton, and John Middleton. To them I assign full authority to search and inquire for all doctors, bachelors, and scholars who hold, teach, maintain, and defend those Conclusions either in or out of the schools."

Courtenay, observing Rygge's scarcely hidden reluctance to comply, smiled again to himself. He felt certain that previous instructions to Rygge along this line had been carried out in a dilatory manner. *Now* he would see results!

On November 24 Philip Repyngton came before those gathered at St. Frideswide's. He dreaded this appearance, for he knew he stood before some who had heard him preach the doctrines he was recanting. He held, as instructed, a copy of the four Gospels, on top of which lay the document he was required to read aloud. He cleared his throat, hesitated a moment, then read:

"I, Philip Repyngton, canon of the house of Leicester, curse and abjure all these heresies and errors underwritten, condemned and reproved by you most reverend Father, condemning both them and the authors of them, and swear by these holy Evangelists which I hold in my hand, never by any way or by any persuasions of men to defend or hold as true any of the said Conclusions. All who stand contrary to this faith I pronounce, with their doctrine and followers, worthy of everlasting curse. Subscribed with mine own hand and with mine own accord, Philip Repyngton."

After dismissing Repyngton, Courtenay's prize victim was ushered in. John Aston had been apprehended preaching just west of the Severn, working his way back toward Worcester.

"John Aston, student of divinity at this university," intoned Courtenay, swelling with satisfaction, "you stand before this body to be examined on the Conclusions upon which your previous replies proved unsatisfactory. You will give attention as the Conclusions are again read. Perhaps you are better able to give thoughtful and proper answers upon this occasion."

Aston listened as patiently as possible to the reading of the articles. He gave his answers, making the wording as ambiguous as possible. To the articles on the sacrament he refused to give a reply. On this he held to his statement, "I am too simple and ignorant to understand these matters. Therefore, I cannot give any clear or distinct answers."

After some quibbling, the court agreed to accept his statements for the articles upon which he had given answer. They insisted that he must give a reply upon the remaining matters.

In exasperation, the archbishop said, "I assign you to Dr. Rygge and others of his choosing. They will instruct you in this mystery and prepare you to answer when the session resumes."

Aston sat meekly with his mentors during the dinner hour, giving every indication of attentiveness. He was actually making a decision as to what course he would follow. He declared, after due instruction, that he stood convinced by the learned doctors. Thanking them, he excused himself and went to find the bishops.

Someone informed him that the bishops still lingered in the refectory, since the hallway was blocked by undergraduates who congregated there at this time of day. Aston elbowed his way through and burst into the refectory.

Bowing low, he said, "I am ready to make my submission." He read the recantation which was handed him, the same form as that which Repyngton had read. Signing and returning it to the archbishop, he said, "I deny that, after consecration, the substance of bread and wine remain in the sacrament. I beg you to accept my humble apology for my insolence at Blackfriars."

Murmurs of approval swept across the room at this display of humility. The archbishop dismissed him with the order that he appear before him in three days' time to receive his absolution.

Aston groaned at the delay. He found Repyngton and Bedeman, but they were uncomfortable in his presence. Repyngton, with his doctorate in theology, would remain at Oxford and lecture. Bedeman would pursue his studies.

On the appointed day Aston knelt before the archbishop and received absolution. Before nightfall he left Oxford with no desire or expectation of returning. He had remained silent when Repyngton and Bedeford spoke of their plans.

Not yet certain where he would go, he knew he must lose himself from the public eye for a time. He thought ruefully of what he had been forced to do. "I am not happy to have gone through the form of making that recantation. Had I refused, it would have meant prison and perhaps worse—and certainly no more preaching. I wish I could slip in to Lutterworth for a brief visit, but I dare not. It would endanger Wycliffe. Hearing of these abjurations will go hard with him."

Plodding on through the night, he wrestled with his conscience. "It was the best thing to do. God understands the mental reservation with which I acted. He will forgive me. I cannot give up preaching. As Wycliffe says, it is the most important occupation of a priest. I may have to dodge Courtenay's men for the rest of my life, but I will preach Christ until he takes me to himself."

After a time he came upon a deserted chapel in which he could spend a few hours resting. "No one must know the way I take," he said, "or I will be watched. I must go where I will not be recognized." Wrapping his cloak tightly about him, he shivered in the deep November cold. "If only Wycliffe could know how it is with me," he said with a sigh. "He will believe I have really deserted to the enemy!"

9. December 1382—Affliction

On December 6, 1382, with the king's authorization, Bishop Spenser formally proclaimed the crusade against the antipope. The timing was propitious, for a week earlier the French had won a great victory over Ghent at Roosebeke. This increased the danger felt earlier by the wool traders, whose representatives had been expelled from Flanders along with priests who claimed loyalty to Urban. An order went out instructing all sheriffs across the realm to gather bows and arrows for arming the crusade.

This, added to the heavy burden of hearing of the abjuration of the men at Oxford, brought Wycliffe almost to despair. He wrote in haste, keeping several articles going at once. To Purvey he could dictate the main ideas and leave it to him to fill in the details. He began dictating some of his work to other helpers eager for any contact with him, but he had to go more slowly.

Not only did he make vigorous attacks on the crusade, but he belabored Courtenay and the bishops for persecuting his Poor Priests. At the call for bows and arrows, he said, "How well I remember the plight of the serfs at Ludgershall when a like demand was put upon them. Men were forced to deliver a certain number of arrows before other work was done. Neglected crops often meant hunger for their families."

He grieved not overmuch at the fall of Bedeman. "He was never strong," he recalled. "Repyngton probably could not face being cut off from the church and isolation from friends. He has good qualities; I hate to lose him."

He suffered most over Aston's fall. "The best preacher of all! The others delivered themselves to the authorities, but Aston did not come voluntarily. I wish I knew the details of his trial. What could have made him recant? And where is he now?"

Purvey's concern for his master increased. "You are pushing yourself too hard," he cried. "You take these things too much to heart. Can't you let up a little and leave it to the Lord?"

"You've got it backwards, Purvey. The Lord has left the battle to me, and I seem to fight alone. There's the damnable crusade and all the evils connected with it, besides the desertion of my trusted men to the foe. How can the younger, less experienced men be expected to hold out in face of this?"

Wycliffe began getting up at night, pacing the floor, railing against those responsible for the swelling tide of evil. This, Purvey knew, could not continue indefinitely. The third week in December what he had feared took place.

Purvey found him where he had collapsed on the floor during his midnight pacing. Terrified, Purvey called loudly for help. Horne was the first to arrive. They carried their master to his bed, not knowing whether he was dead or alive. As Purvey considered the advisability of administering last rites, Horne cried, "He's breathing—he moved!"

He opened his eyes and stared in wonder. "Where am I? What happened?" he asked. Purvey hastily cleared the room, except for Horne. They sought to calm the stricken man and to determine the seriousness of the consequences. He had suffered some kind of stroke, but it was impossible to tell the extent of the damage.

Within days he made a fair recovery. His mental faculties were not affected, and the only persistent physical disability was in his left leg. It remained partially paralyzed.

"I'll have to resign myself to being a cripple," he said, "dependent upon others for getting about!"

"It won't continue that bad," said Purvey. "With a staff, you'll manage. Besides, we are here when you do need help."

"Since I spend most of my time at my desk, I suppose it will handicap me little."

On Christmas morning Purvey entered Wycliffe's room with a smile. "I have two pieces of news. The first you will not like, but the second will take the sting from the first. On December 21 Bishop Spenser preached a sermon at St. Paul's to mark the formal opening of the crusade. That, you expected. The second item is that

Aston has disappeared. Immediately after receiving absolution from the archbishop, he left without a word to anyone. He has not been seen since."

Wycliffe pondered this. "You consider that encouraging news? I want to know where Aston is, what he is doing."

"Consider the facts a moment," said Purvey. "Bedeman received a benefice and has permission to continue his studies at Oxford. Repyngton is lecturing in the schools, headed for bigger things, to his way of thinking. But Aston has disappeared."

"I see what you mean. Aston could have remained at Oxford, too. His disappearance means he wants nothing to do with benefices or degrees or position. He intends to lose himself so he may resume his preaching. Yes, Purvey, you have given me a fine Christmas gift! A great burden has lifted from my heart."

"To see you smile is an excellent gift to me," cried Purvey. "It has been many days since we saw *that* bit of sunshine."

Writing continued. Realizing that what had happened could happen again, Wycliffe could not afford to slow down.

10. January-March 1383—Oxford News

Oxford being crushed by Courtenay preyed on Wycliffe's mind. "The friars are in control now," he said, "the seculars silenced and helpless." This drove him to renewed attacks on the friars.

In mid-January William Thorpe, one of his very young former students, one still studying at Oxford, appeared at the rectory, to Wycliffe's great joy.

"Tell me all you can about matters at the university," he said. "What has happened in the last few months distresses me."

The young man smiled. "As bad as things are they could be worse. The most severe loss suffered was that of your presence. It is true the archbishop has silenced the open teaching of your doctrines and driven away those most active in spreading them.

"All 'heresy' seems quieted, but that is only a seeming. Beneath the surface your doctrines are still taught to small groups, ones and twos. You would be surprised at how many are thus engaged. Your writings have not all been confiscated. They are copied and passed on. This is true of the English Bible as well. Some individuals make their own copies, but the scriveners in Catte Street remain busily at work on the same, undisturbed."

Wycliffe, still in a weakened condition from his stroke, wept. "How happy you make me," he said. "I shed tears of joy."

Thorpe was reluctant to leave. "I remain devoted to you as my master," he said, "though separated from you. The learning I received from you and Hereford changed my life, and is what I intend to teach and live by for the rest of my days, God willing. If I find it not possible to remain longer at Oxford, I should like, with your kind permission, to return here to sit again at your feet. Perhaps I might even be useful in some small way."

Wycliffe sent him off with his blessing and another of the smiles that were all too rare these days.

11. March-September 1383—Spenser's Crusade

Bishop Spenser, in his role of papal nuncio, made a great show of publishing Urban's bull from his palace at Charing, marking one step nearer the entrance of England into the bloody battles already under way on the Continent.

Wycliffe cried in agony, "Spenser is no bishop. He was ever a soldier, nay, not just a soldier, but a butcher.

He was applauded for the part he played in putting down the peasants in 1381, but the details of his action make one shudder."

Wycliffe worked himself up into a fury. Purvey tried to calm him, reminding him that he might bring further injury upon his weak body. He was not to be restrained.

"He took a group of peasants to Wymondham, and, after they had been confessed, had them beheaded. What right has such a man to be called a bishop, a man of God, a follower of Christ? Now he goes at the behest of one false pope to fight against another. How many will be slaughtered in the disgraceful contest?"

Spenser was granted the privilege of commanding the crusade. Orders went out for men ready to join a crusade for the defense of holy church and the realm of England to assemble with all speed. Affairs moved with exasperating slowness. Spenser had difficulty getting supplies and men together.

Finally the archbishop sent out a general appeal to his suffragans. He managed to get the greatest response from the friars, to whom Wycliffe referred as "the pope's whelps." They went in all directions enthusiastically preaching the crusade. They were granted the privilege of hearing confessions in every parish. Anyone who had contemplated a visit to the Holy Sepulchre or the tombs of the Apostles could make a money payment for the war against the antipope instead. For this he would be granted plenary remission of his sins.

This stirred Wycliffe to indignant protest, but it proved a successful means of helping finance the crusade. The bishops amassed an unbelievable amount of money.

Men and women, rich and poor, gave even beyond their estate, so great was the desire to obtain absolution for themselves and friends who were already dead.

Many paid the expenses of men at arms or archers to go in their place. Others agreed to go themselves on the crusade.

Finally, on May 17, Spenser led the army across the Channel. As the crusade moved into action on the Continent, Wycliffe battled against the cause with his pen. As news came in, his temper flared. "Upon landing, the slaughter is already under way! At Dunkirk our fine bishop has killed men by many thousands!"

Worse was to follow. At Gravelines, Spenser pillaged a monastery and left no living soul in the town. The carnage continued, with terrible bloodshed on both sides. Spenser was driven to the coast, losing town after town. Some of the knights grew so disgusted at Spenser's leadership that they made terms with the enemy, receiving in return large sums of gold.

By the end of September it was obvious that the crusade was a dismal failure. Spenser returned in disgrace. When Parliament convened, he was impeached and deprived of his temporalities.

12. April-September 1383—Aston Preaches

From Oxford, John Aston had traveled east. In Hertfordshire he sought Sir John Montague, who resided at a manor at Shenley, which had come to him through his wife. He had heard of Aston's abjuration and, understanding his dilemma, received him warmly and gave a sympathetic ear to his story.

"I came here," said Aston, "because I felt sure of a welcome. I need time to gather myself together and plan for the future. I made no statement before I left Oxford as to my plans. Courtenay will expect me to return to the west, that being my home and the area in which I have spent so much time preaching. By coming east instead, perhaps I have thrown him off the trail."

Sir John gave this some thought. "The fact that you left secretly," he said, "will arouse the archbishop's suspicions. It will incline him to doubt the sincerity of your recantation, and he will consider that your movements bear watching. You will do well to stay out of reach. Remain here as long as you like."

Aston appreciated Sir John's hospitality, but with the passing weeks he grew restless. It was time to move on.

"Will you pay a visit to Lutterworth?" asked Sir John.

"Not yet," said Aston, with a sigh. "Later perhaps."

"Not too much later, Aston. Wycliffe's time may not be long. The stroke he suffered left him much weakened. He's driving himself mercilessly, trying to finish his work before time runs out."

"I've thought of that," said Aston. "I *must* see him again, but not quite yet."

"I suppose Courtenay expects you to go there, and will have his men watching. Perhaps you are wise to wait."

Aston followed a route which took him around Oxford. He sought towns in which he had friends who would offer shelter for a day or two. Some of these were old friends from Oxford, some were priests who secretly held to Wycliffe's doctrines, and some were people who had heard him preach and accepted his teaching.

"I dare not stay in one place long," he said to one of these friends. "It is not as if I were a fugitive, for I was absolved and restored to the church. But my aim is to reach my own country and preach. Until then I do not want to be recognized."

His conscience still troubled him. He argued with himself. "What else could I have done except abjure? Had I not, I would now lie in the archbishop's prison. What good would that do?"

Back would come the reply of his conscience. "It still remains that you *lied*. You swore that you believed something you do *not* believe. Is that an example for those who look to you for spiritual guidance? What will people to whom you preached think? You know this has wounded Wycliffe deeply. He counted on you."

His reply to this varied little. "I know that I sinned, but I have confessed my sin, and God has forgiven me. If we confess our sin and turn from it, he forgives, for Christ's sake."

Another voice would sometimes insert itself into his thinking, a voice he did not like. He felt sure it was not his conscience speaking. He found it disturbing. *You have not confessed to a priest*, accused this voice. *Surely that, and doing penance, is necessary for you to be truly forgiven.*

At last he realized that this voice was from the devil. "No!" he cried. "Confession to a priest is not necessary. Wycliffe convinced us of that. Sins are forgiven by God alone. No priest has the power of absolution. It is a device by which the clergy deceive the people and deprive them of their wealth. Wycliffe calls it simony, for granting absolution for money payment is actually selling spiritual benefits."

He found it difficult to turn a deaf ear to the pleas that he preach. Preaching was his life, but he wanted to put more distance between Courtenay and himself first. When he let himself be perfectly honest, he knew that part of the reason he could not yet preach was the spiritual battle within. He had to be sure God had forgiven him, and he had to forgive himself.

"I can't undo the wrong I have done to the cause of Christ," he admitted. "Scars will remain on some lives. All I can do is pray for those I have weakened or injured by my action."

He moved slowly to the west. When he reached the borders of Worcestershire, he began to preach, and with every sermon, his zeal increased. The old passion for the proclamation of the Word returned. Village after village heard his voice, and through him the voice of God. He aimed to establish in each village little groups who would meet together to read the tracts and Scripture portions he left with them.

"What I need," he said, "is copies of the Gospels and other portions in English. That must wait until I visit Lutterworth!"

He spent spring and summer west of the Severn. In the remote villages scattered through that area he found willing listeners, and the threat of being tracked by the archbishop's men was less. If he was not sure of the priest in a village, he slipped in, gathered a crowd, preached, and slipped away before the priest knew he was there. Often he found a welcome from the priest and even preached in the parish church.

In September he crossed the river and preached in villages near Worcester and toward Gloucester. Since the bishop was out of the diocese, and he need expect no trouble from that source, he decided to preach in Gloucester, where he had many friends. They spread the word, and a great crowd gathered on September 21.

Aston, in a daring move, slipped in at the last moment. He preached a sermon which gripped the hearts and minds of his listeners. He expressed his uncompromising views as to the crusade, which had failed so miserably. He had no kinder words for Spenser nor for the two popes than Wycliffe had. It was a message his hearers would long remember.

Now he must return to remoter western regions, for news of this venture would be reported to the authorities. "I hope Wycliffe hears of it," he said, "and knows I am preaching."

13. September 1383—Hereford at Rome

On the day that Aston preached in Gloucester, Nicholas Hereford sat, a dejected figure, in a prison cell hundreds of miles away. His thoughts returned, as they had innumerable times, to events of the previous months. *Why did it turn out like this?*

His difficulties began long before he reached Rome. He ran into delays all the way. Fortunately his money held out, for money opened doors and removed obstacles.

He groaned as he rose to his feet. "If only I could multiply that dwindling supply, this door might open," he cried, giving the iron door a savage kick. "It would take more than a pittance to oil this lock and grease these rusty hinges."

Crossing the Alps at the approach of winter had been impossible. He had been forced to remain in southern France and wait impatiently for spring. He filled the weary weeks writing and dispatching innumerable letters and tracts toward England, not knowing whether any would reach the intended destination.

When he at last reached Rome, his first disillusionment came when he found he would be dealing with cardinals rather than the pope. A personal audience with Urban VI seemed an impossibility. Even getting his documents into proper hands was no easy matter.

Other matters took precedence over his plea. He haunted the ante-room of the council chamber, but was completely ignored. Eventually he received a call to appear. *Now*, he thought, *I may expect a fair hearing, a chance to defend myself and the Conclusions verbally, if clarification of what I have written is required.* With all confidence he went in to face the cardinals.

His confidence quickly evaporated. Angry eyes bored into him. He could almost feel them draw back as if his presence in the room was a pollution. One of the judges rose and, in a tone of thundering rage, cried, "Nicholas Hereford, do you dare to admit to holding the damnable heresies contained in these pages?"

Hereford hastened to reply, "But the statements are *not* heresies! If you will only let me give an explanation..."

They silenced him before he could go further. He was given no time to speak a word in his own defense, much less to explain the Conclusions. Before he could recover from this injustice, he was declared a heretic with recommendation of the death sentence.

Still suffering from shock, he stood at last before the pope. Urban VI agreed with the judgment of the cardinals. In an oily tone he said, "We in our mercy, which is undeserved, commute the death sentence to life imprisonment."

Without further ado Hereford was conducted to the cell he now occupied. The pope's prison, the dungeon beneath San Angelo Castle, was not noted for its comforts. He had been here more than three months.

In the daily pacing of the cell he counted his steps, determined to keep his body fit. Today he raged in even stronger terms against Urban VI than he had heard Wycliffe use.

"Why did I expect to find justice at the court of the Fiend? I should have known I would end up in such a place as this."

He looked up at the small window high on the wall. "Why put bars in a window that only a crawling insect could reach? Even the rats who share my habitation cannot climb to that height."

Despite his angry words about the window, it was one thing that helped him keep his sanity. It seemed to be only slightly above the ground-level outside, so the

light it admitted was minimal. But during the late afternoon when the sun was setting the light was better.
Once in a while the sun's rays shone directly in, lighting
up the opposite wall with its beams.

By a few words each day he established a friendly relationship with the guard who brought his food. He now
determined to try to put into action a plan he had made.

When the first of his two daily meals arrived, he
detained the guard with a few pleasantries. He suggested that it might be to the man's advantage to obtain
for him a few writing materials. As they talked, Hereford
jingled a couple of coins in his hand to hasten the decision. Agreement was quickly reached.

Hereford felt what was almost a tremor of joy.
"Hope!" he cried. "Something to hope for! I never
thought I would hunger so for parchment and pen and
ink. What a difference it will make! I can't begrudge the
depletion of my small fund of money."

He glanced at the unsavory mess the guard had
brought. Seizing the bowl, he ate every bite, then rose
and continued his pacing with a new energy. *I almost feel
that I still belong to the human race. If he brings what I asked,
I'll consider it a token that I will not spend the rest of my days
in this stinking hole. That thought must remain with me and be
in my prayers.*

The next day and the next he waited. The guard
kept delaying, pointing out that it was a difficult assign-
ment he had undertaken. Then he said it would cost
more than Hereford had offered. Hereford saw that his
game was a play for more money. Grudgingly he agreed
to the higher price, but refused to deliver payment until
the materials were in his hands.

Infuriated by the delay, Hereford wanted to swear at
the man, but that would end his chances of getting what
had become an obsession. Still, having this bit of hope

helped keep him going. Each morning he woke with the thought, *Maybe today...*

Then one night the hope died. The rats scurried about, biting each other and squealing. He could not sleep. He thought of the months he had been there, of the possible years ahead.

"I am deceiving myself," he cried. "I shall never escape from this horrible place. Year will succeed year until I lose count, and I will rot here, forgotten by friend and foe alike. It would have been better to stay and face Courtenay. Nothing he could subject me to could be worse than this."

He stumbled to his feet and felt his way to the opposite wall. The outline of the barred window was barely discernible. He lurched back to sit on the side of the narrow platform which served as a bed and, putting his head in his hands, slipped into the greatest depths of despair he had ever known.

14. October 1383—Brut Visits

Brut walked into the room unannounced. Wycliffe, deep in study, was unaware of his presence until Brut touched his arm and asked softly, "Can you spare a minute for an old friend?"

In his excitement, Wycliffe tried to rise, but Brut restrained him with a hand on his shoulder. "I'll turn your chair to face me," he said, as he dragged a chair from Purvey's desk.

Wycliffe was too overcome by emotion to speak for some moments. He looked at Brut with glistening eyes. "Brut, how I have longed to see you! A burden has lain heavy on my heart that I did not even know where you were. It has been so long!"

It was a happy day as the old friends tried to catch up all that had taken place since they last met. Brut had preached constantly, dodging about to escape Courtenay's men. He found acceptance into many pulpits, unordained though he was. He was shocked over Wycliffe's condition, but tried to make light of it.

He had not seen the completed English Bible. "We must call Purvey in," said Wycliffe. "He is helping our semi-trained apprentice-copyists today. Semi-trained did I say? They are by way of becoming professional, with the experience they get."

Purvey proudly produced a bound volume of the Bible. Brut held it in his hands for a moment. Without a word he rose, placed the book on Purvey's desk, and drew up a chair. For some time he turned the pages, stopping to read here and there.

Smiling at the look of mingled awe and delight on Brut's face, Wycliffe turned back to his own work. Considerable time slipped away before Brut tore himself away from the book.

At last he raised a glowing face and cried, "Magnificent! Think what this will mean to knights and nobles who, though familiar with Latin, never take time to read God's law! Priests who know little Latin—and there are many—will now be able to read it not only for themselves but to their parishioners."

Then a slight shadow crossed his face. He cast a hesitant glance at Wycliffe, then at Purvey.

"What is it, Brut?" asked Wycliffe. "You obviously have more to say. Out with it!"

He relaxed visibly, then smiled. "I may speak frankly. As marvelous as this work is, I find a flaw. You intended it to be as nearly word for word from the Latin as possible."

"Some," said Wycliffe, "would consider a change of the word order equivalent to changing the Word of God. I wanted to avoid criticism. I instructed Hereford to follow along those lines."

"He did a good job, but Hereford is a pedant, and he achieved a style which I find stiff and awkward in places. One must remember that the Scriptures were not originally given in Latin. When God spoke through Moses and the prophets, the language in which it was written was not Latin. Jesus spoke to the multitudes and to the disciples in the common language, and it was not Latin. I am not sure that Jerome, in translating the Scriptures into Latin, followed a word for word order."

Wycliffe and Purvey exchanged glances. "We have discussed this matter," said Wycliffe. "While this translation is useful, far better than having none, there are deficiencies."

Brut showed relief at this admission. "At places the meaning is obscured or even altered by the method used. For instance, in 1 Samuel 2 we read in the Latin, *Dominum formidabunt adversarii eius*, which we know has the meaning, '*The adversaries of the Lord should dread him.*' It is here rendered, '*The Lord shall dread the adversaries of him,*' changing the meaning completely. We do not use in English the word order of Latin."

"Perhaps it was a mistake to go about it as we did," said Wycliffe. "There was pressure, and the work was done in much haste. The remedy will be a revision in which the translating is by thoughts and sentences rather than word for word. That will be Purvey's continuing project for some time to come."

Purvey gave silent assent.

Brut had a story which brought a bit of lightness and laughter. "I have not been back to Oxford since Courtenay undertook to put out the fires of 'heresy,' but I hear things.

"Chancellor Rygge submitted to the archbishop's demands, but obviously not entirely. Last spring he obtained a writ against an obscure priest demanding that he make amends to holy church for contempt and wrongdoing. What he did does not matter, but only his name, which was John Dodford. Now you may recall..."

Wycliffe burst in. "John Dodford is the prior of St. Frideswide's!"

"Quite right," said Brut, with a smile. "Whether it was an honest error or done intentionally, the wrong John Dodford was seized and imprisoned. It afforded the seculars great delight to see the prior thus humiliated. They laughed more heartily when the king himself had to intervene to obtain the prior's release."

Wycliffe wiped away tears of laughter. "It must have turned out just as Rygge intended. It does me good to know that Rygge is there, and that he is able to get in an occasional blow."

"You must come more often, Brut," said Purvey. "That is the first time he has laughed in months. We even have a hard time getting an occasional smile."

"These are sober times," said Wycliffe, "and little to make one laugh. It is well that you can lift my spirits with a story like that, Brut, since you can't coax me out for a walk. *That* would do my soul good, if it were possible. There are good walks around Lutterworth, but I shall never take them again."

"Seeing that pile of manuscripts, I doubt I could lure you away were you physically able," said Brut.

"I expect to preach on Sunday," said Wycliffe. "Will you be staying until then?"

"If you preach in the morning, I may stay. I need to be in Leicester before nightfall. I saw Swinderby at Coventry, where he is preaching, since things got too dangerous at Leicester. He urged that by all means I should preach there."

Purvey put in a word. "He insists on preaching. I tell him it is too much for him, but he won't listen."

"I have become a stubborn old man," said Wycliffe. "I see no reason why I should not preach as long as someone can help me into the pulpit. This leg is not much for mounting steps."

"Did I tell you," asked Brut, "that I barely missed contact with Aston a fortnight ago?"

"No!" cried Wycliffe. "Where is he? Is he all right? My concern for him has been great."

"He's all right. Preaching all over the west. It was at Gloucester I missed him. He made bold to preach there on September 21, and, from all reports, it was quite a sermon. His preaching is apparently as fiery as ever. Until then he had been preaching in small towns, villages, and hamlets, mostly west of the Severn, with no sign of Courtenay knowing where he was."

Wycliffe sighed. "That he preached at Gloucester will not be kept hidden. Courtenay doubtless assumes he is in the west. Aston is pretty adept at dodging the authorities, so perhaps he'll manage. What were you doing in Gloucester?"

"I have friends there who had sent me word that pulpits were open to me. I preached three times to large congregations. It's not the same for me as for Aston. No one is looking for me."

"Exercise reasonable or *extraordinary* care. Courtenay's net will reach farther as time goes on. He's determined to put a stop to 'heretical' preaching by unlicensed preachers. You know by now that we have no need to go among the heathen to die a martyr's death. We've only to preach persistently the law of Christ in the hearing of rich and worldly prelates, and we'll have a flourishing martyrdom, if our faith and patience hold."

"I'll be careful," replied Brut. "I have no desire to seek a martyr's death. I doubt that fate is in store for any in England. Punishment, yes, but death? Will it come to that?"

"Mark my words," said Wycliffe, "it *will* come to that. If not sooner, then later. It is sure to come."

On a bright Sunday morning in late October, Wycliffe limped from the rectory into St. Mary's church to stand before his parishioners. Horne conducted the service until time for the sermon, when Purvey and Horne helped Wycliffe into the pulpit.

The English Bible lay open at John's Gospel. He took as his text Christ's words to Peter: *"Feed my sheep."* After repeating his text more than once, he looked into the faces of his people. He knew them well, and his heart went out in love to them.

"Christ taught the Apostles to feed his sheep in pastures of holy Writ, not in rotten pastures of fables and lies of men. But because a good shepherd should keep his sheep from wolves, defend them from scabs, and from rending, Christ bade Peter thrice that he should keep his sheep. Christ taught not his shepherd to raise a crusade and kill his sheep and his lambs and despoil them of their goods. This is Antichrist's teaching the Fiend has brought in, and by this it is known that these are not Peter's vicars."

It was a familiar theme, and they had heard most of it before, but he felt the necessity of emphasizing the difference between those who followed the true Shepherd and those who listened to the voice of the hireling. They might forget his words, but they would never forget his anger against all that was false and led men astray, or his strenuous upholding of all that was true—of Truth itself as embodied in Jesus Christ.

Wycliffe found himself physically and emotionally exhausted when the hour was over. Brut made ready to leave for Leicester soon after their return to the rectory. Wycliffe clung to him as if he would not let him go. This was one of his oldest, truest friends. They had shared much through many years. It was in Wycliffe's mind, and doubtless in Brut's as well, that they might not meet again on this earth. It was not an easy parting.

15. November 1383—Aston and Wycliffe

Wycliffe's enemies kept at him. They wrote against his doctrines and opposed the tracts appearing in the bookstalls. He received a letter needling him about his call to Rome by Pope Gregory XI. The writer insisted that the summons still hung over his head, even though Urban VI was now pope. He threatened to write a letter to Urban, asking him to renew the citation, since neither king nor archbishop was acting against a noted heretic.

This stirred Wycliffe to high excitement. Purvey tried to convince him that he should ignore the troublesome letter.

"No, Purvey, that is not the best course," insisted Wycliffe. "I shall write a tract which should be called *de citationibus frivolis.* You must see, Purvey, that all such frivolous citations are illegal. They come neither from God nor from civil lords, but from Satan. I have long seen the wisdom of dispensing with canon law. I have even less use for papal interference. Both these must give place to rule by the Gospel."

Purvey realized what was coming and assembled writing materials. With pen in hand he waited for the order to write.

"Write what I have just said, Purvey. Put in that I issue a call to those knights of the shires who support my doctrine, urging them to stand forth as soldiers of Christ, acting against the false antichrist who sets himself up as lord of their lives."

He added further statements, giving Purvey time to make notes which he would expand and organize for the finished piece.

"Now get this closing sentence just as I give it to you. 'So a certain feeble and lame man, cited to the curia, replies that he is prevented by a royal prohibition. The King of Kings has effectually willed it that he shall not go.'"

He then turned to his own desk and seized an earlier sermon to which he was making changes and additions upon points where his views varied from earlier ones. He flew from one task to another. As his body weakened, his mental powers increased. Fortunately, interruptions did not upset him, for they were frequent.

William Smith came from Leicester with copies of Gospels and tracts. Some months earlier he had said to Wycliffe, "Since Buckingham refuses to license me to preach, may I not be useful in transcribing the Word? I *do* preach, but not as often nor as openly as before. I have a writing hand that could be put to use." He had shown considerable skill and kept a steady stream of books feeding into the outlets Wycliffe had established.

"Smith, you are a blessing," cried Wycliffe. "Those Gospels and tracts are just in time to go into the hands of Poor Priests who will come in any day now for a new supply. We keep a number of people at copying here, but it is an endless task."

Purvey smiled and said, "If he would just hold up on the new writing, we might be able to catch up on the Scripture copies and sermon outlines for the Poor Priests."

"But without new riches pouring forth from that matchless mind," said Smith, "we'd be the poorer." With a fond look at Wycliffe, he continued, "Let him keep writing. We can't produce it, but we can copy and distribute it. The power of the written word is great, and it reaches more people than the spoken word."

"You saw Brut last month, no doubt," said Wycliffe.

"Indeed, we welcomed him with open arms. Many in Leicester profited by his messages, for he preached twice. We soon hurried him off, for the abbey men serve as watchmen for the bishop."

Smith departed with more manuscripts. "He's a professional," said Purvey. "Faster and more accurate than our fellows here."

"I spoke to Brut of martyrs, but Smith has put his life on the line numbers of times with his fiery preaching. It is my guess that threats from the bishop will not stop him. God uses such men. And his value to us as a copyist is inestimable."

Again he took up his pen to bring up to date his present views on war. Always he had opposed it, had felt there must be another way to settle disputes. Spenser's crusade, with its horrors, cruelties, senseless destruction of life, had led him to furious opposition to any war. He saw more clearly the suffering and impoverishment it brought with nothing good achieved.

He turned the usual sharp edge of his writing toward the clergy. Despoiling over-rich clergy was preferable to pillaging and despoiling France. Furthermore, fighting priests were unfit to pray, preach, or administer sacraments.

This was bold writing, for the southern coast was in imminent danger of attack, and Richard II was calling frantically for men to fight for their country.

Winter had swiftly succeeded autumn. Purvey moved Wycliffe's desk nearer the fire and made sure that logs were available to keep the fire going, hardly letting it die down for the night. Winds howled around the chimney, sometimes blowing smoke back into the room. Yet Wycliffe continued his work.

On a stormy night in late November, with sleet blasting against the walls, a knock came at the door. "Some poor stranger seeks shelter," said Wycliffe. "See to his needs, Horne."

The door opened to admit a bedraggled figure in a dripping cloak, hood drawn over his face, frozen fingers clutching a staff. Horne led him to the fire. The hood fell back, revealing not a stranger but a familiar face. John Aston stood there.

Dumb with astonishment, Wycliffe could only gape. Aston cried, "A fine welcome you offer a man who has traversed many a mile for the pleasure of your company! Icy winds, driving rain with sleet—enough to send a man back where he came from!"

"Aston, Aston!" cried Wycliffe. "How I have longed to see you come in that door, but I never dreamed of looking for you on such a night!"

In short order he was provided dry clothing and given a chair close to Wycliffe near the roaring fire, upon which another log was thrown. He partook gratefully of hot food and drink. Purvey and Horne had the grace to leave the two alone.

Aston's eyes sought Wycliffe's and held. Then he dropped his eyes. Softly Wycliffe said, "Well, Aston, tell me about it."

The telling was not easy, but the words tumbled out. The hour grew late, but they talked on. They probed the deep places and dug out dark fears and the remainder of guilt. Wycliffe bared the hurt he himself felt, the suffering he endured on Aston's account. Then in an outpouring of prayer the touch of the Holy Spirit brought healing and wholeness. Neither would again mention Aston's fall. The bond between them seemed stronger than ever.

Aston stayed the next day, and the next. The rectory was a busy place with copyists engaged in their important work. Yet he found calm and peace, a needed interlude.

He told Wycliffe he had waited to visit him, wanting to make sure the timing was right. At last he had decided he *must* come, regardless of timing or weather. He had dodged through forest paths and scattered hamlets to reach Lutterworth unrecognized.

Wycliffe treasured each hour. He listened eagerly to Aston's account of preaching ventures and adventures.

"Courtenay no doubt assumed," said Aston, "from the time of my disappearance from Oxford, that I would return to preaching. However, until he had some report of the content, he could do nothing. He has heard rumors, I am sure, but until the Gloucester sermon, no accurate report would have reached him."

"And he found it impossible to trace you," said Wycliffe, "since you move so frequently. It is risky for you to be here."

"That risk, however great, I consider negligible, in view of the privilege of being with you. I feared the danger in which it might involve you, if it were known that you harbored me."

"Have no thought of that. You are not the only 'wanted' man to come here. This is a safe haven, at least for the present. Even if your presence endangered us, you would still be welcome."

As they sat at table with the other members of the household, Wycliffe said, "You will observe that I do not follow the abstemious program of eating of former years. The body, as the house of the soul, must be under control, but I have come to realize that too frugal use of food can contribute to sickness."

"I wish you had made this discovery earlier," said Aston. "It might have meant better health for you now."

"Even before my stroke last year rheumatism racked my body. I am not sure that better eating would have prevented either that or the stroke. Mustard plasters provide the only relief I find for rheumatism, and even that remedy sometimes fails.

"As for food, I have concluded that it is permissible for one priest to entertain another temperately. That is quite a different thing from the banquets some bishops and priests give. I consider these as out of place as riding a saddled cow. In the Lord's Prayer we ask for bread, not larks or other delicacies."

On Aston's second day the weather grew colder, but cleared. Yew trees, beeches, and limes around the rectory and in the churchyard, sheathed in ice, sparkled in the sunlight.

Purvey walked with Aston to St. Mary's Church. They entered by the south porch and walked to the west end of the nave. Aston stood quietly for a few moments, fixing in his mind the feel of this house of worship. Then he advanced toward the chancel.

Observing the high pulpit, he asked, "Does he still preach?"

"Less and less frequently. It is difficult for him to get up into the pulpit, even with our help. Standing to preach must be quite exhausting, though he never complains."

"How much longer can he last, at the pace he keeps up?"

Purvey sighed. "Only God knows. I sometimes think that only the sheer will to continue keeps life in his body."

"He is so frail. Obviously his work is not yet finished, or God would not keep him here. He must suffer much more than he admits. He mentioned his bouts with rheumatism."

"The longer he continues to write," said Purvey, "the more violent he gets in his attacks on the evils in the church. In tract after tract, in Latin or in English, he rages against the pope, the friars, the bishops and especially the archbishop—the whole polity of the church. He once said his call was like Jeremiah's—to tear down and destroy. And like Jeremiah he would have little chance to plant and build up. That is all too true."

"To give his life to a cause, only to see little impact made, so little change brought about must be desolating. He has a clear vision of the evils and of the changes needed to bring the church back to what it should be, but those in a position to act refuse to listen. He stands so alone. In future years all he has fought for will be accomplished—but he will not see it."

"The time remaining to him cannot be long," said Purvey, as they returned to the rectory. "It is left to us to continue the battle. How many of us who have fought alongside him will be strong enough to continue once he is gone?"

Aston spent the last hours alone with Wycliffe. They read from the English Bible and prayed for its distribution and usefulness in bringing truth to a destitute people. They spent time in the companionable silence close friends know so well.

He left at nightfall. "I can move along the main roads and get past Rugby and perhaps as far as Coventry before dawn. Night travel is not bad when I know the route. I'll find friends at Coventry, perhaps even Swinderby. Then on back to the west."

Wycliffe provided him with a warmer cloak than the one in which he arrived. Purvey made up as large a packet of Gospels and tracts as he could carry.

Again it was a difficult parting. Aston said, "I'll come again when the way seems clear," but both he and Wycliffe knew he would not return. His work lay in distant parts, and he must not risk another visit here. The fate of a relapsed heretic was worse than either of them wanted to dwell upon. No burnings had occurred in England, but there were other forms of punishment.

Wycliffe spent most of the night in prayer for his friend.

16. December 1384—Constant Writing

Word finally came. "So Hereford rots in Antichrist's damnable prison," cried Wycliffe. "He should not have gone. He was foolish to expect Urban to listen to the truth. Barring a miracle, he'll end his days in that filthy dungeon."

"Still, there are miracles," said Purvey.

Wycliffe's only reply was additional spewings of venom against the pope. "I see," he said, "how God uses even something as wicked as Spenser's crusade to some advantage. The cursed crusade originated with the arch-enemy of God, acting through the friars, but it has been the means of exposing openly the hypocrisy and worldliness of the pope.

"It made clear the need, in conformity with the law of Christ, of doing away with a pope altogether, and acknowledging that there is but one living Head of the Church militant, Jesus Christ, the bishop of souls. The truth has been revealed that the papacy is not the shepherd of the church, but her betrayer, a foe against which all true soldiers of Christ must unite."

An ominous feeling as to his own end grew upon him. To friends he wrote, "*I am oppressed by the belief that persecution and a horrible death threaten me. I am able to look forward to this, however, as the celestial recompense of perseverance. I trust that by the mercy of God after this short life I shall receive a superabundant reward.*"

Copies of the Bible were in demand. Already more than one knight had ordered a copy of the whole Bible. Professional scriveners at Paternoster Row in London turned out beautiful work on vellum with artistic initial letters in red and with designs in blue decorating the margins. The binding was of tawed leather over thin sheets of fine wood. This pleased Wycliffe enormously. He insisted that Smith and his other copyists leave blank places for the initial letters and for the decorative designs in the margins. "These can be added later by someone with artistic talents," he said. "There must be uniformity."

Holding a copy of the Gospel of Matthew in his hand, he said reflectively, "Horne, when I first conceived the idea of putting the whole of Scripture into the English language, I had in mind mostly priests and bishops, with the better educated noblemen."

"How much easier it is to accomplish my purposes now that I have an English Bible," said Horne. "Not only is study of the Word more fruitful, but my preaching attains new depths. Too, when I read the lesson for the day, my hearers can understand."

"That important use is only the beginning. Some would say the ordinary man cannot read and understand the teachings of the Bible by himself. That is a false view. You preach the truth to our people here, Horne, but many priests and prelates do not."

"Again and again the Poor Priests relate how the people are blessed by the simple reading of the Word," said Horne.

"When there is no Poor Priest to read, a man must read for himself. The New Testament is open to the understanding of even simple men, as to the points most needful to salvation. Every man must have access to the Bible, either to read for himself or, if he cannot read, to hearing it read. Thus may the Holy Spirit teach the Scripture as Christ opened it to his Apostles."

Wycliffe struggled to complete his great work, *Trialogus*, which was a comprehensive treatise of final views on most of the subjects upon which he had written. His haste stemmed from fear that death might come before he completed it.

He dealt with three ideas, which he personified: *Alithia* (Truth), *Pseudis* (Falsehood), and *Phronecis* (Wisdom), who debated among themselves.

This device permitted him to express his own views and at the same time demonstrate the falsity of the erroneous views so prevalent. In his stand for the importance of Scripture he wrote, "Were there a hundred popes and all the friars turned into cardinals, their opinions in matters of faith should be accepted only insofar as they are founded on Scripture."

In his earlier days he had leaned toward extreme realism. Now he warned against this as he spoke of ideas, saying, "I confess that I am ignorant of much because of the loftiness of the subject, but in the fatherland I shall see clearly, as I believe, the views which now I only stammer."

17. January-February 1384—Winter Worries

The new year came in with a snowstorm and bitter cold which settled down for a long stay. A little corps of gallant men remained at work copying, even with fingers almost too stiff to hold a pen. Purvey spent his time between supervising this work and his place close beside Wycliffe with his own pen in hand.

Wycliffe suffered excruciating pain from his old enemy, rheumatism. Mustard plasters no longer relieved it. His lame leg troubled him, and he had increasingly less use of it. As his body grew weaker, his mind grew more alert. Except when the pain was extreme, he continued to make notes, revise, write, and dictate.

As winter dragged on, he longed for spring. "Purvey," he said, "I must see the bluebells. They won't bloom before May, but I will be better and feel less pain when I can walk through them in the churchyard. Even my lame leg may become stronger."

One day as he delivered vituperations against the pope, he saw Purvey wince. "Purvey, I know my vehement language offends you, but you must understand that it only echoes the violence with which the two heads of Antichrist curse each other."

"It is just that I fear the constant use of such language may hurt your cause," said Purvey.

"I feel justified in use of such terms," insisted Wycliffe. "It's the bloody wars, which they call crusades, of which I think now. How can any language be too strong for use in this connection? All war is evil, but a war waged by a pope for his own advancement stands condemned as the work of Antichrist. All the pleadings in its favor are but lies of Satan. The pope has rejected Christ, so Christendom, especially the secular lords, must reject him and restore the church to its primitive poverty."

18. May-August 1384—Bluebells

"Do you feel up to a walk across the churchyard?" asked Purvey one May morning. "You spoke earlier of bluebells, and they are in full bloom now."

With Purvey's help he rose and limped across to the door. "I am weaker than I thought," he said. "Maybe a bit later."

"No," said Purvey, "we must go now, or the flowers will be past their prime. Let me get you back to your chair and call one of the others. We can carry you in the chair. A simple matter."

Wycliffe began to object, then acquiesced with as good grace as he could muster. "I may as well accept my helpless condition and admit it will not improve. How difficult it is to lose one's independence and submit to the ignominy of being a burden!"

"Let's hear no talk of being a burden," said Purvey. "We count it a privilege to serve you in any way, great or small."

Horne and Purvey took up the chair and followed the path along the south side of the church, across the west end beside the tower, on past the yews and hollies to a large beech tree facing an open meadow which was a fantastic glory of bluebells.

"We'll set you here in the shade," said Purvey, "and you can feast your eyes on the bluebells to your heart's content."

"No," said Wycliffe, "set me down in their midst so I can feel myself a part of them. The sunshine will perhaps penetrate to the depths of my aging bones and rejuvenate them."

"Shall we leave you alone for a while?"

"By all means. I can spare an hour for this. It will be like the walks Brut and I took at Oxford to restore us to life."

Left alone he settled back to drink in the beauty. "Ah," he cried, as he spied the hawthorn hedgerow at the edge of the meadow, "the May blossoms, too, are at their height. Such profuse blooms mean a plenteous supply of haws for the birds, come winter." He called the delicate flowers by the common name, given because they generally appeared in May.

Settled once more at his desk, he felt in high spirits and eager to work. "I believe I am actually stronger," he said.

In July, William Thorpe returned. "I have left Oxford for good," he said. "Though, as I told you before, your works are still quietly circulated and read, no public debate can be held on points of your doctrine. The freedom of discussion Oxford knew has withered under Courtenay's mandates. The seculars feel restricted, while the regulars exult over the state of affairs."

He fit in well as he joined the other copyists. "I've been preaching for several weeks," he said. "People are eager to listen to reading and exposition of the Scripture in English. Courtenay's men seem to be on the alert though, and they warned me that I had no license to preach."

"What of the English Scriptures?" asked Wycliffe.

"No order has gone out at Oxford banning these," said Thorpe. "The scriveners in Catte Street continue to make copies. As long as a market exists, they will work. The Gospels are in great demand, and orders for a complete Bible have been placed."

"Courtenay will seek a way to stop that," said Purvey. "It will be difficult for him to label it 'heresy,' unless he can find a point at which he can pretend that a misinterpretation of the Vulgate has crept in. Your name is not attached, nor that of any of the translators, though he knows whence it came."

"The archbishop would do well to listen to Jerome's words: 'So read thou holy writ that the words that thou readest be God's blessed law, that commanded it not only to be read but also that readers should keep it in their works. What profit is it to read things to be done and not fulfil them in deed? As a clean mirror of life the lesson of holy writ is to be had, that all that is good may be made better, and that what is evil may be amended.'"

"And it was Jerome," said Thorpe, "who put the Scripture into the common language of his day—Latin—that the people might *read* and *keep* the word, even as he bade them."

"He would approve of our doing the same in our day," said Purvey.

After the outing to see the bluebells Purvey tried to persuade Wycliffe to be transported in the same manner to church.

"No," said Wycliffe, "I must not give up altogether. With your help I am able to walk to the house of the Lord for worship. It is possible I shall not preach again, though I hate to face that fact, but I must continue to walk as long as I am able."

It was the only time of week he ventured forth, and it was a laborious procedure. He would never admit the pain it caused, not so much from the paralyzed leg as from the increasingly sensitive joints.

Clutching his staff in his left hand and leaning upon Purvey on the right, he gritted his teeth and slowly advanced along the short distance, entering by the priest's door directly into the chancel. This shortened the journey and saved him the ordeal of climbing the few steps from the nave into the chancel.

Summer drew to an end. He finished the *Trialogus* and felt a part of his burden lift. He entrusted the copying of this work to William Smith in Leicester. "It is safer," he said, "not to send it off to Oxford or London, as things now are. After we have a few copies, perhaps the Paternoster Row scriveners in London can make copies for wider distribution."

Purvey expressed doubts as to this latter suggestion. "It might be too easy for it to come to Courtenay's notice in London," he said, "but we shall see. Smith should produce several copies within a reasonable time. I shall do the corrections. Any copyist, no matter how skilled, makes errors."

19. September-December 1384—Final Writings

Thorpe seized every opportunity for contact with Wycliffe. From copying he absorbed much of what was coming from the master, but he wanted more. He persuaded Wycliffe to let him be among those to whom he dictated some of the tracts. Thorpe called this "sitting at Wycliffe's feet." Amid the dictation came intervals of conversation, and he treasured what he imbibed from this.

In spite of bodily weakness and painful joints Wycliffe continued writing. He wrote on the old topics, and he turned to some he had scarcely mentioned before.

"I must write about the sacraments, Purvey," he said. "I admit the value of sacraments, but the church lives not in sacraments invented by the satraps of Antichrist but in definite faith in the Lord Jesus."

He reiterated his doctrine of the Eucharist. He denied the necessity of confession to a priest, but admitted its desirability in some cases. Turning aside momentarily from the sacraments, he thundered a strong condemnation of the sale of indulgences and the practice of simony.

He spoke so rapidly that Purvey had to call a halt so he could catch up. "You say," said Purvey, "that the sacraments can be administered by any of the predestinate. How are we to know who is predestinate?"

"Don't quibble, Purvey. No one can know for sure, but there are signs which indicate a person's status. I add that the king should provide that a priest reside in every parish church in England. The idea that a layman *may* administer the sacraments is one which will not be accepted in the foreseeable future. In the meantime, we must be practical. The king must make provision."

He did not know why he felt impatient with Purvey. "An unworthy priest must be removed," he continued. "As I often say, a priest must live like Christ, a life of poverty. As for the service, I find no confirmation in the

Gospel for many prayers, continual singing, confessions and other ceremonies. Preaching is the chief thing, far more important than even the mass."

"You'll find much opposition to that last point."

"I find opposition to much that I hold. Truth is never popular. That is no reason to abstain from voicing it."

Suddenly he recognized his querulous tone as an indication of extreme weariness. "I'm sorry, Purvey. You are good to remain patient with a tired old man. Let us stop for a rest."

As autumn moved into winter, the periods of rest became more frequent. Yet Wycliffe would never lay the pen down or stop dictating for long. He was like a man driven. There was no hint of discouragement, only the urgency to finish a task for which he knew time was limited.

Horne carried on the duties of the parish ministry but spent what free time he found at Wycliffe's side. Purvey remained with him almost constantly, while Thorpe slipped in whenever he could. All were aware that the master weakened physically day by day.

"Purvey," he said one December morning, "I shall have to leave the work unfinished. You who outlive me must carry on the battle, but it may not be won even in your lifetime. In the end, however, it will all come to pass.

"The Bible—God's law, Christ's law—must be recognized as the supreme word by which the church is guided. No papal word, no tradition in opposition to it can stand. The top-heavy, unwieldy structure of the ecclesiastical hierarchy must crumble and fall, for it has no foundation in Scripture.

"The Church must be brought back to the simplicity of the early days. The Scriptures must be made available to every man in his own tongue. Preaching of the Word and diligent study of it must lead to holy lives and Christian character. Complete the Bible revision, Purvey, and get it into the hands of the people."

He gave attention now to a treatise called *Opus Evangelicum*. The violence of his language died away. As one who has passed beyond controversy, he moved into a calmness of expression which astounded Purvey and the others.

He began this work with a simple commentary, suitable for use in preaching, on the Sermon on the Mount. He continued to quote liberally from Augustine, Chrysostom, and Grosseteste. He was still at home with most books of his library, so, with a volume before him, he could quickly find the passage he needed.

Christmas day fell on Sunday. Several of the Poor Priests had returned for rest and inspiration and to join in the joyous festival. As the company from the rectory gathered in the church with the parishioners on Christmas morning for the celebration of the mass, an unusual solemnity prevailed. As Wycliffe sat before them, the thought in many hearts was of his fragility, of the mark of suffering etched on his beloved countenance.

"Come, Purvey," he cried on the next morning, "let's get into the second book of *Opus Evengelicum*."

Much of what he wrote was reiteration of his earlier convictions and repetition of charges already made. He could not refrain from expressing again his sympathies with the common people and his desire that serfdom be abolished.

He warned, "The voice of the people is only the voice of God when it is the voice of a people led by the Spirit of God."

As the writing ceased on December 27, Wycliffe exclaimed, "Before the year ends, Purvey, the final work will be completed."

20. December 28-31, 1384—Departure

Wycliffe awoke earlier than usual on the morning of the 28th. He felt remarkably free from pain. "I believe I could walk to the church this morning, Purvey," he said. "The brightness of the sunshine has moderated the cold. I must not give up all efforts to walk, even if I must have help."

Purvey sought to persuade him that it would tax his strength unnecessarily to attempt to walk even the short distance.

"Haven't you learned," said Wycliffe, "that it is useless to argue with a stubborn old man? I intend to walk to church this day of the Holy Innocents."

Purvey gave up. Wycliffe held his staff quite firmly in his left hand, and he leaned less heavily upon Purvey on his right. "I *am* growing stronger," he said. "I must do this more often."

The church was nearly full. Murmurs of surprise could be heard as the rector walked into the chancel with little help from Purvey. He settled into the armchair reserved for his use, smiling as his eyes swept across the faces before him.

He thought to himself, *I could have preached today, had I known I would feel this well. It would be good to preach again.*

The service proceeded to the time of the celebration of the mass. As Horne began the consecration of the bread and wine, Wycliffe thought, *No making of the body of Christ by the priest! A spiritual transformation so that Christ is truly present in the elements to feed our souls even as the bread feeds our bodies. Oh, how real the presence of the blessed Lord!*

Horne reached the point of the elevation of the host. Wycliffe looked on, thinking what a glorious moment it was. Then a feeling of weakness crept over him, a sense of helplessness. In desperation he looked toward Purvey, but even as he caught Purvey's eye, darkness fell, and he slipped to the floor.

Purvey sprang to his side, with Thorpe close behind. A cry of alarm burst across the church. Horne paused in the midst of his sacred duties, but Purvey whispered to him to proceed. Purvey and Thorpe placed Wycliffe's limp form in the chair, leaning it back to keep him firmly in place. Between them they carried him out the priest's door and across to the rectory.

William Feilding sent to Leicester for the doctor. Meanwhile, Wycliffe regained consciousness but lay helpless, not able to speak. The doctor examined him and shook his head. "I can do nothing. The end cannot be far off. Only strength of will has kept that frail body going these last months."

Purvey had questions. "Does he suffer? Is his mind clear? Will he be able to speak again?"

"I think," replied the doctor, "that he does not suffer. From the expression in his eyes I would say his mind is clear. He will understand you, but he will probably not speak again."

And so it proved. Purvey remained almost constantly at his side. Thorpe and Horne were often there. Others came and went. Thursday was market day, but much subdued. All Lutterworth, indeed, all the parish, came to bid their beloved rector goodbye. Purvey let them enter, one by one, to touch his lifeless hand, to utter little expressions of love, and to look once more into those eyes so bright even now with understanding.

Tears flowed, but not from his eyes. There was little to read in his expression. Yet what showed combined with the expression of his eyes to reveal peace, love, resignation.

Purvey spoke words of encouragement, of comfort, of reassurance. "Your work will continue; your influence will be felt through the years across the land. The changes you sought will come. This is not the end. It is only the beginning."

Friday passed, and Saturday dawned, the last day of the year. The only change noted was that he seemed to sleep more. When he opened his eyes, he appeared as alert as ever.

Purvey and Thorpe sat with him in the afternoon. Quietness prevailed, interspersed by little ripples of expectancy, of excitement. Wycliffe gave a sigh. Purvey touched him tenderly. "Close your eyes and sleep," he said. *"The eternal God is your resting place, and underneath are the everlasting arms."*

Wycliffe looked at Purvey with an expression of ineffable love, then obediently closed his eyes. He did not wake again. The year ended, and with it the earthly life of John Wycliffe.

The voice long heard in the lecture halls and pulpits of Oxford had been silenced earlier. The pen had continued even to the last to inscribe the truth upon countless pages. Death now silenced the strong, clear voice and stilled forever the pen.

EPILOGUE

On a blustery day three weeks into January, John Purvey rode slowly out of Lutterworth. Horne, the Poor Priests and Thorpe had already left. Purvey was the last. Pausing at the bridge across the river Swift, he took one last look back toward the town. With a sudden pang he recalled the moment ten years earlier when he and Wycliffe had caught their first glimpse of the tower of St. Mary's church from this very spot.

"No looking back!" he cried. Facing the west, he murmured, "Aston, Brut, and Swinderby are out there preaching. Thorpe has gone north. The Poor Priests follow various paths. As I said, we are only at the beginning. The battle for truth to which John Wycliffe gave his life must continue until the victory is won." Purvey's immediate task was the revision of the English Bible.

In that same week Bishop Buckingham installed John Morhouse as parish priest at Lutterworth. The bishop may have cast an uneasy glance at the new grave in the south side of the chancel. He would dismiss his fears with the thought, *Death has solved a thorny problem. That troublemaker can no longer disturb us.*

How wrong he was!

Some call John Wycliffe "Morning Star of the Reformation." In a sense the title is apt. As the brightness of the morning star gleams in the pre-dawn darkness, Wycliffe's life and teaching shed a brilliant radiance in the darkness of his time.

If one cannot be completely satisfied with his theology at all points, it must be remembered that he was a man of his times. He struggled in medieval darkness, and with little insight or encouragement from his contemporaries. No

plaster saint, he was a human being with character flaws—
a violent temper which led to a sometimes shocking viru-
lence in attacking his enemies. Yet he was a man of God,
mightily used.

He contended for the supremacy of Scripture over
tradition and sought removal of the incrustations of an
overgrown ecclesiastical system. He tested the church
against Scripture and battled the error he found. By
emphasizing the priority of preaching and insisting that
an English Bible be available to all, he strove to return
believers to Christlike living and pure doctrine.

Evidence of Lollard activity well into the sixteenth
century is still coming to light. Wycliffe's reformation,
sometimes referred to as the *failed* reformation, was in
fact no failure. It may have been before its time, but it
never died or lost its life force.

Thus the figure of the Morning Star is inadequate.
The morning star gives promise of the coming dawn but
does nothing of itself to bring it. The life and work of
John Wycliffe in the fourteenth century was a most
potent factor in bringing to pass the English
Reformation of the sixteenth century.

The account of the years in between, marked by persecution, repression, and martyrdom, makes another
thrilling story, to appear in a sequel to the present volume.

Select Bibliography

Manuscripts

Archives, The Castle, Lincolnshire
Title deeds of 14th century

Bodleian Library
MS Bodley 647 (Miscellaneous writings by Wycliffe)
MS Bodley 959 (Old Testament to Baruch 3:20)
MS Laud Misc 23 (In praise of Wycliffe)

British Library
Royal 7 B iii (Tracts against Wycliffe)
Cotton Titus D. xix Miscellane A
Royal I C. viii (J Wycliffe, English Bible)

Lambeth Palace Library
MS 25 Bible in English G.a. 3 fol.104
MS 551 Wycliffe Tract c.o.44, 8 vo. 60
MS 1149 Sermons. J. Wycliffe

Reference Library, Lincoln
Ross Manuscripts, Volume IV

Printed Works

Biographical Register of the University of Oxford to A.D. 1500, Vol. 3. Oxford: Clarendon Press, 1959.

Boase, Charles W., *Historic Towns: Oxford*. Longman's Green & Co., 1890, 3rd edition.

Briggs, Asa, *A Social History of England*. New York: Viking Press, 1983.

Bruce, F.F., *History of the English Bible*, Third Edition. New York: Oxford University Press, 1978.

Capes, W.W., *The English Church in the Fourteenth and Fifteenth Centuries*. London: MacMillan and Co., Limited, 1900.

Casswell, Peter J., *The Parish Church of Lutterworth*, (Booklet), Lutterworth, 1978.

Chamberlin, E.R., *The Bad Popes*. New York: Dorset Press, 1969.

Commemorative Booklet, *Wycliffe Six Hundred*. Lutterworth, 1984.

Cowie, Leonard, *The Black Death and Peasants' Revolt*. London: Wayland Publishers, 1972.

Cryer, Mary, *Lambeth Palace* (Booklet). West Sussex: Churchman Publishing Limited, 1988.

Dahmus, Joseph Henry, *The Prosecution of John Wyclif*. New Haven: Yale University Press, 1952.

D'Aubigne, J.H.Merle, *The Reformation in England*, Volume One. Edinburgh: Banner of Truth Trust, 1962.

Deanesly, Margaret, *The Lollard Bible*. Cambridge: 1920.

——*The Significance of the Lollard Bible*. University of London: The Athlone Press, 1951.

Dickens, A.G., *The English Reformation*. London and Glasgow: Fontana/Collins, 1967.

Dictionary of National Biography. Edited by Sir Leslie Stephen and Sir Sidney Lee. Oxford: Oxford Univesity Press, since 1917.

Dyson, A.H., *Lutterworth: John Wycliffe's Town*. Methuen, 1913.

——and S.H. Skillington, *Lutterworth Church and Its Associates*. Leicester: C.H. Gee & Co., 1916.

Evans, Herbert A., *Highways and Byways: In Oxford and the Cotswolds*. McMillan & Co., 1905

Fountain, David, John Wycliffe, *The Dawn of the Reformation*. Southampton: Mayflower Christian Books, 1984.

Fristedt, Sven L., *The Wycliffe Bible, The Principal Problems Connected with Forshall and Madden's Edition*. Part I. Stockholm: Almquist & Wiksells Boktryckeri-A.B., 1953.

Fristedt, Sven L., *The Wycliffe Bible, The Origin of the First Revision as presented in De Salutaribus Documentis*. Part II. Stockholm: Almquist & Wiksell, 1969.

Gilbert, Martin, *Atlas of British History*. New York: Dorset Press, 1985.

Hanawalt, Barbara A., *The Ties that Bound, Peasant Families in Medieval England*. New York, Oxford: Oxford University Press, 1986.

Howard, Donald R., *Chaucer: His Life, His Works, His World*. New York: E.P. Dutton, 1987.

Hudson, Anne, Editor, *English Wycliffite Writings*. Oxford: Clarendon Press, 1983.

—— "John Purvey: A Reconsideration of the Evidence for his Life and Writings." *Viator 12*, 1981. Oxford.

——"A Neglected Wycliffite Text." *Journal of Ecclesiastical History*, Vol. 29, No. 3, July 1978.

——*The Premature Reformation*. Oxford: Clarendon Press, 1988.

——*John Wyclif and his Influence in England*. (Booklet) Lambeth Palace Library, 1984.

Kenny, Anthony, Translator, *On Universals*, (*Tractatus de Universalibus*, by John Wyclif.) Oxford: Clarendon Press, 1985.

——*Wyclif*. Oxford: Oxford University Press, 1985.

——Editor, *Wyclif in his Times*. Oxford, 1986.

LeBas, Charles Webb, *The Life of Wyclif*. New York: J & J Harper, 1832.

Lechler, Gotthard Victor, *John Wycliffe and his English Precursors*. AMS Press reprint of 1884 English Edition.

Leff, Gordon, "John Wyclif: The Path to Dissent." Raleigh Lecture on History, read May 4, 1966. *Proceedings of the British Academy*, Oxford.

Lerner, Robert E., *The Age of Adversity: The Fourteenth Century.* Ithaca and London: Cornell University Press, 1968.

Lewis, John, *The History and the Life and Sufferings of the Reverend and Learned John Wyclif.* Oxford: Clarendon Press, 1820. Reprinted New York: AMS Press, Inc., 1973.

Lupton, Lewis, *Wyclif's Wicket,* Vol. XVI in *History of the Geneva Bible.* Foxton near Cambridge: Burlington Press, 1984.

McFarlane, K.B., *John Wycliffe and the Beginnings of English Non-Conformity.* London: English Universities Press Ltd at St. Paul's House, 1952.

Morgan, Kenneth O., Editor, *The Oxford Illustrated History of Britain.* Oxford, New York: Oxford University Press, 1984.

Packe, Michael, *King Edward III.* London: Routledge & Kegan Paul, 1983.

Page, John T., "John Wiclif and Lutterworth," *Bygone Leicestershire,* S.R. Publishers, 1969.

Paget, Guy, *Leicestershire.* Leicester: Hale, 1950.

Parker, G.H.W., *The Morning Star.* Vol. III in *The Paternoster Church History,* Gen. Ed. F.F. Bruce. London: The Paternoster Press, 1965.

Platt, C., *The English Medieval Town.* London: Granada Publishing, 1976.

Pritchett, H.D. *John de Wycliffe: The Hamlet of Wycliffe, Family and Birthplace of the Reformer.* Revised 1938. Darlington and Stockton Times.

Robertson, Edwin, *Wycliffe: Morning Star of the Reformation.* Basingstoke, Hants: Marshalls, 1984.

Robson, John Adam, *Wyclif and the Oxford Schools.* Cambridge: Cambridge University Press, 1961.

Rowling, Marjorie, *Everyday Life in Medieval Times.* New York: Dorset Press, 1987.

Schaff, Philip, *History of the Christian Church,* Volume VI, The Middle Ages. Grand Rapids: Wm. B. Eerdmans Publ. Co., 1989. Reprint from Charles Scribner's Sons, 1910.

Stacey, John, *Wyclif and Reform*. London: Lutterworth Press, 1964.

Strawley, J.H., *Robert Grosseteste*, Bishop of Lincoln, 1235-1253. Lincoln Minster Pamphlets, No. 7. Reprint 1966.

Trevelyan, George M., *England in the Age of Wyclif*. New York and London: Johnson Reprint Corporation, 1966. Reprinted from Longmans, Green and Co., 1912.

Tuchman, Barbara W., *A Distant Mirror, The Calamitous 14th Century*. New York: Alfred A. Knopf, 1984.

Vaughan, Robert, *John de Wycliffe, D.D., A Monograph*. London: Seeleys, 1853.

——Editor, *Tracts and Treatises of John de Wycliffe, D.D.* London: The Wycliffe Society, 1845.

Watkinson, W.L., *John Wicklif*. Mobile, Alabama: R.E. Publications.

Workman, H.B., *The Dawn of the Reformation: The Age of Wyclif*, Volume I. London: Charles H. Kelly, 1901.

——*The Dawn of the Reformation: The Age of Hus*, Volume II. London: Charles H. Kelly, 1902.

——*John Wyclif: A Study of the English Medieval Church*, Volumes I and II. Hamden, Connecticut: Archon Books, 1966. Reprint from Oxford: Clarendon Press, 1926.

Writings of the Rev. and Learned John Wickliff. London: The Religious Tract Society, 1831.

"Wycliffe", *History of Yorkshire North Riding*. 1914. pp. 138-142.

WYCLIF & his followers. (Booklet prepared for An Exhibition to mark the 600th anniversary of the death of John Wyclif.) Oxford: Bodleian Library, 1984.

To order additional copies of

THE MAN WITH THE LONG SHADOW

please send $16.95
plus $3.95 shipping and handling to:

Clara H. Stuart
313 Walnut Street
Marks, MS 38646

*Quantity Discounts are Available

To order by phone,
have your credit card ready and call

1-800-917-BOOK